THE REVOLUTIONARY ORIGINS
OF MODERN JAPAN

Thomas M. Huber

THE REVOLUTIONARY ORIGINS
OF MODERN JAPAN

STANFORD UNIVERSITY PRESS

Stanford, California

Published with the assistance of the
Andrew W. Mellon Foundation

Stanford University Press
Stanford, California
© 1981 by the Board of Trustees of the
Leland Stanford Junior University
Printed in the United States of America
Cloth ISBN 0-8047-1048-1
Paper ISBN 0-8047-1755-9
Original Printing 1981
Last figure below indicates year of this printing:
98   97   96   95   94   93   92   91   90   89

To my parents

Acknowledgments

I AM GRATEFUL to Tetsuo Najita and H. D. Harootunian for helpful suggestions offered in the early stages of this work. My gratitude is also extended to Conrad Totman for providing valuable insights into the political environment of the 1860's, and to Irwin Scheiner for giving much useful advice on style. I am indebted to Bitō Masahide for kindly allowing me to participate in his seminar on Tokugawa thought during my stay in Japan as a Fulbright-Hays scholar between 1971 and 1974. Satō Seizaburō and Inoue Isao were most helpful at that time in contributing both ideas and information on materials. Umezawa Hideo generously aided me by drawing upon his knowledge of Yoshida Shōin's writings. Sakai Yūkichi gave much stimulation and encouragement in our discussions while the research work was in progress, and Otsubo Kazuo provided congenial instruction in Japanese in the early days of my stay in Japan. I wish also to express my appreciation to the History Department of Stanford University for subsidizing the preparation of one of the later drafts of this work during my service there in 1976–77. Finally, thanks are due to E. S. Cope, Dov Ospovat, Sam Yamashita, Arif Dirlik, and the countless other friends and associates whose thoughtful suggestions have enriched this work over the years.

T.M.H.

Contents

Note on Dates

THE pre-Meiji dates in the text below are all based on the lunar calendar. Intercalary months are indicated with a small case "i." When a series of numbers is used to express a date, for example 4/15/61, these numbers represent the month, day, and year, respectively, in accordance with the usual practice in American English. For stylistic reasons, English month names are sometimes used for the months of corresponding number in the lunar calendar: "January" for the first month, "February" for the second month, and so on, in the same manner that contemporary Japanese dates are rendered in English. The lunar year usually begins sometime in February by the Gregorian calendar, so that as a rule of thumb, four to seven weeks must be added to a lunar date to yield its Gregorian equivalent.

CHAPTER ONE

Introduction

THE CREATION of the Meiji Restoration government in 1868, and the sweeping reforms that followed, constitute the most dramatic event in Japan's modern history. Within a decade Japanese leaders established a system of universal education, formed a modern army and navy, and recruited an efficient administrative bureaucracy, both nationally and locally. They developed a network of telegraph and rail communications, and laid the broad fiscal and financial foundations that were needed for rapid industrialization. The Restoration transformed Japan into a modern society by the standards of the day, and rescued her alone among her Asian neighbors from the bondage of colonialism, and from the feudal encumbrances of her own past.

Western scholarship on Japan has been at pains to explain why this amazing transformation happened to take place, and in recent decades a scholarly consensus on the question has emerged. Since it is my purpose to reopen this issue by offering a differing analysis of the Restoration experience, let us begin by examining the basic assumptions of what is now the most commonly accepted view. First, it is argued by scholars that the leading restorationists, those who seized power in 1868 and set about constructing the new regime, were enlightened statesmen motivated by a shared concern over the growing threat of Western power. Since most of them came from the samurai hierarchy's middle and upper portions, and were therefore already privileged under the old order, social and class grievances played little part in bringing them to act.

Rather, it was their traditional loyalty to domain and nation, daimyo and emperor, that spurred the Meiji leaders to action after Perry's fleet arrived in 1853.

Second, the political turbulence of the 1850's and 1860's is seen by historians as unrelated to the institutional reforms worked out by statesmen after 1868. The strife-ridden decade of the 1860's represented little more than two false starts: xenophobic terrorism (1860–63) and militant loyalty to domain (1863–68). According to the established view, these exhausted impulses gave way after 1868 to a more sophisticated, pragmatic nationalism.

Third, the Meiji reforms after 1868 are seen as being primarily imitative. Having no clear program other than the desire not to be overborne by the West, Meiji leaders understandably turned to the West to discover how Japan might best be strengthened against the Western challenge. Being rational bureaucrats as well as nationalists, when they found economic and social institutions in the West that served their purposes, they simply imported them.

The now widely accepted explanation represented by these three assumptions is ptolemaic in the sense that each set of occurrences in the crucial Restoration years has to be accounted for by a different principle of historical motion. Is it really likely that the fanaticism of the early 1860's simply vanished, or that the leaders who fought so hard from 1864 to 1868 to establish the hegemony of their own domains would work just as hard in 1869 to disestablish those same domains? (There is a paradox in this view that parallels that of the Japanese Marxist thesis, advanced in the 1920's, that "lower-class samurai" abolished the samurai class and the Tokugawa Bakufu in order to preserve as much of the feudal order as possible!) Something seems to be missing from this approach. Either the substance of public life in this period was disjointed to a very unusual degree, or else there was some underlying historical principle giving unity to the events of this era that has somehow escaped scholarly analysis.

I shall argue in these pages that the three propositions stated above are fundamentally mistaken. They are mistaken because they do not adequately explain either the extraordinary events that led up to the Restoration or the massive changes that followed it. I will try to offer fresh concepts that may more satisfactorily explain Japan's great transformation, and will present a new hypothesis with respect to the central cause and mechanism of that transformation.

The premises of this study are as follows. First, the Restoration leadership acted on behalf of a distinctive social category or class, namely Japan's early modern service intelligentsia. Second, the leading members of this class in late Bakuhan society were both materially deprived and spiritually tormented by the workings of an antiquated system of aristocratic privilege and lavish ceremonial waste. Third, these leaders refashioned elements of their own intellectual tradition to construct iconoclastic and compelling ideological support for their social complaints. Fourth, on the basis of empirical principles derived from these traditional sources, the reformist leaders developed notions of social change similar to those implemented in Meiji, and evolved a coherent social program some years before they had meaningful access to Western models. Fifth, the seemingly disjointed violence of the Bakumatsu period reflected what was in reality a continuous escalation of political hostilities, during which reformers were driven to rely in succession on polemic, terror, and civil warfare in their relentless struggle against conservative power. Sixth, the Meiji transformation represented the actual implementation of reforms and reformist principles that had been advocated for decades by Japan's indigenous service intelligentsia.

In sum, I shall argue that the Meiji Restoration was in essence a blow struck at pervasive patterns of social injustice by a frustrated and ultimately embattled service intelligentsia. It was a domestic affair, in which the Western challenge figured only as a convenient instrumentality, used by the reformers to win broader approval for the basic structural changes they had long favored.

Twenty-five years ago, when Tokugawa Japan was typically seen as a "feudal" and relatively backward society, this kind of explanation could not have been easily sustained. In recent years, how-

4 Introduction

ever, scholars such as Ronald Dore, John Hall, Conrad Totman, Tetsuo Najita, and Thomas C. Smith have shown that late Tokugawa institutions and thought were more highly developed in every sphere than had previously been believed. This book, which pursues some of the implications of their revealing studies in the context of the Meiji Restoration, is greatly indebted to their work.

Intelligentsia-oriented analysis has long been familiar in European historiography, where a political intelligentsia commonly figures as the leading element or "vanguard" of a bourgeois or proletarian movement. Japan's insurgent intelligentsia did not conform to this pattern; although motivated in part by idealistic perceptions, it was the vanguard primarily of itself. Whatever benefits its triumph may have gained for other groups, its own interests and perceptions were the main dynamic force behind Japan's modern transformation. (One of the intelligentsia's perceived interests was, however, the welfare of the whole national community, for reasons that will be discussed below.) The case of the Restoration is thus an interesting one in theoretical terms, suggesting as it does that the bureaucratization processes emphasized by Weber may tell us more about some revolutionary upheavals than is revealed by the proletarianization processes described by Marx. This study will allow us ultimately to explore some of the complex issues raised by this suggestion.

In the pages that follow I will make the above arguments by examining the political careers of a prominent group of Restoration leaders known as the Chōshū activists. Chōshū was one of the larger "outer" domains of the Tokugawa system, and in the decades after the Restoration several of her sons came to dominate the highest levels of the new government. Men like Kido Kōin, Itō Hirobumi, Yamagata Aritomo, and Inoue Kaoru wrote the new constitution, founded the new military, created a modern diplomatic corps, and in general supervised the building of the new society.

Earlier, these men had been members of a larger group of militant restorationist sympathizers in Chōshū. This larger group had been continuously active in the movement for reform from the 1850's on. They figured prominently in the terrorism of 1860–63, and it was their mobilization of the Chōshū army in 1866 that brought the Bakufu to its knees. The Chōshū reformers were perhaps the most vigorous and effective opponents of the Tokugawa regime, and it was their actions that ultimately proved decisive in bringing it down.

My main concern is with relating the Chōshū activists' social origins to their values, goals, motives, and strategies in the 1850's and 1860's. I will concentrate in particular on the Sonjuku group, a political association of several dozen persons within the Chōshū movement that produced Itō and the Meiji statesmen. During the 1850's, the famous teacher Yoshida Shōin ran a school called the Shōka Sonjuku in the Chōshū capital of Hagi. Itō and the others were at one time students of this school.

The Sonjuku group was characterized by a high degree of political engagement throughout, and the casualty rate among its members was high. Three men in succession served as its leaders between 1853 and 1868, and each man perished doing so. The martyrdom of these leaders was for their companions part of a larger pattern of political endeavor, however, and it is the purpose of this study to grasp the essential "cause" of the Restoration by revealing what that endeavor was.

My findings take the form of a sequence of political biographies, one for each of these three remarkable leaders. Chapters 2 through 4 deal with the early life, thought, and leadership of Yoshida Shōin, prior to his execution by the Bakufu in 1859. Chapters 5 and 6 explore the promising early career of the young physician Kusaka Genzui, and the years of his political leadership from Yoshida's death in 1859 until his own in a hail of rifle fire at the Forbidden Gate in 1864. Chapters 7 and 8 set forth the early life and political career of Takasugi Shinsaku, who finally led the reorganized Chōshū military to victory against vastly superior conservative forces in the years between 1864 and 1867. The implications of these events are discussed in Chapter 9.

This treatment will show that the Meiji transformation was

accomplished only after a long and daring political insurgency, by men dedicated to reformist principles that were articulated in the 1850's and even earlier. It was over these principles, representing as they did the vision of a new society and the aspirations of a new social class, that the bitter struggles of the 1860's were waged, and for the sake of these principles that the Chōshū men and others put their lives at risk. The Chōshū leaders probably did not see themselves at first as being the foremost champions of these new values, but when fortune so decreed, they proved worthy of the task. In this book the origins of the Meiji state are characterized as revolutionary. If the explanation offered here is correct, they were nothing less.

CHAPTER TWO

The Early Life of Yoshida Shōin

YOSHIDA Shōin was a schoolteacher. He was also one of the more brilliant political thinkers that Japanese society has ever produced. His brilliance, however, was in sharp contrast to the shabby circumstances in which Tokugawa society obliged him to live. Shōin's whole existence, from his earliest years, was submerged, involuntarily, in an intense discipline, all for the sake of lord and domain, and the peculiar set of priorities to which Bakuhan society was heir. In exchange for his sacrificial dedication, the Tokugawa order gave back to Shōin a marginal existence of poverty and obscurity. In the end he devoted his considerable intelligence and his whole soul to transforming the Tokugawa world. The story of Shōin's early life is a mundane story, but its essential conditions were shared by tens of thousands of "lower-class samurai" throughout Japan. In this at first unpresuming saga are to be found the wellsprings of the Meiji rebellion.

Yoshida Shōin is one of a half-dozen men whose names are indissolubly linked with the Meiji Restoration. Many scholarly observers feel that Shōin was somehow an essential manifestation of the spirit of his age. At the same time, however, few believe that he influenced the course of events in a direct way, because his later years were marred by a succession of tragic failures. He tried unsuccessfully to board Commodore Perry's flagship in 1854 for the purpose of studying in America. He attempted to assassinate the Bakufu's powerful police representative in Kyoto in 1858, an audacious course of action that led to his early death. Scholars have concluded from this that Shōin was an impractical idealist, a leader with much charisma but one who lacked meaningful political goals.

Still, the circumstances of Shōin's early years do not suggest the formation of a romantic extremist. His education, though unusually rigorous, was conventional. The images of Shōin that emerge from most accounts of his early youth reveal a gentle young man with an immense appetite for knowledge. Never did he defy authority except where it seemed necessary to extend his education beyond the customary limits. He was a voracious reader, an observant traveler, and a sensitive educator. In many respects, Shōin was the epitome of what a young scholar-samurai in Tokugawa Japan was expected to be. How could he have made the transition from the compliant, mild-mannered scholar described by the biographers of his youth to the extremist of the 1850's described by historians?

Yoshida Shōin's education was his life. Because of an accident of inheritance, he was thrust at the age of five into an environment of accelerated educational expectations. This milieu seems to have forged within him an imperative of intellectual achievement that would last the rest of his life and would in itself do much to shape his future.

Shōin was born in 1830, the second son of Sugi Yūrinosuke, a Chōshū samurai of modest rank (*mukyūdōri*) and 26 koku of income. Yūrinosuke had two younger brothers, Yoshida Daisuke and Tamaki Bunnoshin (see Figure 1). At the age of four, Shōin was adopted by his uncle Daisuke. Although Daisuke was then only twenty-eight, he was already in ill health and died a year later. This left Shōin as the legal head of the Yoshida house, with a stipend of 57 koku.

The practice of adopting younger sons from the Sugi house into the Yoshida line had been established for generations before Shōin's birth, probably because of the straitened financial cir-

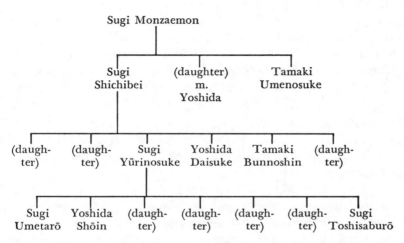

Figure 1. Patrilineal genealogy of the Sugi family from the generation of Yoshida Shōin's great-grandfather Sugi Monzaemon. SOURCE: *Yoshida Shōin zenshū*, ed. Yamaguchi ken kyōiku kai, 12 vols. (Tokyo, 1940), 1: 69–72.

cumstances in which service samurai like the Sugis found themselves. To stave off insolvency, the Sugis controlled two additional hereditary lineages, the Tamaki line and the Yoshida line. The oldest male offspring of the Sugi house in each generation became the Sugi heir. Younger sons (or, if need be, sons-in-law) were then adopted as heirs of their uncles in the Tamaki or Yoshida lines, as Shōin was. This pattern required the incumbent in the Yoshida line, and in most generations in the Tamaki line, to remain unmarried, in order not to obstruct a Sugi succession. Each of the three hereditary lines carried with it only a modest stipend, the total sum of which could support the Sugis and the two collateral uncles in modest comfort, but would have been insufficient to support three separate households in each generation.[1]

Daisuke's premature death left Shōin with a difficult obligation. The Yoshida house had a proud tradition of instructing the daimyo and his retainers in the subtleties of the Yamaga school of military studies, and indeed, from the *han* government's point of view, this was the raison d'être of the Yoshida house.* It was the Yoshidas' duty to supply an instructor in Yamaga military studies at all times, but now the head of the house was a small boy who was obviously unequal to the task. To avoid embarrassing the family, Tamaki Bunnoshin, the younger of Shōin's two uncles, took upon himself the responsibility of accelerating the boy's education. Two months after Daisuke's death, the han confirmed Shōin's succession and appointed four men, including Tamaki, to represent the Yoshida house as instructors during his minority.[2]

Scholars who have examined Shōin's youth agree that his early education was both intense and severe.[3] Whether because of this severity or in spite of it, Shōin was remarkably responsive to his mentor's expansive instruction. By the age of eight he was ready to study Mencius, and Tamaki decided he could appear without disgrace at the han academy, the Meirinkan. So in the first month of 1838 Shōin donned his Confucian robe and went up to the Meirinkan as an apprentice instructor. He apparently performed adequately, because in November 1839, at the age of nine, he was vested with a provisional instructorship in Yamaga learning. The han then dismissed the four "representative instructors" who had served in his place and replaced them with three "supervisors," one of whom was the prominent official Yamada Uemon. At the same time Shōin also continued his studies at home and helped with the farming by which the Sugis supplemented their slender income.

The following year the Chōshū daimyo Mōri Takachika, just back from Edo, invited various teachers of the military and literary arts to the domainal castle. The Mōri were the descendants

---

* The Yamaga school of military studies was based on the theoretical writings of Yamaga Sokō, a political thinker who is best known as one of the initial formulators of Bushidō, the "Way of the Samurai." The traditional duties of the Yoshida house had to do with interpreting Yamaga's ideas, especially those embodied in the *Bukyō zensho* ("Complete Writings on Military Education," 1656). The founder of the Yoshida line, and Yoshida Shōin's lineal ancestor six generations back, was Yoshida Tomonosuke, who had studied with Yamaga Sokō's son, Fujisuke Takamoto. Tomonosuke was evidently given samurai status by Chōshū around 1700, well after the onset of the long Tokugawa Peace. Thus the Yoshida house never had held its rank by dint of military service in the remote past. The Yoshidas were samurai of the brush.

of the warlord Mōri Terumoto, who in earlier days had built a vast regime in western Japan by force of arms, founded Hiroshima as its capital, and fought as an equal against the Tokugawas. One of the daimyo's traditional duties was to keep morale in the domain high by periodically conferring his personal praise and encouragement on each of its official activities.

Shōin, who was now ten, went up to the castle with the others and delivered a lecture to Takachika on the *Bukyōzensho*, Yamaga Sokō's collection of essays on military strategy. Somewhat taken aback by the young boy's unexpected skill, Takachika, then only twenty-one himself, asked Shōin who had educated him. Shōin diffidently replied that Tamaki Bunnoshin had.[4] Twice thereafter, at two-year intervals, Takachika invited Shōin back to the palace to lecture on Yamaga's writings. At Takachika's request, the boy supplemented his performance on the first occasion by a demonstration of extemporaneous poetry and on the second by a lecture on Sun Tzu, the ancient Chinese writer on warfare.[5]

During Shōin's teens, his education continued under his han-appointed supervisors and such other teachers as the Meirinkan environment had to offer. In addition to the Chinese classics, he acquired a smattering of horsemanship, traditional gunnery, and Western bivouac techniques. Through his supervisor Yamada Uemon he is said to have gained his first knowledge of the Western presence in Asia.[6] In January 1848, at the age of eighteen, Shōin was promoted to the position of independent instructor at the Meirinkan. The school's buildings were scheduled for a complete renovation in 1849, and Shōin was probably consulted on this occasion, along with the other instructors. He took advantage of his newly acquired authority to present to the han government on 10/4/48 a lengthy opinion paper on the reform of the academy. This work marked the earliest expression of his major reformist interests.[7]

In 1850 Shōin left home to travel in Kyūshū for the purpose of broadening his experience.[8] For a three-month period he visited Hirado, Nagasaki, Kumamoto, and other cities. In Nagasaki, Dutch sailors invited him aboard their ship, showed him about, and afterward treated him to rum and bread. In Kumamoto, Shōin met and befriended Miyabe Teizō, a student of Western learning, who like Shōin would later become active in Bakumatsu politics.[9] Shōin also discovered in Kyūshū some of the classics of restorationism. Under the tutelage of another acquaintance, Hayama Sanai of Hirado, he read Aizawa Yasushi's *Shinron* ("New Thesis") and works by the radical reformers Takano Chōei, Watanabe Kazan, Rai Sanyō, and Ōshio Heihachirō. He read during his trip some eighty other volumes (*maki*) as well, on the Opium War, Western gunnery, and geography.[10]

By the last month of 1850, however, Shōin had returned to Hagi and the humdrum duties of a Yamaga military studies teacher. On 1/15/51 he formally initiated daimyo Mōri Takachika into the Yamaga school and received a crested cloak and some money in appreciation. In February he lectured to the daimyo on Confucius and submitted to the government a memorial "on avoidance of decay in the training of letters and arms."[11] Shōin's continued scholarly proximity to the daimyo suggests that he was close to the Chōshū governmental establishment in these years.

A new opportunity to escape routine presented itself only two months later when Shōin was allowed to accompany the daimyo's party to Edo to further his studies there. This stay in Edo would prove to be an extremely formative one for Shōin. Some of the foremost scholars and proponents of reform in the Bakumatsu period were in the metropolis at this time, and Shōin would meet a number of them while pursuing his education. He continued his Yamaga studies under the Edo master Yamaga Motomizu, studied swordsmanship with the Chōshū samurai Hiraoka Yasabei, and also took advantage of educational opportunities within the Chōshū han compound.

During this period Shōin sometimes went to visit Sakuma Shōzan, the celebrated teacher of Dutch studies and gunnery who had established his private school in Edo only the year before. Shōin was deeply impressed with Sakuma, the only man in his adult life that he would refer to as "my teacher" (*waga shi*). He summed up his perceptions of the great reformist scholar in a letter written in 1851 to his uncle and former tutor, Tamaki Bunnoshin: "The person called Sakuma Shōzan is an extraordinary man of really heroic proportions. . . . Those who enter his school to study gunnery he compels also to study the Chinese classics, and those who enter to study the Chinese classics he compels also to study gunnery." Sakuma had broad political interests, Shōin reported, and could read Western books, so well in fact that "he lectured from the original text."[12]

The intellectual competition and stimulation of the capital were much greater than any Shōin had known in Hagi, and he soon found himself wishing to expand his knowledge into several entirely new spheres. In a letter of 8/17/51 to his older brother Sugi Umetarō, he lamented that his "scholarship up to now had amounted to nothing more than distinguishing characters in a text." Three broad areas, he felt, demanded his further attention: history, Chinese classics, and military studies. He considered his prior historical studies to have been particularly inadequate. "To start with, I do not know one thing about history," he claimed. As for Confucian classics, Shōin proposed to study further the Four Books and Five Classics, as well as works from the T'ang, Sung, Ming, and Ch'ing. His third category, "military studies," was broad; it included "world studies" (*yochigaku*), gunnery, Western military writings, and mathematics.[13]

Shōin felt that to master these subjects he needed much more time. He asked his brother to petition the han government to allow him an extended period of freedom from his hereditary duties so that he could continue his studies in Edo. This letter was a milestone for Shōin. It marked the point at which the educational imperatives of the Sugi house had come to have a logic of their own that transcended the narrow feudal uses they were initially intended to serve. Indeed, they had perhaps begun already to serve a larger cause.

By his twenty-first year, Shōin had resolved to master a whole new body of learning that would span much of the human experience as his culture knew it. Although his ambitious intellectual pursuits at this time seem oddly disparate, future events would show that he was in fact striving to comprehend just one thing: the dynamics of political community. This was the key, the vital underlying theme, that linked such diverse areas as native histories, the ancient political philosophers, and Western military techniques; each of these would yield some truth about the way politics worked or could be influenced.

The first twenty years of Shōin's life represented an intense educational preparation. Always outdistancing his knowledge, however, was his curiosity, his compelling desire to understand still more. This trait, acquired somehow during the demanding years of his early youth, would in itself do much to shape his later destiny, in both its tragic and heroic dimensions.

FLIGHT

Although the Chōshū government showed little interest in the long-term continuance of Shōin's studies, he was still impatient for firm assurances that his education could progress. He therefore resolved to protest the han's unresponsiveness with an assertive gesture that, although unorthodox, was ultimately effective. On 12/14/51 he set out on a tour of northern Japan, to broaden further his knowledge of the country and his experience. He had been granted permission from the han authorities on 7/23 to make the trip, but departed nevertheless without waiting to receive a certificate of permission from the han government. This made him technically guilty of "fleeing the han" (dappan), a serious offense.

During his four-month trip to the Northeast, Shōin kept a journal in which his growing interest in the diverse aspects of political community was constantly evident.[14] He spent a month in Mito, visiting with the elderly political thinker Aizawa Yasushi and others, then set out toward the northwest, accompanied now by his old acquaintance Miyabe Teizō.[15] At Sado Island, on 2/29, Shōin took the trouble to "shed his coat" and "enter the shafts" of the great Sado gold mine to see exactly how the mining operations were carried on.[16] He and Teizō then went north along the coast to Akita, where Shōin noted that the price of rice was low while all other prices were high, a condition that worked great hardship on the agriculturalists there. They proceeded to Nambu han, where Shōin observed the famous horses raised in this territory and noted how they were marketed to ensure governmental profit.

By 3/5 they reached Tappizaki on the Hokkaidō straits. Although the straits were only eight miles wide, foreign ships sailed through freely, and Shōin was surprised and dismayed that they were allowed to do so without any recognition of the authorities through whose waters they passed. He then visited five Japanized Ainu villages in the same vicinity. "These Ainu are people," he candidly recorded. Despite their distinctive racial characteristics, they were not essentially different from ordinary Japanese people. He felt that with appropriate education the native peoples of Hokkaidō and the northern islands could be fully assimilated into the Japanese population.[17]

This series of seemingly insignificant observations is important for an assessment of Shōin's political attitudes. Shōin's journal shows that he had a keen and tireless interest in the conduct of public affairs. His methodical notations were the work, not of a romantic who ignored political reality, but rather of a man who walked the length of the country to observe firsthand the diversity of political realities that the realm had to offer.

Shōin and Teizō returned to Edo early in the fourth month, by way of Sendai and Wakamatsu. Shōin stayed inconspicuously in the city until 4/10, then turned himself in to the han authorities at Chōshū's Sakurada compound. For deserting the han he was ordered to return immediately to Hagi and to confine himself to the Sugi house until further disposition should be made of his case.[18] He arrived in Hagi on 5/12/52 and took up a life of confinement in the Sugi household. He had been traveling or living in Edo almost continuously for twenty months, during the course of which he had toured on foot what was then the whole country, from Nagasaki to Aomori.

In the end, Shōin's flight to the Northeast proved costly but successful. On 12/9/52 the han government announced his penalty: he would lose his samurai status and the stipend of 57 koku that went with it, and his father Sugi Yūrinosuke would be appointed his guardian. The daimyo himself is said to have felt regret for Shōin's dappan, however. He and his advisers probably understood what Shōin was trying to do. He therefore took Yūrinosuke aside, admonished him for his son's behavior, and then granted Shōin ten years of leisure in which he might study freely in any part of the country.[19]

By his defiant conduct Shōin had finally elicited some tacit cooperation from the han government in his effort to throw off his humdrum house duties and enter a more challenging intellectual world. He would thereafter have the opportunity to live his life in intellectual terms that were not confined by narrow hereditary obligation.

After the daimyo formally gave his approval on 1/16/53 for Shōin to "study abroad," Shōin was on his way to Edo within ten days. He made this trip, too, last several months, and used the time as before to learn of persons and things along the way. On 5/24 Shōin arrived in Edo, where he immediately set about renewing his contacts, especially with Sakuma Shōzan, the scholar to whom he had been most drawn during his earlier stay in the metropolis in 1851.[20] His object was to seek new horizons in learning, and soon after his arrival an astounding opportunity to do this seemed to open before him.

BOARDING PERRY'S FLAGSHIP

Shōin's entering the capital at this time would enable him to participate in one of the most extraordinary dramas in Japan's modern history—the arrival of Commodore Perry. He would take part in this event not only as an earnest observer but also as a would-be passenger. Nothing better reveals Shōin's ultimate commitment to political knowledge than his carefully planned but still hazardous attempt in 1854 to study in America.

On 6/3/53 four ships of the American Pacific squadron under Commodore Matthew Perry steamed into Edo Bay and dropped anchor at Uraga. Their purpose was to open Japan to Western

influence, by force if necessary, and to secure Japanese cooperation in accommodating the growing needs of American navigation
in the Pacific. So when Shōin paid a routine call at Sakuma Shōzan's school on 6/4, he was astonished to hear that Sakuma had
already left with some of his students to inspect the black ships
at Uraga. Shōin hastened after them and then remained on the
coast with Sakuma for almost a week, scrutinizing the equipment
and activities of the Americans.[21] For several more weeks thereafter he reflected on what this foreign intrusion might mean for
Japan's future.

Two months after the Uraga experience Shōin presented to the
Chōshū daimyo a memorial entitled "Some Confidential Advice"
("Shokyū shigen"), in which he revised some of the reforms he had
proposed for Chōshū in 1848 so that for the first time they would
be applicable to national institutions.[22] This event appears to be
of little significance compared to the fact of Perry's arrival; yet it
was part of a reformist impulse that would later have a massive
impact on Japanese society, an impact with even more intrinsic
significance, perhaps, than Perry's appearance itself.

Shōin grasped another opportunity at this time that went beyond the submission of memorials. Sakuma Shōzan had long considered the desirability of sending students to the West. He now
applied to the Bakufu for permission to do this, through his friend
Kawaji Toshiakira, a Bakufu superintendent of finance. Sakuma
submitted to Kawaji a list of promising candidates that included
Yoshida Shōin's name. When the Bakufu's response was negative,
Sakuma and Shōin resolved that Shōin should go to study in the
West in spite of Bakufu intransigence, a gesture that, though not
without risk, would at the very least force the issue into open public debate.[23]

Sakuma provided money for Shōin's trip, and gave him a poem
of encouragement on 9/18/53. Shōin then set out for Nagasaki,
where he hoped to take passage with Putiatin's fleet, which had
recently put in there. He missed the Russians by several days and
arrived back in Edo in December. One benefit of this Nagasaki

trip was that he had been able to renew his friendship and discuss reformist ideas at length with Yokoi Shōnan and Miyabe Teizō, with whom he stayed for six days in Kumamoto.[24]

The American squadron returned to Shimoda in the spring, and on the night of 3/27/54, after elaborate preparation, Shōin rowed out to Perry's flagship and boarded. Wearing his best kimono, polished, polite, and doing his best to please, he requested that he be taken to America and allowed to study there. Although he made a very favorable impression on the expedition's translator, S. Wells Williams, the Americans, unable to make up their minds whether Shōin was acting out of admiration for America or as a Bakufu spy, put him back ashore under cover of darkness in the small hours of the morning.[25]

Shōin, frustrated, was determined nevertheless to force the Bakufu to come to grips in public discussion with the impropriety of its emigration laws, a result he achieved the next day by giving himself up. Going abroad to study, salutary as it might appear, was a capital offense. Sakuma Shōzan's poem of encouragement was found among Shōin's effects, and Sakuma, too, was promptly arrested.[26]

Sakuma Shōzan and his student were soon summoned to appear before the Bakufu's interrogators. Sakuma, a sometime adviser to the shogunate, did not apologize for the rash act of his student as expected but instead voiced unequivocal criticism of the Bakufu's rigid and anachronistic emigration policy. Although impressed by the sincerity of this distinguished and articulate scholar, the interrogators recommended execution. At this point, however, Sakuma's friend Kawaji Toshiakira intervened and obtained clemency for the two men. In September both were released to house arrest in their respective han, a lenient punishment for an emigration attempt. On 9/18 Shōin was turned over to his own domain and moved to Chōshū's Azabu Hall.[27]

During their five-month imprisonment in Edo, Shōin the activist and Sakuma the reformer were placed in adjoining cells separated only by bars. Though scholars by calling, they were not allowed books or paper in prison, and they relied on each other's company to pass the time. For five months, day and night, they were together in the most inescapable sense, and they absorbed many of each other's ideas. After they were released to different authorities and separated, Shōin wrote a long apologia for his conduct called the "Record from Prison" ("Yūshūroku"), and Sakuma wrote one called the "Record of My Errors" ("Seikenroku"). Perhaps not surprisingly, long passages in these two works were similar in both expression and content.

It has been customary in the past to make a distinction between rational reformers like Sakuma Shōzan and romantic extremists like Yoshida Shōin. Drawing a sharp analytical line between these two men may be misleading, however. Their close cooperation in 1853 and 1854 suggests that whatever their later differences in political style, both men shared the same reformist goals, just as both shared the same scholarly vocation. Shōin's students, too, would maintain close ties with Sakuma even after their teacher's death.

A compatibility of goals is strongly indicated, for example, by Sakuma's response to Shōin's "Record from Prison" of 11/54. In this work Shōin suggested several fairly drastic innovations, including moving the Bakufu government to Kyoto and establishing there a new national academy to teach Western languages and technology. When he was finally shown a copy of these startling recommendations in 8/55, Sakuma replied in this way: "While in prison I wrote the 'Record of My Errors.' . . . Now Shōin has sent me his 'Record from Prison.' The concepts in it are entirely the same as mine. Ah, while separated by three thousand miles, he has had thoughts like my own such as I had not hoped for. . . . His having progressed so far was unimaginable."[28] Shōin the romantic extremist and Sakuma the rational reformer had more in common than has sometimes been supposed.

Shōin was allowed to remain in Edo for only a few weeks before the han authorities sent him back to Hagi, this time rather inelegantly in a prisoner's portable cage. Shōin's literary education served him well on this occasion. He passed the long days on the road by composing poetry for himself, fifty-seven pieces in all—an unusual pastime for a criminal in transit.[29]

Yet Shōin's conduct, viewed strictly as the activity of a student and scholar, was also unusual: he had broken the law. He did so because he had a breadth of vision and a desire for new knowledge that went beyond that of all but very few of his contemporaries. More than others, too, he seems to have harbored a certain dauntlessness. He risked the Bakufu's ire if he failed to reach America, and faced the certainty of other hardships if he succeeded. Perhaps the accelerated educational experiences of Shōin's earliest years had accustomed him to making large personal sacrifices in pursuit of learning. But whatever his innermost rationale, there is no question that access to a new community of truth in the West was his objective, and that in his quest for it he betrayed no lack of physical or psychological courage.

SHŌIN IN PRISON

After his emigration attempt, Shōin spent fourteen months in prison. The long, uninterrupted days of this period allowed Shōin to achieve an intensity of scholarly concentration unsurpassed by any other interval in his life. An examination of his work during these months shows the extent to which his determination to explore all aspects of political knowledge had by this time reached a mature phase.

The Bakufu had been lenient when it sentenced Shōin for his attempt to leave the country in 1854. It prescribed that the offenders, a half-dozen including suspected accomplices, be released to their respective domains and placed under house arrest rather than be executed as required by Bakufu law. Although Sakuma was allowed to return to his home by the Matsushiro government, Chōshū authorities placed Shōin in Noyama prison in October 1854, and held him there for over a year.[30]

During his stay in prison, Yoshida Shōin sought to expand his intellectual frontiers with a systematic rigor. He kept lists filling several short volumes of the titles he read, and these monthly bibliographies seem to have replaced diaries during the period of his imprisonment, perhaps because apart from his scholarship all of his days were the same. He explored a remarkable quantity of material: 106 volumes in his first nine weeks, then 512 more by the time of his release in 12/55, or about 40 volumes per month. His brother Umetarō carried books in and out of prison by the armful.[31] Shōin's readings included works by the reformist thinkers Aizawa Yasushi, Rai Sanyō, and Fujita Tōko, and also works dealing with the West, especially Wei Yüan's *Gazetteer of Maritime Nations* (*Hai-kuo t'u-chih*), which he cited repeatedly. Miscellaneous items from the classical corpus appeared on Shōin's lists, including T'ang and Sung poets and the ancient military writer Sun Tzu.[32]

Above all else, however, Shōin was preoccupied with fundamental questions of political theory. He read widely in Mencius, read Chu Hsi, and examined various commentaries on Mencius and on Confucius' *Analects*. Innumerable histories of China, Japan, and even the West found a place in his bibliographic catalog.[33] Shōin seems to have studied the history of polity in the same spirit that an architect studies the history of architecture, that is, in order to achieve a sense of its potentialities. Many of these works would find their way in later years into the curriculum of Shōin's renowned private academy, the Shōka Sonjuku.

If Shōin's readings during his months at Noyama were substantial, so were his writings, and even his personal contacts with other scholars. From prison he sent papers to Kido Kōin, Miyabe Teizō, and many others. He left a lengthy collection of essays, of which his "Questions and Answers in Prison" ("Gokusha mondō") was one of the better known. Shōin also wrote his "Record from Prison" during this period. The "Record," completed late in 1854, was an apologia for his efforts to go abroad, supplemented with broad suggestions for reform and with some imperial history.[34] In addition, he had some contact with his acquaintance Gesshō, the "coastal defense" priest, in 3/55, and later conducted a furious exchange of ideas with the loyalist priest Utsunomiya Mokurin, who came to Hagi on 9/13.[35]

Naturally enough, Shōin also gradually discovered his fellow prisoners, of whom there were eleven in the compact prison. He established mutual instruction among them as a means of filling the time. He chose two of the men with the requisite skills to lead the others in poetry sessions, and had a third teach calligraphy. Shōin participated in these classes himself as a student. Nor did he abandon the friends he made in prison when he left Noyama. The jailer's son he welcomed as a student at his school, and he later was responsible for the release of several of the inmates who had been kept immured in Noyama mostly by official neglect.[36]

When Shōin's moods or his companions' questions moved him to do so, he talked informally about public events or about the classics that he read. Although these discussions probably began as a way to alleviate the general boredom, Shōin was soon describing them as "lectures on Mencius." By 6/13/55 these talks had become a regular lecture series with a momentum of their own, as Shōin related successive passages from Mencius to current issues and events and used Mencian rationale to advocate far-reaching institutional reforms. He cited Mencian doctrine to justify the overthrow of governments that ignored the people's needs, and made the case that persons of ability from all over Japan should be recruited into the government of Chōshū han in order to improve the welfare of the people.

Shōin's lectures were exciting for the lecturer and for the listeners as well. So compelling were they that even the jailer and his son attended. When Shōin presented copies of these talks to Yamagata Taika, the most prominent Neo-Confucian scholar in Chōshū, Yamagata found them so well grounded in orthodox arguments, and yet so inflammatory, that he undertook to refute the whole series, passage by passage. Shōin was beginning to make his mark now. His ideological impact was, if anything, greater after he became a prisoner than it had been when he was an official full-time scholar.[37]

THE SHŌKA SONJUKU

In the three years following his release from Noyama in 12/55, Shōin would reach the pinnacle of his career as an educator. In those years he would establish his celebrated private academy, the Shōka Sonjuku. The quality of instruction there would reveal the values he held most dear and confirm his own identity. It was through his activities at the Shōka Sonjuku more than in any other realm that Yoshida Shōin would earn his place in history.

One of the major questions that confront scholars investigating Shōin's life, that of whether he had any specific influence on the Restoration outcome, can be resolved only with respect to his activities at the Sonjuku. Ultimately the academy proved to be the sole viable instrument of Shōin's political will. Whether or not he effectively shaped the conduct of Restoration activists and statesmen can be assessed only by examining who his students were, and what and how he actually taught them.

Another analytical difficulty that Shōin's biographers have faced is that of reconciling the conflicting images of Shōin as a highly emotional extremist on the one hand and as a mild-mannered scholar on the other. Much light may be shed on this question, too, by scrutinizing the mixture of charismatic loyalty, political engagement, and rigorous scholarship that Shōin cultivated among his students at the Sonjuku.

When Shōin was released from prison into domiciliary arrest at the Sugi house on 12/15/55, he took over the educational functions that had intermittently been carried on there, and the name under which they were performed: *Shōka sonjuku*, the "Private Academy of the Village Under the Pines." The first Sonjuku had been run by Tamaki Bunnoshin from 1842 until 1848, when official duties prevented him from teaching. In 1853 the name Shōka Sonjuku was adopted by Shōin's maternal uncle Kubo Gorōemon for the small private classes he was teaching at his nearby home in Matsumoto. After Shōin's release, some of the young people who had been studying with Kubo began to visit him for educational help. Shōin's counseling role was gradually expanded until all the functions of the little academy at Kubo's were transferred to him at the Sugi compound.[38] In order to accommodate the growing number of pupils, the Sugis refurbished a storage cabin near their house for use as a school.[39]

The philosophy of education that Shōin wished to implement at the Sonjuku is reflected in a set of principles he wrote at the time. In 1855, while Shōin was still in prison, his cousin and student Tamaki Hikosuke (1841–65) wrote to him concerning his coming-of-age ceremony and queried him about the "way of the adult." Shōin wrote in response a thoughtful set of maxims, "The Seven Principles of a Gentleman" ("Shiki shichi-soku"). The first two of these dealt with the supreme importance of loyalty to community, in general and in particular. The remaining five were concerned with justice, honesty, and sociability:

3. Nothing is more important than justice for the way of the gentleman *(shi)*. Justice is brought about by courage, and courage grows when one stands for what is just.
4. Honesty and avoidance of deception are important to the conduct of the gentleman. To cover errors by artifice is a cause for shame. Rather all should dispense fairness.
5. One who is not versed in mankind's past and present, who does not take the sages as one's teachers, is just a bumpkin. To become intimate with the sages' writings is something a true gentleman *(kunshi)* does.
6. In order to achieve virtue and advance one's ability, much advantage lies in enjoying the friendship of many exemplary persons. Therefore the true gentleman places a high value on broad acquaintanceship.
7. Observe the principle of the phrase "die and then give up." Cleave indomitably to perseverance and achievement. Otherwise one's life will be devoid of grace and skill *(jutsu naki nari)*.[40]

These "Principles" almost certainly corresponded to the virtues Shōin sought to instill in his students at the Sonjuku. A gentleman, according to Shōin's maxims, was a man who was loyal to his country and family, just, honest, literate, sociable, and determined. What Shōin described in these few lines seems to have been an idealized version of a certain type of person whose vocation lay in the sphere of public service. The living models for this ideal, of course, would have been the administrators and scholars that he knew, men like his father Yūrinosuke or his uncle Tamaki Bunnoshin.

The gentleman that Shōin evoked had to delicately maintain many, and sometimes conflicting, virtues. For example, the gentleman had to be highly literate in the classics, the "writings of the sages," yet harbor no ambivalence of competing ideas when the time came to "stand for what is just." The standards by which Shōin measured a gentleman were comprehensive. He required not only that a man be devoted to his community but that he be resolute in action as well as capable of thought.

Moreover, Shōin regarded these virtues as existing independently of social rank. A prospective student could expect no relaxation of the instructor's high standards on account of his lineage. Shōin ignored samurai rank in the admission of students to his school and in the treatment of them after admission. The sons of farmers and craftsmen attended as well as samurai of the lowest ranks.

The young men who came to the Shōka Sonjuku collided immediately with the rigorous standards that Shōin derived from his ideal image of the gentleman as public servant. A few of them, like Kusaka Genzui, a hereditary physician of low rank, were eager for political action but gave little thought to deliberative preparation or practical strategy. These wished to "stand for what is just" without first investigating what "justice" in a given situation was. In 1856, after returning from his own trip around Kyūshū, where the reformer Miyabe Teizō had told him about Shōin, Kusaka wrote to him, seeking admission to the Sonjuku: "I was born in the country of Japan, and I eat the rice of Japan. Therefore I am Japanese. Nonetheless, Japan at present is pitiful. . . . I think the time has come when we might well kill the American envoy and show a firm attitude. What do you think of this?"[41] Shōin's reply was blunt: "Your argument drifts and the sense of it is shallow. . . . In the world in every place and for every person, there are things that must be done. . . . If you do not consider this, and haughtily offer great plans for the realm, even with mouth afire and lips aflame, I do not see what good it will do. It is on this point that your argument drifts."[42]

Shōin buttressed this with another letter to Kusaka six weeks later. He made explicit the passion for thorough observation, pragmatism, and careful deliberation that would characterize the activities of the Sonjuku group in the years ahead, and of which a more mature Kusaka would be the foremost practitioner: "Great men in arranging the affairs of the realm . . . place a high premium on accomplishing their purpose, and therefore perfect their strategies, observe the dynamics of the time, and familiarize themselves in detail with real opportunities. . . . I want you to open your heart and your mind, to depart from the abuse of empty words, and to return to the realm of practice."[43] Kusaka did not understand the dependence of action on thought, a defect Shōin intended to correct.

Much more common than students of Kusaka's type, however, were young men who were interested in cultivating the intellect but who gave no real thought to their public responsibilities. Watanabe Kōzō, one of Shōin's students who later entered the Meiji government, described this phenomenon in later years:

> When students came to [Shōin] for the first time he would invariably ask for what purpose they wished to study. They would usually reply that they could not read adequately and wished to develop this skill. To this the teacher would reply, "It will not do to become a scholar. It is real action that is of utmost importance for a person. If you apply yourself to your studies and at the same time devote yourself to real affairs, you will come naturally to be able to read." The word "real action" (*jikkō*) was constantly on his lips.[44]

Shōin told his new students in plain terms that scholarship was of value not for itself but for the impact it would enable a man to have on real affairs. Here again he was determined to make clear the dynamic relationship between thought and action. The course of action chosen must proceed from investigation and thought, and the courses of thought one chose must be selected according to, and assimilated in terms of, their applicability in real affairs. Both scholarship and action were to be used to achieve desirable results in the world, an imperative that was based in turn on loyalty to the community.

An appreciation for the interdependence of thought and action, and a readiness to use both for the amelioration of society, would prove in later years to be important attributes of the activists who came out of the Sonjuku experience. These men would strive successfully in the 1860's and 1870's to restructure the entire political community. It is not unlikely that their fitness for this task derived in large measure from their uncompromising exposure at the Shōka Sonjuku to Yoshida Shōin's multifaceted ideal of the true gentleman.

LIFE IN THE SONJUKU

Much may be learned about the style and character of education at the Sonjuku by considering the routine, the attitudes, and the habits that Shōin fostered there. Although life at the school had many sides, there was a certain order to it, and the key to that order was Shōin's vision of what he wanted his students to become. How, then, did Shōin translate his complex ideal into educational practice?

Despite the stern attitude that Shōin took toward new students, many young men came to study with him, more than seventy in all. According to the student Watanabe Kōzō, this was in part because of the prevailing belief that a course of study at Shōin's school would help one obtain a satisfactory post in the government. Among the Hagi public, Shōin's reputation as a scholar was justifiably high. He had been a child prodigy at the Meirinkan, was unusually well traveled, and had studied with some of the foremost scholars in Edo. For an ambitious young samurai, an occasional appearance at Shōin's school was probably de rigueur.[45]

Shōin assumed that the young men who came to him would be responsibly self-motivated, and avoided petty regulation. When a student arrived at the Sonjuku in the morning, he greeted the instructor, and when he left for the day he repeated this courtesy. These two gestures were the only formal ceremony at the school. Students could even come and go as they wished. The elaborate and carefully graded ritual observances practiced at the Meirinkan were conspicuously absent from the Sonjuku, though many of the

Sonjuku students, because of their rank, either were or had been enrolled at the Meirinkan.[46]

The schedule at the Sonjuku varied from day to day according to Shōin's estimation of the students' needs. On some days he lectured to them. Most of the time, however, the students read independently. With the instructor's guidance, each student chose his own texts from the books housed at the Sonjuku or from the library of his own family. The students would then read on their own, and Shōin would go from one to another, giving assistance or advice.[47]

Shōin's selection of materials was highly eclectic, reflecting his desire to give his wards the broadest intellectual exposure possible. The Sonjuku curriculum spanned what had become the three standard cultural spheres of progressive Bakumatsu scholarship: Chinese learning, Japanese learning, and Western learning. In the field of the Chinese classics, Shōin used Confucius' *Analects* and Mencius, commentaries by both Chu Hsi and Wang Yang-ming, and also discussions of the classics by Itō Jinsai, Ogyū Sorai, and many other Japanese writers of his own era. For Japanese studies Shōin used especially Motoori Norinaga's *Kojiki den*, but also the Mito scholars and the works of Rai Sanyō. As for affairs of the West, Shōin used as his point of departure Wei Yüan's *Gazetteer of Maritime Nations*.[48] This curriculum mirrored, of course, Shōin's own wide-ranging readings of earlier years.

The instructor encouraged his students to practice composition. "People who read books should spend half of their mental energy writing," he would say. To enhance his own prose style, Shōin read endless volumes of poetry, and he urged his students to emulate this habit as well. The composition of poetry, however, was not encouraged at the Sonjuku, because, like playing chess, practicing the tea ceremony, and painting, it was "an elegant accomplishment" with aristocratic overtones and of no practical use. Nevertheless, Shōin himself was quick at the writing of poetry. For him personally his taste for composing verse evidently outweighed his distaste for poetry's aristocratic associations.[49]

Shōin's concentration on texts was complemented by his interest in maps. He taught his wards to read political history while looking at a map, so that they might comprehend "changes past and present, far or near," in detail. "There are no men divorced from the earth and no events divorced from men," he told them. "If you want to study human affairs, first look at the geography involved."[50]

Scholarly activities at the Sonjuku were sometimes interrupted by animated discussions of history or the classics, which could go on until dawn. At other times Shōin would encourage the students to take him on in informal argument: "There were dry fields around the Sugi house. In the spring and summer the teacher would go out to remove the weeds, and the students would all follow along to help. While weeding, the teacher would carry on discussions of reading methods or of history. He could not easily prevail over his students in these discussions, and that is what he enjoyed."[51] However formidable he may have been in these sessions, the overall impression Shōin left on his students was one of gentleness and courtesy. According to the student and Meiji bureaucrat Watanabe Kōzō, "He never used harsh words and was not a person to joke at others' expense. He was a gentle person. . . . I know of no occasion on which he became angry. He was kind toward people, was open, and used courteous language toward everyone."[52] Yoshida Shōin was mild-mannered in his daily relationships. Watanabe pointed out that he wrote reproofs more easily than he spoke them, however. It should be remembered, too, that Shōin's mild disposition would not prevent him from later advocating political operations that were bold and assertive in the extreme.

Shōin's popularity as an educator reflected in part his skillful use of positive reinforcement. On one occasion a student privately told Shōin of his fears that his memory was inferior to that of the others: "The teacher replied that memory came naturally on repetition and that scholarship like other enterprises ought not be done hastily. Moreover, he said, those who remembered well at first had a disadvantage in that they tended to become lazy at reviewing."[53] Shōin used this occasion of a student's serious self-doubts to administer a large dose of encouragement laced with good advice.

Another anecdote in this vein further reveals Shōin's educational style. The instructor was "chary of time" and eager that all of his students make the best possible use of the leisure they had. During the long New Year's holiday, a student named Okada Kōsaku, at ten the youngest of the Sonjuku students, came to the school in search of a book. Shōin showed openly that he was impressed with the lad's diligence and gave him a special selection. Later on he made a point of praising him warmly in the presence of the others.[54]

There were several diversions from the academic regimen in the Sonjuku. One of these was lunch. Each student was expected to bring a lunchbox. When one did not, he would start for home at lunchtime. At just that moment Shōin would appear and invite the student to join the Sugis in the family kitchen. "The Sugi house busied itself actively out of solicitude for such matters."[55]

The Sugi family provided the Sonjuku students with a building, books, and an instructor, in addition to occasional meals. The students, instead of paying regular fees, were expected to assist in whatever farm work Shōin himself usually did. That meant weeding, threshing, and doing occasional errands.[56] The weeding and threshing were more than just a way of helping out the Sugi family: Shōin regarded this kind of work as a part of the students' program of physical exercise, and he saw to it that they applied themselves to such activities frequently.[57]

For Shōin, physical education was not equated with swordsmanship; so he did not demand a growing proficiency in fencing from his students as the domainal academies did. Instead he was concerned to teach them elementary Western infantry formations and the manual of arms.

Shōin emphasized Western arms and methods of encampment. . . . The teacher, leading his students, would line them up beside the house or along a riverbank, and with bamboo poles in place of guns, he would teach them the ways of drilling with a rifle. At such times the teacher himself would give the commands. When the students went as far as

Obata [a suburb northeast of Hagi] to practice, the teacher could not go along, being under house arrest. Sometimes the students were led by Iida Seihaku [the eldest of them].[58]

This regular drill may explain why the Kiheitai paramilitary units formed by Takasugi and other Sonjuku students later on in 1863 would be organized swiftly and smoothly along the lines of Western rifle companies.

Another departure from strictly academic activity was provided by the many visitors to the Sonjuku: "The instructor's acquaintanceship was extremely broad. . . . It was not simply confined to scholars, but included doctors, painters, experts in the military arts, and Shinto and Buddhist priests. As for farmers, artisans, and merchants, men from among them of enthusiasm or of developed proficiency, men who excelled in their ability or craft, all of these did not refrain from visiting the instructor."[59] Shōin, like most alert educators, understood that broad socializing was an essential part of "advancing one's ability." During the Sonjuku years he shared his acquaintances with his students as a part of their education. Sometimes he would send them elsewhere to learn from other lecturers, as he once did when the priest Gesshō gave a temple lecture series in Hagi.[60]

The activities carried out at the Shōka Sonjuku were highly diverse. They ranged from "association with exemplary persons" to rifle drill to Confucian learning. Yet this disparate program had a certain internal coherence. Each part of it, in one way or another, helped prepare a man for public service. Association with others brought not only an accustomed ease in socializing but also a means of broadening one's awareness and many friendly personal contacts that might serve as a basis for joining forces later on. Military drill helped preserve physical stamina, nourished a confident esprit, and imparted a basic knowledge of some of the mechanics of military force, force being always a potential policy instrument. At the same time, Shōin set an example of gentleness for his students, probably as a matter of personal disposition but perhaps also so that they might learn the patience and tolerance necessary for the smooth operation of any joint enterprise.

Above all, Shōin strove to impart to his students the knowledge and the intellectual skills that they might later find essential. He exposed them to a wide range of scholarship, encouraged them to develop their capacity for written expression, and taught them to sharpen their articulateness in brisk discussions. In so doing, he made the Shōka Sonjuku a school for public men, regarded by the han's ambitious young and many others as a stepping-stone to high office in the domain.

SCHOLARS AND PHYSICIANS

Members of the Shōka Sonjuku shared certain attributes that make it possible to view them as a distinctive social category, even though the often-used term "lower-class samurai" does not adequately describe what this social category was. Almost all of the students came from the ranks of Chōshū's austere and highly educated service strata. A careful examination of the social composition of the Shōka Sonjuku may furnish the key not only to the motives of the Chōshū activists but also to the constellation of loyalties and interests that propelled the Restoration movement as a whole.

Most of the Sonjuku students either came from the families of professional administrators, physicians, or priests, or had full samurai rank with less than 200 koku of income, or both. A rank with less than 200 koku usually meant in itself that a samurai had been given a rigorous literary education such as might fit him for an administrative or other service post.

To gain a clearer sense of what this rank of less than 200 koku meant, it will be helpful to review the structure of the samurai hierarchy in Chōshū (see Table 1). Chōshū had some 11,000 samurai altogether: just over 2,700 samurai proper (shi), some 3,000 foot soldiers (sotsu), and about 5,700 rear vassals (baishin). These same samurai had stipends that ranged from zero to 16,000 koku of rice. Within the top category of shi there were seventeen further gradations, each with a different number of members and sometimes a considerable range of income within the rank.[61] The most preferred positions in the domain were reserved for shi

TABLE I

The Samurai Hierarchy in Chōshū

Rank and rank grouping	No. of families	Income range in koku[a]
1–17. Shi (SAMURAI PROPER)		
1. Ichimon (daimyo houses)	6	
2. Eidai karō (elders)	2	6,000–16,000
3. Yorigumi (Near Group)	62	250–5,000
4. Ōgumi (Great Group)[b]	1,378	40–1,600
With over 100 koku	569	101–1,600
With under 100 koku	809	40–100
5. Funategumi	29	
6. Enkintsuki	216	13–105
7. Jishagumi	87	
8. Takajō	7	
9. Mukyūdōri	512	10–100
10. Sentō	50	
11. Zempu	25	
12. Edo Kachi	75	
13. Chi Kachi	55	
14. Sanjūnindōri	55	10–40
15. Jinsō	39	
16. Ōsaka sentō	1	
17. Shiko	118	10–40
TOTAL	2,717	10–16,000
18. Sotsu (FOOT SOLDIERS, ashigaru, chūgen)	2,958	0–10
TOTAL shi AND sotsu	5,675	0–16,000
19. Baishin (REAR VASSALS)[c]	ca. 5,700	
GRAND TOTAL	ca. 11,000	0–16,000

SOURCES: Yoshida Shōin zenshū, ed. Yamaguchi ken kyōiku kai, 12 vols. (Tokyo, 1940), 5: 99–100; Suematsu Kenchō, Bōchō kaitenshi, 2 vols. (Tokyo, 1967 [1921]), 1: 13–14; Kimura Motoi, "Hagi han zaichi kashin dan ni tsuite," Shigaku zasshi, 62, no. 8 (Aug. 1953): 27–50.
[a]Data on income are unavailable for rank nos. 5, 7, 8, 10, 11, 12, 13, 15, 16, and 19.
[b]The breakdown into "over 100 koku" and "under 100 koku" was made by Suematsu Kenchō in 1921. My own research suggests that the politically crucial dividing line was in the range of 200–400 koku: families with over 400 koku clearly tended to oppose reform; families with under 200 clearly tended to support it; families with between 200 and 400 koku might support or oppose. See below, pp. 184–92.
[c]Some baishin had incomes that were quite high, i.e. their hierarchy mirrored that of the main han. On the whole, however, their incomes were lower than those of the corresponding main group categories.

of Near Group rank (yorigumi) and for the most highly stipended persons in the Great Group stratum, namely, those receiving more than 200 koku. These positions were preferred both because they required little toil and because the prestige and material benefits they conferred were lavish. Few shi were eligible for these lucrative posts, so that they were in practice the hereditary prerogative of a few aristocratic families.

Beneath these privileged few were much larger numbers of "lower" shi, several thousand families, who actually carried on the business of the domain. Such persons received less than 200 koku of income, and most received under 100 koku. The Sonjuku students who were samurai came from these lower staff echelons. At this lower level, available candidates outnumbered positions in a much greater proportion, and appointment depended on actual competence. In other words, most shi with only modest hereditary stipends, if they wished their houses to survive, were forced into a frantic competition for posts. Although these posts were at the middle and lower levels of the administration where the actual work was done, they were not well remunerated. Still, the importance of this work was understood, and it was considered an honor to hold such a position. In the process of this demanding vocational competition, almost all of the modestly stipended samurai involved in it acquired intensely professional skills and attitudes, including an interest in enterprises like the Shōka Sonjuku.*

Men of shi rank, of high income or low (but no other social group), were automatically admitted to the domainal academy, the Meirinkan, at public expense. There they were taught the "literary and martial arts." There they became engaged in the intellectual competition that would determine whether they received an official post or not, and there also the crucial question was decided of whether a young man's family stipend would be significantly increased or drastically reduced during his lifetime. His family's very livelihood was at stake. Consequently, men of full samurai rank but penuriously small stipends had both a great incentive and an exceptional opportunity to develop difficult

* Although no thorough study of recruitment patterns and rank in Chōshū is currently available, the configuration described here conforms closely to the configuration that John Hall has described for Okayama, and that probably prevailed in all late Tokugawa domains. See John W. Hall, "The Ikeda House and Its Retainers in Bizen," in John W. Hall and Marius B. Jansen, eds., *Studies in the Institutional History of Early Modern Japan* (Princeton, N.J., 1968), p. 87.

literary and technical skills. Shi rank with a low stipend meant that a person was extremely likely to have subjected himself to a starkly competitive professional education. In light of this situation, let us consider the Sonjuku students' social origins. The fullest available list of Sonjuku students is Shōin's account of who dined with the Sugi family on what days.[62] Umihara Tōru, in a recent book, has identified seventy-two of these students (see Table 2). His list reveals that forty were shi with stipends of less than 200 koku, whereas thirteen were sotsu and baishin, classes that were also partially educated and profes-

TABLE 2

Social Origins of Seventy-two Shōka Sonjuku Students

Rank (samurai) or vocation (non-samurai)	Number	Percent[a]
SAMURAI		
Shi		
Ōgumi[b]	27[c]	37.5%
Ichidai enkin	3	4.2
Jishagumi	4	5.6
Mukyūdōri	5	6.9
Sanjūnindōri	1	1.4
TOTAL *shi*	40	55.6%
Sotsu		
Ashigaru (kumi moto)	4	5.6%
Chūgen (kuramoto tsuki)	1	1.4
Baishin		
Baishin, chihōgumi, and misc.	8	11.1
TOTAL *sotsu* AND *baishin*	13	18.1%
NON-SAMURAI[d]		
Han physicians	3	4.2%
Private physicians	3	4.2
Priests	3	4.2
Townsmen (*chōnin*)	4	5.6
Unclear	6	8.3
TOTAL NON-SAMURAI	19	26.5%

SOURCE: Table 18 in Umihara Tōru, *Meiji ishin to kyōiku* (Tokyo, 1972).
[a]Percentages do not total 100, because of rounding.
[b]Under 200 koku of income.
[c]Includes two "han samurai" (*hanshi*).
[d]Includes persons who may be samurai but identify themselves by other than samurai rank.

sionalized even though their members were not automatically admitted to the Meirinkan. The rest were physicians, priests, and townsmen.[63]

Kurihara Ryūichi and Umetani Noboru have also described the social origins of the Sonjuku students. Kurihara explored the background of thirty-two students who subsequently became politically active and found that thirteen were samurai of shi rank, thirteen were of lesser samurai rank (four being *ashigaru*, three *chūgen*, and six baishin), and six were non-samurai (two being from han physician families, two from private physician families, and one each from families of potters and fish dealers).* Umetani has listed the origins of what he considered to be the fifteen leading Sonjuku students (see Table 3). All were of samurai rank: nine were shi and six were sotsu. (The nine shi, despite their high rank, had extremely modest incomes.)[64]

Despite some minor discrepancies, owing to the use of slightly different categories, the data of Umihara, Kurihara, and Umetani are basically in agreement. Members of the Sonjuku group were drawn almost exclusively from this slender, almost impoverished, educated service stratum of Chōshū society. Sonjuku members of non-samurai origin were drawn from the professions of physician or priest, or from among townsmen. Those who were samurai were predominantly of modestly stipended shi rank. That is, they received less than 200 koku of income and belonged to the stratum in which intellectual competition for scarce posts was most intense. Samurai of over 200 koku were absent, and samurai of less than shi rank were drastically underrepresented, given the fact that they constituted three-quarters of the domain's samurai population.

The social identity of Sonjuku students is almost unmistakable. Their ranks and educational opportunities were quite high, even

---

* These calculations are based on the biographical information on the students given by Kurihara Ryūichi in Naramoto Tatsuya et al., eds., *Yoshida Shōin to sono monka* (Tokyo, 1973), pp. 141–51. Kurihara provides information on 40 men. Of these, 8 are excluded from my calculations because their affiliation with the Sonjuku was either pre- or post-Shōin, or in some other way peripheral. The 8 are Sugi Umetarō, Kido Kōin, Akagawa Awami, Kaneko Shigenosuke, Kuchiba Tokusuke, Iida Seihaku, Dairaku Gentarō, and Nogi Maresuke.

The Early Life of Yoshida Shōin

TABLE 3

Rank, Name, and Stipend of Fifteen Leading Shōka Sonjuku Students

Rank and name	Stipend in koku	Rank and name	Stipend in koku
Ōgumi		*Ashigaru*	
Fukuhara Mataichi	82	Irie Sugizo[a]	≤10
Kido Kōin	90	Nomura Wasaku	≤10
Maebara Issei	47	Shinagawa Yajirō	≤10
Nakatani Masasuke[a]	160	Yoshida Tomimaro	≤10
Okabe Tomitarō	40	*Chūgen*	
Takasugi Shinsaku	150	Itō Hirobumi	≤10
Jishagumi		Yamagata Aritomo	≤10
Kusaka Genzui	25		
Mukyūdōri			
Ariyoshi Kumajirō	21		
Terajima Chūzaburō	70		

SOURCE: Umetani Noboru, "Meiji ishinshi ni okeru Chōshū han no seijiteki dōkō," in Sakata Yoshio, ed., *Meiji ishinshi no mondaiten* (Tokyo, 1962), p. 325.

NOTE: The range of income is 0–160 koku; the mean is 50 koku (calculated by assuming that the last six students had their maximum possible income of 10 koku).

[a] Also a physician.

though their incomes were usually very low. Members of Chōshū's service intelligentsia, they were without exception men of modest means whose lives, nevertheless, were heavily invested in those intellectual and social disciplines that were essential to their community's survival. An awareness of this makes it possible to link social motives directly to many of the reforms that would later be imposed by the Chōshū leadership, both at home and, ultimately, throughout Japan.

MINISTERS AND BUREAUCRATS

The later careers of the Sonjuku students also reflect on the social character of the group, and make clear the high level not only of their ability but also of their public involvement. Being a Sonjuku student was dangerous, and that danger sprang from political engagement.

Of the thirty-two original Sonjuku students who became politically active in the 1860's, only half lived to see the Meiji peace in 1870 (see Table 4). Shōin himself died trying to implement a strategy of direct action, and thereafter, too, each paramilitary

38   The Early Life of Yoshida Shōin

TABLE 4

Political-Career End Point of Thirty-two Sonjuku Students

Political-career end point	No.	Percent	Average age in 1853
Cause of death of students who died before 1870:			
1. Died of natural causes	4	12.5%	24.3
2. Died at the Ikedaya Inn, 6/64, under Bakufu attack	2	6.3	18.5
3. Died at the Forbidden Gate, 7/64	4	12.5	17.3
4. Died in combat between 1865 and 1869	3	9.4	18.0
5. Political suicides	3	9.4	20.7
TOTAL	16	50.0%	
Highest career achievement of students who died after 1870:			
6. Became Yamaguchi (Chōshū) prefectural officials	2	6.3%	33.5
7. Became governors of other prefectures	2	6.3	24
8. Officials in Meiji government below ministerial level	4	12.5	15.7
9. Officials in Meiji government at ministerial level or above	5	15.6	16.4
10. Involved in antigovernmental activities	2	6.3	30.5
11. Left politics before 1870	1	3.1	16
TOTAL	16	50.0%	

SOURCE: Naramoto Tatsuya et al., eds., *Yoshida Shōin to sono monka* (Tokyo, 1973), pp. 141–51.

NOTE: The students by category, with their ages in 1858, are as follows: (1) Ikutari Ryōsuke, 22; Tsuchiya Shōkai, 29; Takasugi Shinsaku, 19; Nakatane Masasuke, 27. (2) Yoshida Toshimaro, 17; Sugiyama Matsusuke, 20. (3) Ariyoshi Kumajirō, 16; Kusaka Genzui, 18; Terajima Chūzaburō, 15; Irie Sugizō, 20. (4) Komai Masagorō, 17; Tokiyama Naohachi, 20; Tamaki Hikosuke, 17. (5) Matsuura Shōdō, 21; Ōtani Shigeki, 20; Akane Taketo, 21. (6) Okabe Tomitarō, 28; Ono Tamehara, 39. (7) Kubo Seitarō, 26; Saitō Eizō, 22. (8) Onodera Shinnojō, age unknown; Okabe Shigenosuke, 16; Amano Gomin, 17; Watanabe Kōzō, 14. (9) Itō Hirobumi, 17; Yamagata Aritomo, 20; Shinagawa Yajirō, 15; Nomura Wasaku, 16; Yamada Akiyoshi, 14. (10) Tominaga Yurin, 37; Maebara Issei, 24. (11) Mashino Tokumin, 16.

tentative took its toll in lives. Sonjuku activists died when the Bakufu's special police, the Shinsengumi, attacked the Ikedaya Inn in June 1864. More died at the Forbidden Gate the following month, and each major campaign by the *shotai* military in the years from 1865 to 1869 took at least one Sonjuku life. These casualties accounted for nine of the original group of thirty-two, and political suicides claimed three more.

Among the Sonjuku students who lived beyond 1870, political struggles were also not abandoned. Thirteen of the sixteen survivors held prefectural or national office after the Restoration. Five of these, including Itō Hirobumi and Yamagata Aritomo, moved into posts in the new government at the ministerial level or above, where in the 1870's and 1880's they helped to shape the new institutions of the state.

There was no clear difference in age or activities between the group that died in combat and the group that became the senior statesmen of the Meiji government. The men who came to dominate the Meiji hierarchy—Itō, Yamagata, Shinagawa, and a number of others—had been among the most vulnerable of the Sonjuku's paramilitary commanders, were often exposed to death, and seem to have differed from some of their less fortunate colleagues only in that they did not happen to be overtaken by it. It is likely that many of those who perished would also have manifested an effective vocation for high public office had they lived.

GREAT EXPECTATIONS

There is some evidence that Yoshida Shōin had prepared the Sonjuku students as a political cadre from the beginning. This possibility is indicated by a letter that Shōin wrote to Kusaka Genzui in 1856. Shōin would brook no abstention from ultimate responsibility for the political outcome in Genzui:

Concerning . . . the current of events past and present, being deeply doubtful is not enough. Because men born under Heaven differ from inanimate objects, one must, in accordance with morality and justice, take the responsibility on oneself, and for the sake of posterity assume the task. . . . Devoting one's mind to the realm and one's life to the people, and acceding to the Way of the Sages, one takes the first step into eternity.[65]

Shōin insisted to Kusaka that this ultimate responsibility for the welfare of his society was not figurative, and had to be achieved out of one's own real-life situation, however unpromising it may have seemed:

When discussing, one must start from oneself and where one is. This is only honesty. . . . As I must speak from the standpoint of a prisoner, you must speak from the standpoint of a [young] physician. . . . How many people are willing to die following you? How many people are willing to contribute their efforts for you? How many people are willing to give funds to help you? The sages are honored not for their words but for their real accomplishments.[66]

Shōin may have held up these standards not only to Genzui but to himself. Where would he, Shōin, acquire the power to guide the destiny of the realm, or find men prepared "to die following him"? The answer, of course, may have been the Shōka Sonjuku. Whether intentionally or not, Shōin created in the Sonjuku a resourceful political cadre. In the end his students became men who, like the Ancient Sages, were "honored . . . for their real accomplishments."

There are many aspects of Yoshida Shōin's youth that suggest he was not merely the romantic extremist that later episodes of his life seem to indicate he was. He was subjected to an unusually rigorous academic preparation. He became well read and well traveled early in life. He acquired an insatiable appetite for knowledge, especially knowledge relating to public affairs and political theory. It is not unlikely that Shōin's later role in the Restoration movement was somehow motivated and shaped by his relentless early educational experiences.

Although there was no political involvement as such during the period of Shōin's youth, there were nevertheless numerous activities that suggest the conduct of someone with practical political concerns. In his years of study and travel he maintained contacts with dozens of other persons who shared his political interests. He was closest to his teacher, Sakuma Shōzan, but was also on good terms with Yokoi Shōnan and Aizawa Yasushi. He knew well many of the most prominent reformers of the pre-Restoration period.

Shōin shared both his assiduously acquired knowledge and his practical political values with a group of gifted and promising younger men. These younger men, like their teacher, came from the austere and literate ranks of Chōshū's service intelligentsia. They included Kido Kōin, Itō Hirobumi, and Yamagata Aritomo, the same persons who, with their Satsuma colleagues, would later become the architects of a new Japan. Yoshida Shōin would not be present to implement the particular results of the Meiji Restoration. Still, he may have exercised a considerable influence on the outcome of the Restoration by having educated in public values many of the men who later would actually supervise the Meiji reforms.

CHAPTER THREE

Yoshida and Ideological Reconstruction

ONE OF THE greatest obstacles a historical observer faces in trying to find continuities in Bakumatsu politics is that there appears to have existed no written plan for the sweeping institutional reforms that were finally realized in the 1870's. Surely if massive reforms were intended from the start, there would have been some kind of design for them, and this design would have been visible long before the reforms were implemented. One of the most striking features of Yoshida Shōin's thought is that he was struggling to create such a blueprint for major reform, and that as his life progressed, these plans increasingly resembled the Meiji reforms of the 1870's. This aspect of Shōin's writings may provide an important clue to the theoretical origins of the Meiji transformation and help to establish some lines of historical continuity through the turbulent Bakumatsu years.

One can also find in the thought of Yoshida Shōin sophisticated ideological structures built and used by him to justify the drastic institutional changes he proposed. Moreover, his ideas can be seen to have collided with an equally sophisticated conservative ideology. The contours of this conflict were clearly visible in the long, bitter debate over Mencius' thought that took place between Yoshida Shōin and the established conservative scholar Yamagata Taika in 1855 and 1856.

These structural and ideological innovations in Shōin's thought were both linked to patterns of social grievance. Shōin often articulated a sharp complaint against men who were "noble," men who were "inner retainers," or "men of large stipend"—categories from which he felt he was socially excluded, samurai though he was. He made a number of proposals for diminishing the perquisites of such persons in ways that would not adversely affect ordinary servants of the polity like himself. There emerge in the pages of Shōin's work the dim outlines of an immense social struggle, not over the rights of samurai and commoner, but rather over the rights of great and lowly among samurai.

A careful perusal of Shōin's thought will reveal that already in the 1850's there were present in the reformist movement in Chōshū an evolving blueprint for social change, a distinct pattern of major ideological innovation, and pronounced discontents that were clearly related both to the reformers' own anomalous social condition and to other structural absurdities of the status quo.

REFORM OF THE ACADEMY AND DOMAIN

Yoshida Shōin's reformist premises were first developed in the institutional microcosm of Chōshū's official academy, the Meirin-kan, then later applied to the successively larger contexts of the Chōshū government and the national government. Shōin advocated ideas that were shockingly unorthodox: Chōshū should use in its government only the best men, even if they hailed from some distant province or were the sons of lowly farmers and tradesmen. He favored putting an end to lavish spending by the privileged few and also proposed a massive infusion of Western technology for the Chōshū military.

An emphasis on real ability echoed throughout Shōin's work. In 1848 he began his ten-year pilgrimage as a reformist thinker by recommending that all privileges and perquisites at the Meirin-kan be allocated on a basis of actual ability, not hereditary rank as in the past. On 10/4/48, some ten months after being promoted at the age of eighteen to the post of instructor at the school, Shōin submitted to the han government a memorial entitled "On Revival of the Meirinkan" ("Meirinkan osaikō ni tsuki kizuki sho"). Its main thrust was that scholarly recognition should be given only for achievement, and that the sons of higher-ranking families should no longer be given automatic precedence. "If we institute unprecedented rewards and punishments, such that favor and prestige do not enter in, we will be able to reform the old customs," he wrote. Shōin claimed that in this way better morale and performance could be achieved among the students.[1]

Shōin next applied this principle of merit over birth to the recruitment practices of the Chōshū government, in ways that would make the whole population of Japan eligible. He began in 1848 by requesting that han posts be open to Chōshū samurai of all levels on the basis of ability.[2] By 1855 he was asking that posts be opened to able samurai of other domains as well, a proposal that ignored the centuries-old precedent of choosing officials only from among a domain's own samurai: "If Chōshū invited into its government men of the whole realm who have technical skills, talent, or learning, she would have a fund of talent (*jinzai*) without peer in all of Japan. This would give Chōshū the moral authority to lead all of the realm. Among the han of the four directions, what han would not look up to ours?"[3]

In 1858 Shōin escalated his petitioning again. In his memorial of 1/6, "Words of a Madman" ("Kyōfu no gen"), he urged that the Chōshū government appoint only the most accomplished candidates, even if they were the sons of lowly artisans or farmers. Stretching the rules of eligibility somewhat was an accepted practice, but Shōin argued that the rules should be stretched much further, to include not only samurai from other han but also "farmers, craftsmen, and merchants," that is, persons from any of Tokugawa Japan's four social classes:

If there is no suitable man in the nobility, you take a man from among the Near vassals. This is customary in today's system of eligibility. Expanding on this principle for the sake of discussion, would it not be desirable, if there is no man among the Near vassals, to take someone from the Great Group, the Far and Near samurai, the Unsalaried, the foot soldiers, or even to take someone from among the farmers, craftsmen, or merchants? While regarding Chōshū as important, would it not be desirable to recruit even men who are not of Chōshū?*

* *Yoshida Shōin zenshū*, ed. Yamaguchi ken kyōiku kai, 12 vols. (Tokyo, 1940), 5: 99–100. The Japanese terms for the English rank names given here are

Although cautiously stated, this passage amounted to a provocative demand for universal eligibility on the basis of ability alone and indicated a bold disregard for all of the traditional class distinctions. In ten brief years, Yoshida Shōin had progressed from asking that merit be recognized among students at the Meirinkan to the radical position of asking that merit be the only basis of recruitment into the han government. This evolutionary expansion in Shōin's expectations would soon lead him to demand similar reforms for new national institutions as well.

Implicit in Shōin's acceptance of individuals on the basis of ability was his downgrading of privileges accorded by birth. If merit were the proper criterion both for winning public recognition and for holding office, then the large hereditary incomes at the top of the samurai hierarchy had no social validity whatsoever. In 1868 Shōin's followers would abolish such incomes by a governmental directive that wiped out 90 percent of all hereditary stipends in Chōshū above the meager 100-koku level.[4]

Although Shōin never openly advocated such a simple solution, and perhaps could not have in the political climate of the 1850's, he nevertheless did urge stringent curbs on aristocratic consumption. In order to justify this, he sometimes dwelled on what he believed to be the principal vice of Chōshū's late-Tokugawa notables—vanity. In his Meirinkan memorial of 1848, Shōin had roundly criticized "persons of large stipend," describing them as men "who are preoccupied with maintaining the superficialities of their rank or who adhere to pastimes and fads, and are negligent of their training in letters and arms."[5] He then offered some unflattering words about the manners of such samurai, who represented a cultural milieu very different from his own:

Men of large stipend should reduce the number of their attendants. At the same time, it is necessary to praise those who practice simplicity, and disparage those who practice pomp. . . . The devotion of the samurai

---

as follows: Nobility, *kizokuichimon* and *eidai karō*; Near Group vassals, *yorigumi* (6,200–250 koku); Great Group vassals, *ōgumi* (1,600–40 koku); Far and Near samurai, *enkin* (150–30 koku); Unsalaried, *mukyū* (60 koku and below); foot soldiers, *kachi* (20 koku and below) and *ashigaru* (10 koku and below).

must surely be shallow in those who dedicate their minds to pursuit of personal appearance, clothes, and hair styles. . . .
Some men buy at a high price paintings or calligraphy which have no practical value. Some men acquire tea vessels, flower vases, carafes, and the like at high price and are proud of this. It is like the play of little girls, and men of high purpose can only heave a deep sigh. . . . The buying and selling of [rare] tea vessels and paintings should be stopped. Perhaps if they were confiscated, conventions of taste could be somewhat reformed. . . .
The above matters are great abuses for the han community and dealing with them is urgent.[6]

Such criticisms were often reiterated in Shōin's work, as was the solution: government intervention and confiscation.

It was the house of the daimyo that set the pace for aristocratic prodigality, and by 1858, Shōin was prepared to question gratuitous consumption in the daimyo's establishment itself (though he exempted the daimyo personally). He charged that "unhealthy customs"—frivolous preoccupations and waste—had "arisen within the women's interior," where "the officials, the pages and such . . . trouble themselves only about fashion and new ways of making up their faces." Concerning "the literary and martial arts, and frugality," the palace officials' attitude was hopeless. Shōin recommended a drastic solution: that the Mōri scale down the operations of their women's interior to the level of the Uesugi, a daimyo house with only a fraction of the Mōri's resources.[7]

For Shōin, the restriction of gratuitous indulgence among the highest hereditary classes represented part of the same effort that merit recruitment represented, namely, the transference of social recognition and resources from less productive persons and activities to more productive ones. Sharply reducing the lavish operations of the women's interior, which involved the social participation of many aristocratic families besides the daimyo's, would have brought relief to the han budget. It would have withdrawn a large fund from aristocratic luxury consumption and made it available for application to other urgent problems faced by the han society.

In addition to the elevation of talent and curbs on aristocratic consumption, Shōin specified the need for costly and technically demanding military reforms at the domain level. Some of his clearest statements on the subject appeared in his "Some Confidential Advice" ("Shokyū shigen") memorial of 8/53. Concerning Chōshū's infantry, Shōin maintained that the han had been beguiled by "the words of artists," whereas in the West the uses of rifle and artillery had been "highly refined for real war." Therefore, he urged that Chōshū "conduct maneuvers daily using Western equipment and discipline." Men "versed in these skills" should be summoned to supervise such activities. Shōin went on to argue that Chōshū must acquire the technology to build Western-style ships and that it should start experimenting immediately with the kind of large-scale cavalry formations that had been used to such advantage in the West.[8] Like his other reforms, Shōin's program for the han military was designed to increase efficiency and relied heavily on "specialists" and on persons "versed in skills."

REFORM AT THE NATIONAL LEVEL

At the same time that Shōin was advocating a wider role for merit in Chōshū, he was also fashioning some startling plans for the government at the national center. He envisioned a reconstituted and revitalized Bakufu to be established near the imperial residence in Kyoto. This new Bakufu would build a great university to draw to the metropolis men of the greatest talent from all of Japan. It would create an oceangoing navy and a modern army. It would reach beyond the seas for new knowledge.

In his "Record from Prison" ("Yūshūroku") of 1854, Shōin had recommended some major departures from the status quo. His object was to reorganize and strengthen the central governmental authority. Shōin urged that the Bakufu be moved from Edo to Kyoto, where it would be closer to the imperial abode, because Kyoto was much less vulnerable than Edo to modern naval bombardment. A new fortified seat of government should be built, one more defensible against contemporary military forces than Edo Castle. Other measures were to be carried out in connection with this relocation of the central government, the most prominent of which was the creation of a great new school to instruct students from various domains in defense-related subjects, including European languages and the "many technical and mechanical methods now being devised in the various countries of the West." In this discussion Shōin urged once again the utilization of "talented men," "excellent persons," and "men of greatest ability."[9]

The concept that a national merit university should be founded in connection with the proposed new governmental seat in Kyoto matured in Shōin's mind in the years following 1854, and reemerged in his "Modest Proposal Continued" ("Zokuguron") of 1858. As he had proposed earlier for the Chōshū bureaucracy, he asked that persons "accomplished in both the literary and martial arts" be admitted to the university regardless of their geographical or social origins, "from the imperial children above to the common people below . . . without discriminating between noble and base."[10] Quite as remarkable as his sweeping commitment to universal eligibility, however, was Shōin's idea that entirely new kinds of activities should be undertaken in the context of the university, including "a hospital and an orphanage," "various forms of manufacturing," "preparing medicines," and "making books." All of these innovative activities were to be funded on a national scale by reliance on prosperous existing agencies, namely, "the various [Buddhist] sects," "the rich of Osaka," "the shogunal house," and "the various lords."[11]

There is more than a suggestion in Shōin's extraordinary vision of the university that he was on the verge of designing a new social order. How such activities as public hospitals and machine manufacturing were to be supported he was not quite sure: he relied at this point on the familiar administrative structure of the academy, and on funding drawn from the treasuries of existing religious, mercantile, and political institutions. His proposals still fell short of the Meiji reforms, but they clearly represented a major step in that direction.

Shōin wanted the relocated central government to organize a new kind of egalitarian, Western-style army. In his "Modest Proposal" ("Guron") of 1858, Shōin offered this formula for the creation of a Bakufu army that could stand up to Western intimidation: "Recruit corresponding to their capability men of stature with respect to martial courage . . . without regard for whether they have a stipend or not, for whether they be samurai or masterless. . . . If we carry out these ideas we will be able both to find excellent commanders and to select superior troops. Even if it should come to war, we would have no cause whatever to be apprehensive."[12]

Shōin developed another category of reform at the national level that had not been entirely appropriate for Chōshū—the increasing of contacts with foreign lands for purposes of information, trade, and security. Shōin was critical of the Bakufu's policy of passively opening the country and urged instead a policy of actively opening it as the best way to deal with the foreign threat. He put this succinctly in one of his policy memorials of 1858: "I think there is no way to sweep away the foreigners unless we cross the seas and trade (*kōkai tsūshi*). . . . American influence must be swept away in accordance with a closed-country policy; yet if we do not base this on an open-country policy, how could we extend and strengthen the power of the nation?"[13]

Shōin expatiated often on the importance of dispatching talented students abroad. While in prison in 1854 for the offense of having tried to study in the West himself, he recommended that "excellent persons" should be sent "to each country" to "pursue the scholarship of that country" and to "purchase books." When they returned, "it would be desirable . . . to make these men instructors at the university."[14] He also thought the various daimyo should fund opportunities for promising candidates to go abroad to study new manufacturing techniques. On their return the students were to disseminate the new methods:

Machinery and technology are advancing [in Western nations] from year to year. In investigating and applying these, Japan and foreign countries are on the same footing. In outlying areas there is much resistance to change in ways of doing things, however. Therefore each daimyo should contribute 10,000 koku, and select one man of ability and send him abroad for three to five years. When one of these after his return produces ingenious ideas and initiates new ways of doing things, he should be sponsored beyond the 10,000 koku to spread these ideas.[15]

Shōin wanted Japan's revitalized central authority to acquire a fleet, establish a presence abroad, and engage in trade: "We must . . . train a navy, and navigate increasingly, without missing a single day between Hokkaidō and Karafuto in the northeast and Tsushima and the Ryūkyūs in the southwest. . . . We must research the conditions of the seas. Then we should visit Korea, Manchuria, and China. In Canton, Australia, and the like, we should establish consulates, have military forces reside there, and investigate local conditions. Then we must profit by trade."[16] Shōin probably took part of his inspiration for these measures from the mercantilist thinking of Honda Toshiaki, Hayashi Shihei, and other late-eighteenth-century writers. He was almost certainly inspired as well by the methods used by England and other Western powers in dealing with Asian nations in his own day.

Shōin's proposals for national reform—the new university, the military, and the activities overseas—had in common that they depended heavily on the selection of new talent and that each represented for its author a more efficient disposition of the realm's social energies in view of its perceived needs. There can be no doubt that in the ensemble, Shōin's reformist ideas represented a thrust toward major institutional change. He insisted that boundaries of class and rank must be ignored in all civil, academic, and military recruitment. He maintained that the indulgences of the uppermost classes had to be curbed, and that entirely new categories of institutional practices, educational, military, and diplomatic, had to be undertaken in the context of a revitalized national government.

THE RESTORATIONIST TENDENCY

Between 1848 and 1858 Shōin fashioned a vision of increasingly more comprehensive institutional reform. This vision grew dramatically over time, and by 1859 was approaching the reforms that actually would be carried out by the Meiji regime a decade later.

The reformist goals of Yoshida Shōin already derived from the same two principles that could be said to inform all of the drastic institutional changes of the 1870's. One of these was the sub-

stitution of merit for birth in allocating preferment and perquisites. The other principle was the rechanneling of communal
energies into creative new activities that would meet the real
needs of the society in the present, while channeling them away
from older activities that served only the sterile conventions of
the feudal past.

The principle of merit recruitment versus birth recruitment
manifested itself one way or another in most of Shōin's proposals
for reform. Many of his demands were simply that merit recruitment should be introduced in some new institutional quarter or
that the scope of it be enlarged. Many of Shōin's projects involved
the second principle, however. His frequent petitioning that aristocratic prodigality be curbed and his requests that hospitals and
orphanages be established are examples of this.

The particular reforms that Shōin advocated followed an
evolutionary course of expansion. The memorialist began in 1848
by advocating that a merit system of preferment including all
Chōshū samurai be initiated by the Chōshū academy and in the
Chōshū bureaucracy generally. Between 1848 and 1858 Shōin had
progressed from prescribing this limited form of merit recruitment for the Meirinkan and Chōshū to advocating unrestricted
national merit recruitment both for the Chōshū bureaucracy and
for the new university, military, and numerous other functions
that he urged be established at a newly constituted national center.
He moved from the sphere of the Chōshū university to that of the
Chōshū bureaucracy, and then to that of a national university.

The logical next step was to advocate replacing the Bakufu
itself by a new national bureaucracy chosen on a merit basis, the
very measure that would serve as the key reform of the Meiji Restoration. Shōin would not live to take this short theoretical step,
but his successors would soon do so. Shōin's student Kusaka Genzui
would offer bureaucratic replacement of the Bakufu as a policy
goal in August 1862.

There were in the 1850's no detailed written plans for the Meiji
Restoration. But there were in the reformist writings of Yoshida
Shōin and other Chōshū activists many proposals that closely

resembled reforms that would be realized in the 1870's, and also a strong developmental tendency that was evolving steadily in the direction of the broader Meiji program. Although the reformers' plans for sweeping structural change were in the 1850's still not complete, nevertheless conceptual preparation for those plans had reached an advanced stage. In theoretical terms they were almost there. There may have been far more continuity in the reformist movement in Chōshū that culminated in the Meiji Restoration than has previously been supposed.

CLASS MOTIVES

Yoshida Shōin was motivated to present his bold reformist designs by collective self-interest—that is, class interest—and by patterns of idealistic social commitment. (The second of these motives will be examined in the following section.)

There is compelling evidence in Shōin's writings that he was motivated by "class" interest in his condition as an intellectual worker. Interspersed in his memorials were many passages asserting that upper-strata samurai were prodigal and incompetent, while impoverished lower-strata samurai were superbly capable. A double standard operated, he said, between upper and lower ranks, which caused the mediocre upper echelons to enjoy vastly more power and wealth than the lower, despite their very dismal qualifications. Shōin was exasperated by this and advocated radical change.

An early presentation of these ideas can be found in Shōin's Meirinkan memorial of 1848:

> One would suppose that since men of large stipend do not manage their houses or have errands relating to clothing and food, they would devote themselves all the more exclusively to study, but contrary to expectation, one hears lately that they are preoccupied with maintaining the superficialities of their rank . . . and are negligent of their studies . . . and of public service. . . . On the other hand, persons of small stipend are distressed, and although it is difficult even with much mending of clothing and goods for them to keep their wives and children, they are diligent in their studies, and one should bestow substantial praise on this kind of man.[17]

There emerges in this text and others a clear image of two kinds of samurai: "men of large stipend" who although they did little of the work were generously provided for, and "men of small stipend" who although they worked hard were nearly impoverished. Shōin commented on social inequalities again in his "Confidential Advice" memorial of 1853. He criticized the injustice of the existing situation in which "inner retainers," though "soft and sycophantic," had better access to the daimyo than "outer retainers," who were "isolated," even though they "excelled in the skills of letters and arms." ("Inner" referred to the highest grades of samurai, who therefore had personal access to the daimyo. "Outer" referred to the numerous grades of samurai below these.) The solution to this problem, according to Shōin, was that "inner vassals should be dealt with more severely, and made to apply themselves to their studies," and that "outer vassals who excel" should be "given a place in the han council." In this way one could "make inner and outer one." Shōin was not asking that the special privileges of inner vassals be extended; rather he was asking that they be abolished to make room for a rigorously uniform merit standard.[18]

Shōin reiterated his verbal assault on privilege at regular intervals. In his "Words of a Madman" memorial of 1858, he allowed that there were a few "able men" among the "great retainers," but unfortunately even these few "immersed their minds in women and drink, and softened their bodies with lavish dwellings and apparel." Instead of relying on these, the government should select promising young men of modest rank, who lived on "barely a few mouthfuls of rice," and send them away to study. When they have "arrived at competence and polished the old usages," they should be "raised into the government as great retainers." In this memorial as in many others, Shōin argued the interests not of the privileged but of the able.[19]

In many of these statements, Shōin described service samurai of modest rank in terms which suggest that, despite their often remarkable accomplishments, they lived close to material want. They were "destitute," or "distressed," or lived on "a few mouthfuls of rice." Not all of the activists in the Sonjuku group that Shōin founded were poverty-stricken, but passages like these suggest that many of them were close to it, and this could have been a factor in their political motivation. Recent scholarship by Kōzō Yamamura suggests that most of the Sonjuku students, though they were highly educated samurai, had incomes that were actually less than those of ordinary carpenters and tatami matmakers.[20]

Other evidence corroborates Shōin's assessment that "outer vassals" often found it difficult to live. Fukuzawa Yūkichi, who became famous as a popularizer of Western ideas in the 1870's and was of lower-samurai origins himself, wrote in 1877 that it was impossible for a typical lower-samurai household with senior and junior dependents to provide "even the necessities of life such as food and clothing" to its members, unless the husband and wife somehow earned money on the side. Consequently many samurai couples "eked out a poor livelihood by odd jobs such as spinning and handicrafts."[21]

Recent scholarship suggests that financial pressures had already compelled many samurai of low stipend to abandon or restrict their family lives. Kōzō Yamamura has discovered that among modestly stipended samurai retainers of the Tokugawa house, celibacy increased sharply over the Tokugawa period, and the number of children born to those who did marry decreased. Yoshida Shōin's own family situation may have reflected this same solution to the problem of chronic indigence. By Shōin's time, no heir to the Yoshida line had taken a wife or sired a child for several generations. Rather Yoshida heirs were provided generation after generation from among the younger sons of the Sugi house, who then remained unmarried through life. Although vocational devotion may have been part of the reason for this sterile arrangement, the specter of poverty probably provided the main incentive for it.[22]

Many analysts of the Bakumatsu era have observed that the leadership of the Meiji Restoration derived predominantly from an elite social category, that of the samurai class. This fact seems to render social interpretations of the Restoration movement problematical insofar as the leaders, who eventually discontinued the hereditary privileges of the samurai, would then have to be seen as having betrayed their own class interests. Still, although Yoshida Shōin was influential as an early Restoration leader, he did not see himself as belonging to a privileged class. Rather he consistently described his social standing by such terms as "distressed," "base," "outer," and "low." Although Shōin was evidently motivated by devotion to the common good, his writings show him also to have been motivated by the sense that he and his colleagues were the victims of a damaging pattern of social inequality.

IDEAL MOTIVES

Although Yoshida Shōin sought reform in connection with the material interests of the service class, it is also almost undeniable that he was motivated by a powerful "ideal" interest in the well-being of the whole society.

The gratifications a man draws from life, and that motivate him generally, are closely associated with his ideal interests and his identity. Everyone has "material" interests—an interest in his own material well-being. Everyone also has "ideal" interests—an interest in the state of the world corresponding to the ideal patterns he finds most satisfying. Once elementary natural needs are met, both material interests and ideal interests operate on the same spectrum of human gratification: the emotional one. Once he is fed and warmed and so on, a man seeks what is emotionally satisfying to him, what is "meaningful." He may seek possessions, or a change in the way his community is organized, or anything else that pleases him. In a society that is not starving, a man's motives for action often derive from his ideal interests. A person's identity is an essential key to this kind of motive. Identity is a man's ideal of himself, of what he is and ought to be. It is therefore the paradigm against which all his actions are valid or not, nourishing or not. Much of the pleasure a man takes from life derives from his seeing that his actions affirm his ideal view of himself. He strives for this satisfying effect. In this way, identity shapes conduct.

Shōin's ideal interests were those of the Mencian "true gentleman" (*kunshi*) and "sage" (*seiken*). In his capacity of political
thinker and activist, Shōin sometimes hinted, in an almost mystical way, that he was in some respects akin to Mencius himself.
For Shōin, being a "true gentleman" meant being committed to
the well-being of "all under heaven," a notion he sometimes referred to simply by the term "loyalty" (*chūkō*). In his "Principles
of a Gentleman" he wrote that "the honor of men who are men
has loyalty . . . as its foundation." These "Principles" were written
as precepts for Shōin's nephew, but he must have applied them
also to himself.[23]

Moreover, Shōin aspired to being a "sage." A sage was a man not
only of good intentions but also of unusual merit and ability. In
his lectures on Mencius of 11/22/55 and 11/24/55, Shōin described
the Mencian sage and the sage's ascendancy over rulers. The ruler's
task was to implement "the will of Heaven," which meant securing
"the blessing of the people."[24] Since rulers were usually inadequate to this lofty task, the burden of righteous rule fell in actu-
ality upon the sage, who for Shōin was someone with superior
knowledge, wisdom, and dedication to the people's welfare. Moreover, the sage was duty-bound to depose any ruler who was unfit.
In some of his memorial writings, Shōin affirmed that everyone
with the sage's qualifications should have the prerogative of advising rulers. In other words, there might be innumerable sages
within a given political community.[25]

The implication of this was that the role that Shōin and others
had to play in society was a very meaningful one indeed. Rulers
were not themselves competent. The welfare of the people, and
indeed all of the benefits of political society, depended on the
capabilities and goodwill of the sages. The well-ruled society was
governed not by a philosopher king, but rather by a king who
served as a figurehead for a large band of virtuous and highly competent philosophers. Needless to say, the sage as described by
Shōin had many of the attributes of the educated and resourceful
samurai administrator. In his lecture of 11/24/55, Shōin went

on to point out, in a circuitous and scholarly way but nevertheless explicitly, that he himself had the qualifications of a sage.[26]

Shōin's aspirations along these lines took a slightly mystical turn in a document that he wrote in prison after his unsuccessful attempt to board Perry's flagship. In order to maintain his resolution and good cheer in moments of discouragement, Shōin created a charismatic identity for himself as a "Valiant Samurai." In 11/54, after seven months of confinement and with no prospect of release in sight, he wrote a somewhat fanciful essay characterizing himself as "Twenty-one Times a Valiant Samurai." A divine figure came to him in a dream and said that he must demonstrate valor twenty-one times. Numerals totaling twenty-one were present in the characters of his name, and his given name at birth had been the fairly common one of "Tora," or tiger, a beast said to have valor. A valorous expectation was thus appropriate. Shōin noted, however, that he was "slight of build" and had "little physical strength." "If I have the valor of a tiger it can only be as a teacher." He had shown valor, he said, by submitting his boldly candid "Confidential Advice" memorial, which put him in political danger, and by seeking to study in America, which landed him in prison. It was clearly still "Heaven's intent," however, that he show valor many times more.[27]

The full significance of all this becomes clear only in light of the fact that in Japanese "Valiant Samurai" (*mōshi*) is an exact homonym for Mencius (*Mōshi*). Graphically, too, the two terms are strikingly similar (see Figure 2). Shōin's meaning was that he

Figure 2. LEFT: *mōshi*, "valiant samurai." RIGHT: *Mōshi*, "Mencius."

had a divine mission to serve Heaven as Mencius had, by providing enlightened counsel to rulers, no matter how unwelcome this was among the powerful, and no matter how hazardous to himself. The "Twenty-one Times a Valiant Samurai" conceit remained part of Shōin's self-awareness for the rest of his life. It appeared regularly in one form or another as the signature on his writings. His five-hundred-volume prison bibliography of 1855 was signed "Twenty-one Times a Savage Tiger," for example.[28] Those around Shōin also willingly adopted the phrase's symbolism. When he was extradited to Edo in 1859, his student Kusaka Genzui wrote a poem for him, dedicating it to "Twenty-one Times a Valiant Teacher."[29] Kido and Itō used the phrase as the epitaph for Shōin's tombstone later that year, and when Takasugi Shinsaku was imprisoned years later, he could still be found writing with admiration about the man who was "Twenty-one Times a Valiant Samurai."

The students of the Shōka Sonjuku were familiar both with Shōin's scholarly association of himself with the Mencian sage and with the slightly mystical Valiant Samurai idea. Together, these images lent to Shōin and his followers a quality of transcendent religiosity that served to buoy the teacher's morale while he lived and the students' morale after his death. Insofar as the members of the Sonjuku group were often under severe psychological stress between 1858 and 1868, this transcendent identity may have contributed significantly to their tenacity and ultimate success.

It is likely that such ideas also represented a source of considerable gratification in themselves, and so served not only as a refuge, but even more importantly as a major basis for the group's motivation. The Chōshū activists were prepared to embark on a hazardous quest to make the world better because as scholars and sages that was their reason for existing. Their belief that they and they alone assured the well-being of society was a source for them of pride, self-respect, and much psychological nourishment. It may have been their only source of this kind of intense satisfaction.

For this reason, social altruism was their highest self-interest, and transcended petty material interest or class interest. This source of emotional gratification would soon fade and be lost, however, if they did not act upon their beliefs in life. Shōin's and his followers' view of themselves as gentlemen and sages constituted an ideal interest, and was in itself a powerful basis for action.

IDEOLOGICAL STRATEGY

Though he devoted much time and energy to the fashioning of proposals for reform, Shōin also made an earnest effort to create for his reformist ideas an intellectual legitimacy that would be persuasive for the Tokugawa public. To provide ideological justification, he used familiar ideas where possible, and molded new ones where necessary. The application of ideology is essential for anyone trying to tailor the conduct of others, because men do not act on a basis of empirical reality, but rather on a basis of the meaning of perceived reality. As a man with a serious interest in ameliorating the institutional structure of his society, Yoshida Shōin developed an ideological equipment for his programs.

The simplest device—one that he used from the beginning to validate his unorthodox pronouncements—was to associate them with passages in both the Chinese and the ancient Japanese classics, thus conferring upon them a kind of scriptural charisma. He grew quite skillful at this practice as the years passed. One of the more remarkable examples may be found in his "Four Urgent Tasks" ("Kyūmu yonjō") memorial of 1858. There he used classical precedents to justify radically increased opportunities for lowly rural administrators. To do this, he cited Mencius, the Book of History (*Shu ching*), the seventh emperor of the earlier Han, and the second and third emperors of the T'ang, among others. At the end of his recommendation, Shōin asserted that all of his innovative suggestions had been developed in detail centuries before in a memorial written by the Sung statesman Su Shih. Su Shih's memorial contained twenty-five sections, of which Shōin quoted five.[30] In this way Shōin sought to add a dimension of historico-mythical legitimacy to his highly unorthodox proposals. He associated them by juxtaposed similarity with what were for his readers specially validated contexts in the past.

To justify his many reformist projects in strictly rational terms, however, Yoshida Shōin needed a theory of institutional empiricism. He did not have far to look. Such theories had existed as a part of Japan's eclectic Neo-Confucian tradition since the days of Ogyū Sorai, over a century before. The contours of Shōin's version are visible in his *Lectures on Mencius* (*Kōmō yowa*) of 1855 and 1856. In his lecture of 6/27/55, Shōin asserted, echoing the Mencian text, that "a man can only be called a ruler when he sustains his people." That is, he would enjoy Heaven's Mandate and be tolerated by the people only if he assured their welfare. Even though the essential object of all government was to achieve "the blessing of the people (*keimin*) of which Mencius speaks," in Chōshū "the hopes of farmers, shopkeepers, and persons who leave home to work" were still not being realized, Shōin noted. He therefore recommended "managing the government so as to rescue the poor, care for the sick, and provide for [homeless] children." Shortly after this statement Shōin urged that "Chōshū invite into its government men of the whole realm who have technical skills, talent, or learning," on a basis of their abilities alone, because it was only such men as these who could manage, rescue, and provide, in such a way as to sustain the people on the ruler's behalf, and thereby satisfy the Mencian ideal.[31]

Here Shōin was using an empirical approach to institutions based securely on the orthodox Mencian concepts of the Mandate of Heaven (*temmei*) and the "people's welfare" (*ammin* usually, though Shōin used *keimin*) to justify what was for Tokugawa society an extraordinary departure from the structural norm. The legitimacy of a regime depended on its concrete success in meeting the people's needs, and on that alone.

Although Shōin did not usually make the ultimate theoretical justification for his unprecedented proposals as explicit as he did in his lecture of 6/27/55, most of his reformist writings assumed this conceptual scheme, and occasionally it showed through. In a letter to his brother on 9/4/53, for example, Shōin wrote that "institutions for the poor, the sick, and children have been established even by the Western barbarians. Contrary to what one would expect, these institutions do not exist in august Yamato to carry out the Way of Blessing to those below. Is this not a great defect?"[32] The validity of an institutional practice, Shōin argued, had nothing to do with a particular tradition and everything to do with empirical results. If existing arrangements did not achieve "the Way of Blessing to those below," they had to be changed, even if this meant taking a lesson from the Westerners. For Shōin, this was what Mencius' Mandate of Heaven meant.

With a social philosopher's genius, Shōin fashioned from elements of his own intellectual tradition an ironclad classical argument for ignoring traditional beliefs about the value of certain institutions and for judging them instead against a universal ideal of performance. That is, he used familiar and accepted classical arguments, temmei and ammin, to attack actual precedent and custom. His readers were already well acquainted with the Mencian principle of the Mandate of Heaven and the obligations it implied for systems of rule. As long as he could persuasively invoke these concepts, he was free to advocate any rationalizing reform he wished, no matter how badly it jarred against custom or embarrassed existing authorities. He was able to condemn the status quo and to demand profound change, but in a way that was philosophically plausible to his contemporaries. To support his reformist proposals, Shōin used orthodox theories to craft a powerful, inconoclastic doctrine of utopian empiricism.

Why he had to develop these uncompromisingly antitraditional ideas will become more apparent if one considers the traditionalism, or historical particularism, that constituted the dominant ideology of the Tokugawa system. The traditionalist view emphasized unquestioning loyalty to one's feudal superior as paramount, usually citing the Confucian Five Relationships to justify this. It held that Japan was different from China because of Japan's long history of warring military houses. This history meant that it had become desirable and necessary from the standpoint of maintaining social order for the whole society to be organized in terms of strong bonds of particular personal loyalties. These bonds extended vertically in gradually converging chains, from samurai, to daimyo, to shogun, to emperor. In Japan, its historical idiosyncrasies being what they were, a man served the whole not by worrying about the whole but by minding his immediate superior. To insist on an abstract classical ideal and ignore Japan's real historical experience was an invitation to catastrophe. All ties extended upward to the emperor anyway; so there need be no concern about one's own small contribution eventually serving the general good.*

This traditionalist current was the main ideological pillar of the Tokugawa status quo in all its arbitrary complexity. What was, was for the best and had to be. Because of the critical ideological function of this brand of particularist thought in legitimizing the status quo, scholars who championed the traditionalist view were maintained in most han academies. The leading advocate of historical particularism at Chōshū's Meirinkan was Yamagata Taika (1781–1866). Yamagata had a national reputation as a Confucian scholar and for many years had been the han's leading Confucianist. Though he had retired from his teaching post by 1855, he continued to be thought of as the Meirinkan's dean of Chinese classical studies.

Yoshida Shōin and Yamagata Taika became engaged in a prolonged and bitter ideological dispute in 1855 and 1856. On 9/18/55, shortly after Shōin had begun to deliver his "Lectures on Mencius," he wrote a letter to Yamagata, politely inviting him to respond.[33] Yamagata accepted this challenge, and over the course of the following year made a caustic reply to each and every one of Shōin's lectures. Yamagata's texts abounded in observations like these:

* Whereas historical particularism served as the prevailing orthodoxy through most of the Edo period, institutional empiricism had coexisted with it in the Tokugawa mind since the days of Ogyū Sorai. The particularistic current, emphasizing personal loyalties, the Five Relationships and so on, was used as the main ideological underpinning of the regime. Institutional rationalism, on the other hand, was used to justify the marginal institutional adjustments to the system that in practice were often necessary.

For samurai [shi] to leave the country of their birth and serve in another country could not be wise, Confucius and Mencius notwithstanding. . . . They would be divorced from people's feelings and events and lead states astray.

Today is different from the [chaotic] Warring States period [1467–1568], and now all staff persons are chosen from the body of samurai who are already stipended in each han. We must rule the country by firmly maintaining the great laws of our forebears without changing them, and govern in response to the opportunities of the times.

Since our han is a great country, even if we do not gather samurai from other han, there would be nothing lacking, would there not?

In our land there are many now who say the Bakufu is hegemon and that the various lords are retainers of the court. This is an error that proceeds from scholars of Chinese learning trying to apply the ciphers of ancient China to the current affairs of our country.[34]

These remarks were directed at Shōin's lecture of 6/27/55, in which he advocated that talented persons from other han should be recruited into the Chōshū government. This would not be wise, Yamagata claimed, because it would bypass particular personal loyalties. Besides that, it was just not done. "The great laws of our forebears" must be maintained, "without changing them." Setting up ideological constructs that justified major institutional changes was just "an error that proceeds from scholars of Chinese learning trying to apply the ciphers of ancient China to the affairs of our country."

Yamagata insisted that basic social change was only an impossible fantasy of dreamy ideologues. His arguments took the form of using immediate historical precedent to refute statements of Shōin's grounded only in empirical observation, the classics, and good sense. He argued from the premise, opposite to Shōin's, that the status quo was satisfactory and immutable. It was perhaps inevitable that Shōin, the radically progressive utopian empiricist, should before long find himself grappling ideologically with Yamagata, the local champion of conservative historical particularism. Yamagata's critique is useful for gaining a sense of the orthodox arguments that Shōin's thought was intended to pierce.

Another major approach used by Yoshida Shōin to vindicate his reformist proposals was his ideology of national salvation from the foreign threat. This structure consisted of three elements:

first, an august emperor, who represented what was best in Japanese society (*sonnō*); second, Westerners, whose power if left unchecked threatened to impair that society (*jōi*); and, third, rationalizing reform, which was the only plausible means of preventing such an eventuality (*jinzai tōyō*). In the memorials written after Perry's arrival in 1853, this scheme was often used by Shōin. Even in his earlier writings he had often explicitly complained of the harmful social complacency brought about by the long Tokugawa peace, and from this point of view, Perry's dramatic and menacing appearance may have been almost welcome to him.[35]

Perry strengthened Shōin's hand. Before Perry, Shōin often had to beg the question of whether his reforms were fundamentally needed. After Perry, he could, and did, assert that if reforms were not undertaken, the entire realm would fall into a demeaning subservience to the West. In this sense it was Perry's guns that suddenly in the 1850's compelled Japan to listen when Shōin and other serious reformers spoke.

Although Shōin rarely mentioned Perry without also reciting his latest agenda of reforms, it is still almost certain that Shōin's interest in the Western presence was not exclusively one of using it to seek social change. As a thinker committed to providing for the "blessing of the people," he had an interest in erecting effective defenses against arbitrary foreign activities. This was an important aspect of assuring the people's welfare. At the same time, it should be remembered that Shōin sought out foreign influences that he judged to be beneficial. He was an enthusiastic and consistent advocate of Western learning, as we have seen, and it was for having been determined to study in America himself that he was made to spend his last four years in confinement.

Still, Shōin's rhetorical strategy often involved his prefacing a set of reformist proposals with a reference to the foreign threat. In his "Record from Prison" of 1854, for example, he outlined a half-dozen breathtaking suggestions for reorganizing the Bakufu itself. Before he made these innovative proposals, however, he gave a brief but chilling account of Japan's two great-power rivals on the sea. These powers, Russia and the United States, threatened to engulf Japan altogether. After alluding to Russia's vast size and proximity, he noted that the Russians "are finally dispatching soldiers and warships to Kamchatka. . . . When these are built up sufficiently, it is just a matter of time before this malignancy reaches Japan." He was no more sanguine about the United States, whose influence, he said, already extended "from the South Pole to the North Pole." So, he asked, "Why would Washington not embrace greater ambitions or be satisfied with this? If they invaded and usurped the wealth of the nation it would be even worse than if the Russians did."[36] To a reader thus terrified by fearful invasions launched from the west, and then from the east, Shōin's highly untraditional proposals may have seemed less drastic, or even moderate in the circumstances.

The other essential element of the salvationist argument was the importance of what was to be saved: the imperial institution and the imperial land. Shōin sometimes accompanied his reformist proposals in the later 1850's with a testimonial to the broad spiritual authority of the imperial house. In his "Confidential Advice" memorial of 1853 he wrote: "Under all of heaven there is no land that is not the monarch's land and to the edges of the sea there is no person who is not the monarch's retainer. . . . Therefore if anyone within the realm endure the insults of the foreigners, the Bakufu should all the more cleanse away the shame of the realm, leading her various lords. In this way it should console the mind of the emperor."[37] Shōin used the emperor as a convenient symbol for the well-being of a jeopardized Japan, a well-being that could be safeguarded only through reform.

Use of the emperor had the further advantage of allowing Shōin to criticize the existing feudal hierarchy without seeming too insubordinate. The traditional view held that public order depended on observing ties of personal loyalty to one's immediate feudal superior. These ties extended upward in long, vertical chains, which ultimately converged on the emperor. Since the emperor represented the general good, the general good could be served simply by one's being loyal to his own superior. Shōin, however, vehemently denied this. He argued rather that his and others' personal loyalty was owed directly to the emperor, thus bypassing all feudal intermediaries. This device permitted him to remain "loyal" and at the same time broadly to condemn existing social structures.[38]

Moreover, for Shōin, the emperor was a Shintoist metaphor for the Will of Heaven in his scheme of Mencian idealism. He made this explicit in his lecture of 7/17/55, for example.[39] (This notion had been a commonplace among Tokugawa scholars since Yamazaki Ansai had developed it in the seventeenth century.) Shōin's object was to have particular loyalties to feudal superiors be owed instead to an abstract ideal of righteous rule, the Will of Heaven, the principle that was the foundation of his institutional empiricism. The emperor was merely a personification of this ideal. Use of the imperial institution as the symbol of a threatened Japan thus blended very well with Shōin's use of the emperor to obviate the powerful hold of feudal particularism on the public mind.

Shōin's reliance on the emperor as part of an ideology of national salvation, like his use of Mencian institutional empiricism and of scriptural charisma, was aimed at fostering an intellectual climate favorable to the reforms he advocated.

ORIGINS AND ANTECEDENTS

Although Yoshida Shōin's reformist proposals and ideological positions were all remarkable, not all aspects of them were new. It will be useful from the standpoint of demonstrating the currency of some of his ideas to indicate the presence in earlier thinkers of certain broad categories of thought that Shōin used.

Shōin's interest in the elevation of talent and other rationalizing measures had been shared by earlier Tokugawa reformers, heretical though the degree of Shōin's application of these ideas was. Greater utilization of talent especially had been advocated by many thinkers after Ogyū Sorai first elaborated the idea in the 1710's. Shōin sometimes argued that active relations with foreign lands and the refurbishing of domestic institutions were both needed because of Japan's involuntary involvement in a pattern of global rivalries on the sea. These notions had been developed earlier by Honda Toshiaki, in his "Confidential Proposals on Political Economy" ("Keise hisaku") of 1798, for example. Honda urged the creation of a merchant marine and the colonization of northern territories. To make Japan internationally competitive, he recommended that "talent throughout the country should be judged and selected according to economic and scientific criteria, as done in the University (*daigakkō*) of London. Out of this screening would emerge the new sages of the future."[40] Numerous passages of Shōin's reformist writings were close in both content and spirit to the work of Honda.

Shōin drew heavily on the reformist ideas of the generation immediately prior to his own. Some of his recommendations for remedying the institutional ills of his own domain were similar to those made in the 1830's by the noted Chōshū reformer Murata Seifu. Shōin received a number of ideas from Sakuma Shōzan, and was probably influenced by Yokoi Shōnan and Fujita Tōko as well. Some of the reforms Shōin outlined for Chōshū's Meirinkan were similar to innovative practices prescribed by Fujita for Mito's han academy, the Kōdōkan.

Some of Yoshida Shōin's ideological constructs, too, had been present in some form in earlier thinkers. The scheme of an august emperor who must be protected from malevolent aliens by domestic reform was initially developed by the later Mito school of historians. Although sometimes reduced to rudimentary slogans by activist youths in subsequent years, the Mito doctrine was itself a cultivated synthesis of Shinto, Sorai learning, and knowledge of the West. Shōin began using Mito ideas soon after discovering them on his tour of Kyūshū in 1850.

The origins of Shōin's institutional empiricism are more difficult to trace to any individual thinker because the concept represented one of many possible variants on a widely articulated theme. Nonetheless, it is safe to assume that the more remote antecedents of Shōin's Mencian rationalism are to be found in the early eighteenth century. Ogyū Sorai had then argued that governmental structures should be judged by whether or not they conformed to the principle of rule he imputed to the Ancient Kings, namely, managing the society so as to achieve a maximum level of "peace and contentment" among the people. Ogyū was already using Shōin's tactic of invoking a classical precedent in order to justify the evaluation of institutions on the basis of whether or not they worked. Other scholars, too, were using this approach by 1800. Although Yoshida Shōin's empiricism of the 1850's, in contrast with Ogyū's, emphasized Mencius' idea of the Mandate of Heaven (temmei) and the allied concept of the "welfare of the people" (ammin), it is reasonable to say in spite of this that Shōin's version was largely a product of the ideologically sophisticated environment in which he was raised.

Many of the component parts of Shōin's thought were inherited from earlier thinkers. Still, the new whole that he created from them was his own. What made Shōin's discourse unique was the dramatic way in which he brought together some of the most powerful elements in the Tokugawa tradition.

Examination of Yoshida Shōin's writings reveals an intellectual weave that is unexpectedly rich. Ambitious programs for institutional change took shape early on in his lectures and essays, and to justify these measures he marshaled complex ideological constructs by which a new organization of society might be understood. Underlying this energetic outburst of creative activity, and propelling it, was Shōin's unique sense of mission as a gentleman and a sage, but also his pervasive sense that the political community in which he lived was critically weakened by an unjust system of hereditary inequalities. Ideas alone would never suffice to realize Shōin's hopes for reform, however: so in 1858 he launched his first efforts to influence national politics directly, an undertaking that would prove hazardous in the extreme.

CHAPTER FOUR

Yoshida's Leadership
1858-1859

YOSHIDA Shōin's bold conduct in 1858 and 1859 has tended to obscure from view his scholarly preoccupation with rationalizing reform and ideological innovation. Some of his actions in these years seem disproportionate when considered apart from the political environment in which they took place. Shōin did all he could to assassinate the Bakufu's powerful police representative in Kyoto, for example. In ordinary circumstances, such actions would have to be regarded as quite extreme.

The circumstances of 1858 and 1859, however, were not ordinary. It was understood that issues of overwhelming importance for the future of the nation were being decided. Conservatives within the Bakufu as well as reformers without had already turned to violence when the usual processes of public discussion had broken down. In this situation, Shōin, too, felt an obligation to act. Deeply disappointed by the Bakufu's failure to commit itself to needed reform in 1858, he ventured for the first time into the harsh world of metropolitan politics.

Although his several efforts to sway the course of events at the national level were daring and imaginative, each ended in failure, and for this reason some observers have dismissed Shōin as being inept as well as extreme. Still, given the milieu in which he actually devised them, Shōin's bold efforts to influence the course of national events were not irresponsible, were not ill-informed, and were not without a vital legacy for the future of the Restorationist movement.

THE ANSEI PURGE

Shōin's political perceptions in 1858 were shaped by the onset of the Ansei repression. As a consequence of Bakufu policies in 1858, the terms of the continuing debate over foreign relations and reform were fatefully altered. The struggle of words gave way to a struggle of a much bitterer sort.

During the latter months of 1857 the Bakufu was under increasing pressure from the American consul Townsend Harris to sign an expanded treaty of friendship and trade, an instrument that would be less advantageous to Japan than the Shimoda arrangements. By the end of the year the Bakufu felt it had no choice but to submit or face American naval retaliation, an eventuality for which it was not prepared.

During the early months of 1858, an interclique struggle took place within the chambers of the Bakufu government in Edo. The visible object of the struggle was the matter of shogunal succession. The real issue, however, was whether Bakufu policies in the late 1850's would take a reformist direction, thus enabling the Tokugawa government to cope more actively with Western power, or take a more conservative stance, in which case even limited reforms would be avoided.

Ii Naosuke, daimyo of Hikone, led the group of Bakufu notables who favored the more conservative approach. Ii's faction supported the young and passive Tokugawa Iemochi as shogunal successor. The moderate reformist faction, including the "able daimyo" of Mito, Owari, and Echizen, put their hopes on the capable reformer Hitotsubashi Yoshinobu. The more conservative party prevailed in this palace struggle, and Ii Naosuke became chancellor *(tairō)* in April.

Ii signed the controversial Harris treaty on June 19, even though he had failed to win court sanction for it. The "able daimyo" were displeased by this, and presented themselves at Chiyoda castle to protest. Their protests went unheeded, and Tokugawa Iemochi was confirmed by the Bakufu council as shogunal successor while at the same time Hitotsubashi supporters were being removed from their posts in the Bakufu administration. Even the "able daimyo," Tokugawa Nariaki of Mito and the others, were placed under house arrest on July 5 for the offense of having visited the castle without permission the month before. This move made conservative control at the top level of the Bakufu hierarchy complete.

Still, forcible suppression of the dissenting lords served only to quicken dissent among many of their retainers. Ordinary service samurai whose reformist heroes were also their daimyo by feudal obligation, especially those of Mito and Echizen, were incensed by what they felt was Ii's high-handedness. Having adopted a policy of arresting moderate reformist leaders, Ii was left with little choice but to arrest a broad array of their reformist followers as well. This meant putting pressure on individual han governments to hand over their own dissidents.

Suppression also meant the arrest and execution of many of the samurai in Edo and Kyoto, cosmopolitan areas under the Bakufu's own jurisdiction. The high-ranking Bakufu official Manabe Akikatsu was dispatched to Kyoto to ensure the enforcement of this policy in the especially sensitive area of the imperial capital. The necessary administrative apparatus was set up in August, and the first arrests were made on a substantial scale the following month.

It was this configuration of conservative repression that has come to be known as the Ansei Purge ("Ansei" being the era name for the period 1854–60). These events would decisively influence Shōin's political thinking over the course of 1858 and 1859.

COMMUNICATION AND STRATEGY

In the early months of 1858 Yoshida Shōin worked quietly and without fanfare to create the far-flung patterns of communication that later would become the cornerstone of the Chōshū movement's political effectiveness. He went further and fashioned a number of concepts that would become an essential part of his followers' diplomatic and military strategies in later years.

During the course of 1858, Shōin began sending his students to Edo and Kyoto to study, and to acquire the broadening experiences of travel. By the end of the year, nine of his handpicked protégés were in the vicinity of the two capitals or were traveling. Kusaka Genzui, his best student, set out in February, and Matsuura Shōdō followed a few weeks later. In the seventh month, Shōin sent out another group, including Irie Sugizō, Takasugi Shinsaku, Itō Hirobumi, Yamagata Aritomo, and Sugiyama Matsusuke. Onodera Shinnojō went to join the others in the eighth month. For these young men, though they could not know it, this was the beginning of a hazardous ten-year odyssey that many of them would not survive.[1]

Shōin saw to it that his students met the scholars and reformers that he himself had come to know during his travels in the early 1850's. In this way the Sonjuku group in the two capitals inherited a considerable wealth of contacts from their mentor even before their arrival.[2] Also remarkable was the closeness of the relationship Sonjuku students maintained among themselves in spite of their dispersal. With their teacher's encouragement, they kept up a continuous correspondence both with one another and with Shōin himself. This far-flung network of young men with shared goals would later become the basis for highly effective coordinated action in the sphere of national politics.

Of equal importance were the group's activities, carried out under Shōin's supervision, of gathering and disseminating vital political information. Shōin strongly urged each of his students to write to him about any event or practice of political significance.* He bound these reports into a journal that was kept in the Sonjuku and was freely accessible to anyone who came there. Shōin called this chronicle of public affairs the "Long View" ("Bijichōmoku").† In later years the surviving students Amano

---

* See, for example, Shōin's letter to Kusaka Genzui of 6/28/58 in *Yoshida Shōin zenshū*, ed. Yamaguchi ken kyōiku kai, 12 vols. (Tokyo, 1940), 9: 50–51. Genzui asked if he might not make a trip to Siberia to achieve a better knowledge of that area. Shōin replied: "Was it not your job in Edo to grasp the situation in every area and report? Nakatani Masasuke is in charge of Kyoto and Hōjō Genzō is in charge of Nagasaki. The situation is not such that you can throw up Edo and Kyoto to visit the Amur basin." Reporting was Genzui's primary mission.

† *Bijichōmoku*: literally, "flying ears, long eyes."

Gomin and Watanabe Kōzō both maintained that the content of the "Long View" resembled that of modern newspapers. As Watanabe put it in 1931, the "Long View" was a journal "in which were recorded things such as are in the newspapers of today."[3] Under Shōin's guidance, the Sonjuku had become a small public, a political interest group. As such it had need of the political information that in other times and places is provided routinely by various forms of journalism. Faced with the nonexistence of a regular journalistic source of political information, Shōin devised his own techniques for gathering it. The Sonjuku students were thus expected to devote some of their time to serving as a newsletter staff.*

It is difficult to overestimate the importance of this seemingly inconsequential practice. Journalism is a modern political impulse, and the spontaneous appearance of it within the Sonjuku is one possible measure of the level of political sophistication the group had achieved.†

---

* Shōin's students in the metropolis were able observers, and the information they sent was of good quality. Their reports allowed Shōin in a memorial of mid-April 1858, without ever leaving the confines of his own domicile, to anticipate the likelihood that Bakufu authorities would set aside the embarrassing wishes of the court with respect to the Harris treaty and seek instead the opinions of the various daimyo. The Bakufu's decision to do this would be made public in Edo only on 4/25. Or again, when in the eighth month Mito han was given a confidential decree from the court authorizing that han's opposition to Bakufu policies, Shōin, still without leaving his home, had already known about this for six days when the Chōshū government in Hagi was first informed. See *Yoshida Shōin zenshū*, ed. Yamaguchi ken kyōiku kai, 5: 138–39 and 1: 36.

† The spontaneous journalistic appetite of the Sonjuku was almost certainly widely shared by other groups. In the early 1870's scores of newspapers and journals would spring up in Japan and enjoy a thriving business despite the suddenness of their appearance. The unprecedentedly rapid success of the new Japanese press in the 1870's is a phenomenon that is difficult to explain. Part of the explanation may lie, however, in the widespread reliance in the 1860's and before on the private or semipublic newsletter as a source of information. It is perhaps worthy of note in this regard that personal reporting and the circulation of newsletters were the crucial intermediate steps that immediately preceded the establishment of the first newspapers in England. In that case also, the rapid growth of journalistic activities went hand in hand with a deepening of political awareness and participation. See Joseph Frank, *The Beginnings of the English Newspaper, 1620–1660* (Cambridge, Mass., 1961), pp. 2, 19–20.

Shōin used the information he received from his students in 1858 to help influence the decisions of Chōshū policymakers. After hearing of the failure of the reformist movement in the Bakufu, he wrote memorials incessantly, producing a major new document almost every month. These memorials were of two kinds. One group of them, including Shōin's "Modest Proposal" ("Guron"), "Words of a Madman" ("Kyōfu no gen"), and "Four Urgent Tasks" ("Kyūmu yonjō"), spelled out major institutional reforms that were needed at both domainal and national levels. A second set of memorials, including "A Policy Route" ("Taisaku ichidō"), "Discussion of the Great Justice" ("Taigi o gisu"), and "Discussion of Justice in Present Circumstances" ("Jigi ryakuron"), dealt with immediate policy issues, particularly the issue of what Chōshū han's response should be to the Harris treaty question. Shōin had never sought previously to intervene in Chōshū's daily political decisions, and his interest in Chōshū's attitude toward the treaty issue probably sprang from his perception that something much larger was at stake, namely, whether or not the realm would commit itself to the basic reforms that would permit it both to stem Western influence and to eliminate the grave injustices that had long plagued Bakuhan society.

Shōin had always assumed that the Bakufu as the highest authority in the land would eventually become the vehicle for major social reform. He had often written in defense of the Bakufu's basic authority and was doing so even as late as the fifth month of 1858: "All hate the evil conduct of the Tokugawa and some report this to the court. But this is born of flattery toward the court and jealousy toward the Bakufu. If one does not reflect well on this, it can lead to great error."[4] But when the "able daimyo" who made up the moderate reformist faction around Hitotsubashi lost out completely in 1858, the widespread public hopes for Bakufu-led reform were dissolved. When Shōin received the news that Ii Naosuke had signed the Harris treaty on 6/19 without an accompanying gesture of commitment to reform, he concluded that in spite of the confident hope he had placed in it, the Bakufu had finally shown itself incapable of supporting even the limited reformist program of the "able daimyo." In response to this melancholy turn of events, Shōin at last submitted to the Chōshū government an anguished memorial explaining his changed point of view.

Shōin's "Discussion of the Great Justice," presented on 7/13, contained for the first time a sophisticated assault on the Bakufu's basic right to rule. The Bakufu, Shōin claimed, was guilty of a serious violation of the realm's constitutional principles. Not only had it terminated the traditional practice of seclusion out of timidity rather than make the reforms necessary to resist; it had done so in disregard of the court's and many others' wishes that there be no unilateral concessions to the outsiders. The Bakufu had gravely infringed the mandate from the court on which the legitimacy of Bakufu rule depended.[5]

In a second memorial, submitted a few days later, called the "Discussion of Justice in Present Circumstances," Shōin outlined a program of comprehensive resistance to the Bakufu's conservative policies by Chōshū han. This program involved clearly and openly stating Chōshū's opposition to those policies, because of the favorable effect this in itself would have on public opinion. Far more surprising, however, was Shōin's suggestion that a new kind of armed force should be used.[6]

Shōin argued that the han should mobilize commoners to make a show of military force in Kyoto. There were 150,000 able-bodied men among Chōshū's four classes of samurai, farmer, artisan, and merchant, Shōin wrote, and 1 percent of these, 1,500 men, should be summoned from all classes as soldiers. One-third of that force, 500 men, should then be sent to the Kyoto-Ōsaka area so that it might be weighed in the political balance on the reformist side.[7] This recommendation long antedated the formation of the Kiheitai and other commoner military units by Shōin's followers in 1863. Shōin's advice also anticipated Chōshū's sending of the Kiheitai and other forces to Kyoto in 1864 as a means of coping with Bakufu influence there. The creation and bold use of a new commoner military would prove to be a decisive factor in the Chōshū activists' ultimate triumph over conservative forces later in the 1860's.

Two weeks after offering up the "Discussion of Justice," Shōin provided a more concrete demonstration of his commitment to the drastic step of using commoners as soldiers. He invited twenty-six youths from an interior farming village called Heta to his school in Hagi, where he drilled them for seventeen days in Western-style rifle formations. These exercises culminated in maneuvers carried out in the Hagi suburb of Ōihama, in which both the newly instructed farm youths and Shōin's own students participated side by side. Shōin had gone beyond toying with the idea of a new form of military organization and had actually begun drilling commoners in the use of the rifle.[8]

Shōin's activities in 1858 foreshadowed still another later strategy of the Sonjuku students. After having written several memorials to the Chōshū government, Shōin in the ninth month sent a memorial entitled "On the Conditions of the Times" ("Jiseiron") directly to the court noble Ōhara Shigetomi. In it he requested an explicitly anti-Bakufu decree from the court such as would justify independent action by the transient student population, which Shōin referred to as "retainers of the grassy field" (*sōmō no shin*), meaning retainers not locked into the feudal hierarchy in the sense of holding office. The court, he wrote, should authorize youthful activists to assail the Bakufu and its agents. What this meant was political street violence under an umbrella of imperial legitimacy.[9] This concept was a major tactical breakthrough. By relying on it in 1863, Shōin's followers would be able to move national politics in a reformist direction for the first time.

The first nine months of 1858 were a dynamic, formative period for the Chōshū activist movement. During this interval of energetic quest for effective political methods, Yoshida Shōin established the crucial pattern of coordination in dispersal among his students. He taught them how to gather and disseminate essential information, a discipline that produced the journalistic "Long View." He deluged the Chōshū government with memorials chal-

lenging the wisdom of Bakufu policies and interspersed these with
another series of memorials describing a broad panorama of needed
institutional changes. He anticipated both the basic plan of military organization that would sweep the field in 1865 and 1866 and
the political alliance that would hold sway in the national arena
in 1862 and 1863. Yoshida Shōin was one of those romantic dream-
ers that conservatives fear most. His dreams kept coming true.

ACTION

Better known than Yoshida Shōin's work in the first nine months
of 1858 are his efforts in the last three to eliminate the supervisory
agent of the Bakufu police repression in Kyoto, Manabe Akikatsu.
This has often been viewed as a foolhardy course of action. Nevertheless, given the extreme and violent circumstances in which
Shōin made the decision to pursue it, it represented a plausible
tactical approach to an intractable problem. Shōin's decision to
strike at Manabe could not have been more rational. It was deeply
rooted in the harsh realities of national politics that Shōin was
doing his level best to observe and comprehend.

When, in the seventh month of 1858, the Bakufu had placed
Hitotsubashi Yoshinobu and the other great reformist lords under
house arrest, it had only served to make the public outcry against
Bakufu policies more shrill. Ii Naosuke's attempts to manage pub-
lic opinion proved ineffective, and he therefore undertook a campaign of physical repression. So in the ninth month, the Ansei
arrest of Kyoto activists began. The elder loyalist poet Yanagawa
Seigan escaped by natural death on 9/2, but the younger Umeda
Umpin was caught in the Bakufu's net on 9/7. Other critics of the
Ii government were detained in the following weeks, and it was
understood that for many of these, detention would be terminal.
On 9/17 control of loyalist activities in Kyoto was tightened further by the arrival of the Bakufu senior councillor Manabe Akikatsu, the official whom Ii had placed in charge of the Ansei
repression in Kyoto.

The installation of this new regime of direct coercion meant
that Ii felt he had lost the battle of public conscience. Rather than

concede or retrench his policies, Ii chose to move the struggle into the realm of physical force, in which he believed he had the advantage. It was not long, however, before the hardiest elements on the reformist side began rising to the challenge that Ii had offered. Already in the ninth month a plan to blunt the force of the Ansei repression was being formed among a group of students, most of samurai rank, who were living in Kyoto and Edo. The cardinal objective of this plan was the assassination of Chancellor Ii himself. The group embraced some seventy members, including Hashimoto Sanai and Yūri Kōzei, the two Echizen samurai who were at the center. Satsuma was represented by Arima Shinshichi, and Tosa by Hashizume Akihei. Numerous Mito men also shared in the plan. It was their intention that Echizen's Matsudaira Yoshinaga come secretly to Kyoto and then assume police jurisdiction there in the confusion following Ii's projected death. In this connection the group was quietly calling on other activists to prepare an auxiliary plan to assassinate the Bakufu representative in Kyoto, Manabe Akikatsu.[10] Yoshida Shōin was promptly informed of all this through one of the more alert of his young political reporters, Akagawa Naojiro.[11]

At this time Shōin as a political observer had just passed through a period of many months of acute disappointment with the Bakufu's performance. The opportunity for ameliorative adjustment of Bakufu policy offered by the shogunal succession in the fifth and sixth months of 1858 was lost. Moreover, the Bakufu was now detaining and executing the realm's most articulate reformist spokesmen, many of whom, like Umeda Umpin, were personally known to Shōin. In other words, from Shōin's point of view, the Bakufu besides persisting in unwise policies had now embarked on a campaign of political extermination that included even his own friends. This was carrying things too far, and it was now clear to Shōin that some firm stance of opposition was urgently needed.

Shōin's response to the information Akagawa brought him was to cross at last the narrow boundary that separates articulate watchfulness from action. He undertook to construct a plan whereby Chōshū men would accommodate the Echizen group by assassinating Manabe. Like the conservative Ii Naosuke of the Bakufu and the reformist Hashimoto Sanai of Echizen, Shōin saw no other choice. He was now prepared to use force as an instrument of political influence. He enlisted seventeen of his own students, who swore to uphold the assassination prospectus. He then instructed the han government of the Echizen movement, and of his intention to complement it, in two letters written on 11/6/58. One of these letters was for Sufu Masanosuke, leader of the reformist "Justice faction" (*Seigi ha*) in the han government. The other letter was for Maeda Magoemon, a sympathetic high-ranking official, also of the Justice faction. The Justice faction in the Chōshū administration had actively favored institutional reform of various sorts for several decades. The purpose of Shōin's letters to these Justice officials was to enlist the cooperation of the han government in supplying travel orders and arms.[12]

To Sufu, Shōin revealed the news of the Echizen-Mito strategy, and said that it was not worthy for the Mori house to be left behind in the great deeds of loyalism. To Maeda, Shōin outlined what he wanted the government to do. He requested eight cannon from the han arsenal and added a list of the kinds and quantities of ammunition he wanted, 120 rounds in all. Shōin went on to ask that two of his students be sent to Kyoto as quickly as possible to prepare the way for the main group and that a third man be dispatched to Nagasaki and another to the central Kyūshū han of Higo for purposes of political communication.[13]

Shōin has been criticized both for making himself vulnerable by revealing his intentions to the Chōshū government, and also for not trying to make use of the government's resources in his political pursuits. In reality, Shōin did try to mobilize the han government, and he had reason to believe that his efforts would be successful. In his two letters of 11/6, Shōin was acting in accord with a pattern of cooperation that had gradually grown up between himself and the han government in the course of 1858. This pattern had begun with the government furnishing orders for study in Edo to Shōin's students. By the seventh month, it had produced not only a political reconnaissance expedition of

six Sonjuku men to Kyoto that included Itō Hirobumi and Yamagata Aritomo but also the reinstatement of Shōin's credentials as
an instructor in Yamaga learning, which had been in abeyance
since 1852.[14] Nevertheless, Shōin's Manabe expedition was destined never to come about because of the reaction of the han government to his requests for aid.

Shōin's carefully developed plans for Manabe generated adversity in unexpected quarters. Three independent forces opposed
his effort: Sufu Masanosuke, the voice of pragmatism at the han
administrative level; Nagai Uta, a highly placed han conservative; and Shōin's own very vulnerable students who were already
in the Kyoto area. Each of these elements was influenced in one
way or another by the Bakufu's enormous capacity to reward its
friends and punish its enemies. At the same time, none of these
three represented direct Bakufu interference, and none could have
been clearly anticipated. It is a measure of Shōin's influence that
in spite of all this adversity he never found himself politically isolated.

The most decisive opposition came from Sufu Masanosuke, in
response to Shōin's letter of 11/6. Maeda Magoemon, the other
recipient of one of Shōin's letters, appears to have viewed his plan
as suited to the needs of the time.[15] Sufu, on the other hand, as
responsible chief of the Justice faction in the government, was
apprehensive. The problem Sufu faced apropos of Shōin's Kyoto
expedition, whether he sympathized or not, was that of pressure
from the Bakufu. The Ansei Purge had already strengthened the
hand of Sufu's rivals in the so-called "Mundane Views faction"
(*Zokuron ha*), Chōshū's conservative clique. Provoking the Bakufu
could lead to a complete loss of the Justice faction's fragile dominance in the han government. Avoiding such an occurrence was
one of Sufu's responsibilities as leader of his faction.

The influential conservative Nagai Uta had aggravated Sufu's
anxieties in this regard. Nagai had recently been promoted to the
post of direct inspector (*choku metsuke*), and was trying to estab-

lish ties whereby he could personally represent Chōshū to the shogunal authorities. He was eager that Chōshū men not antagonize the Bakufu, and so put pressure on Sufu to restrain Shōin's activism.[16] Whether as a consequence of Nagai's machinations or out of the independent anxieties on Sufu's part about the future of the reformist Justice faction that he headed, the han government under Sufu's direction ordered on 11/29/58 that Shōin strictly observe his house arrest and confine his movements to one room. This did not dampen the ardor of Shōin or those around him, however; so on 12/5 Sufu ordered Shōin's reincarceration at Noyama prison.[17]

Yet not everyone agreed with those who had made the decision for reimprisonment. Rather, Shōin's cause enjoyed vigorous support in some quarters of the Hagi government as well as among his own followers. The Chōshū administration was divided into two parts, one that ran the daily affairs of government in Hagi and one that traveled with the daimyo to Edo. It was this Edo branch that managed interdomainal relations. In general, the Edo branch favored restraining Shōin, while the Hagi branch resisted the policy of reimprisoning him as too extreme.[18]

A bitter struggle took place at the end of November between those who favored reimprisonment and those who opposed it. This was not a case of the government against Shōin's Sonjuku, but rather a case of both the government and the Sonjuku splitting over the tense question of whether Shōin's direct-action approach to Bakufu repression was on the whole desirable. This split followed geographical lines. Students and officials in Edo and Kyoto, who were more vulnerable to Bakufu actions, favored restraint, whereas those in Hagi, who were less vulnerable, tended to favor positive action.

Shōin's uncle Tamaki Bunnoshin, other officials in the Hagi government, and Shōin's students themselves put pressure on Sufu's spokesman, Inoue Yoshirō, to justify the han's policy of incarcerating Shōin. Sufu had earlier declared that "Shōin's teachings are impure and he causes unrest in the human heart," and that he was therefore being jailed. Shōin's supporters raised an outcry over this, believing it could hardly be the true reason. Inoue finally had to admit that the Justice faction leadership had nothing against Shōin or his teachings. Their real reason for confining Shōin was only that Sufu did not want him to do anything that would embarrass the faction and so undermine its precarious dominance in the administration.[19]

Tamaki resigned from his post as a district administrator to protest Shōin's imprisonment. When the government accepted his resignation without a word of objection, he realized that the struggle was lost and urged Shōin to go to prison quietly.[20] Even when Tamaki felt he had exhausted his influence, however, some of Shōin's students still felt they had not used up theirs. Eight of them went to protest to Sufu and Inoue. When the two officials would not meet them, they "kept a noisy vigil through the night." On the following day, the han government arrested all eight.[21]

When the imprisonment order came down on 12/5, Shōin's students had held a farewell party for him at the Sonjuku. The government, however, granted him a reprieve of twenty days to nurse his ailing father, an action that tends to confirm Inoue's statement that the government's intention toward Shōin was to restrain, not to punish. This delay merited another farewell party on 12/26, after which Shōin went off to Noyama prison, accompanied as far as the gate by several students and old friends. Sufu himself, meanwhile, had come under so much criticism in connection with Shōin's reimprisonment that he had to retire temporarily from his post, claiming illness.[22]

Yoshida Shōin was never politically isolated during these troubled days, but rather had many determined sympathizers both within the government and without. Still, the division over the incarceration question that appeared in the Chōshū government was mirrored in a rift that emerged among Shōin's own students. Those living in Hagi supported Shōin's plans to eliminate Manabe. Those who had gone to Kyoto and Edo during 1858 opposed them. The issue that separated the two groups was not one of basic goals, nor was it one of conflicting personalities. The issue was one of political tactics, and each side couched its arguments persuasively in tactical terms.

On 12/11, soon after they had heard of their teacher's proposals and were able to confer on them, Kusaka Genzui, Takasugi Shinsaku, and three others sent him a letter rejecting his assassination plans. The rationale they used was that the time was not opportune. Bakufu officials were "behaving like madmen," and the public was not yet resisting. A public reaction would gradually set in, however, and Chōshū men should wait for that opportunity. This reasoning echoed Shōin's own in his highly critical letters to a younger Kusaka in 1856.[23]

Shōin was not impressed by the use of his own ideas against him, however. In a letter from prison to one of his students in Hagi, dated 1/11/59, Shōin put his reaction this way:

Waiting for the time, uselessly waiting for the time. . . . Without me, even waiting a thousand years, this kind of oppression would never have arisen. With me present, there will always be pressure. Loyalty is not like drinking tea when troubles are elsewhere. If I give up my offensive, enemy pressure will loosen. If I go on the offensive again, opposing attacks will necessarily become severe. The power relation of opposing forces is that kind of thing.[24]

Shōin did not believe as Kusaka and the others did that the Ansei Purge would soon lift in the natural course of things. Rather, he believed it was a reaction to reformist pressure. From this point of view, the only way to avoid the purge was to give up one's commitment to reform. To wait for a time when there could be reformist activism without conservative repression would be to wait perpetually. When the future of the realm seemed in his best judgment to depend on the use of force without delay, Shōin had instructed his modest cadre to act, but the students had refused. They had refused, moreover, on the grounds that the situation was too dangerous for them personally. Shōin was furious.

The students in Edo and Kyoto were also unhappy. Shōin, their teacher, had always seemed a reasonable enough man. Now, however, from a vantage point of safe and comfortable arrest in his own house, he was arranging their involvement in conduct that was extremely dangerous and of uncertain outcome. Unlike the Hagi students, who agreed with Shōin about the desirability of immediate action, the students in Edo and Kyoto lived each day under the scrutiny of the Bakufu, a process that made them more sensitive than their Hagi brethren to the Bakufu police power. Nonetheless, the rift did not prevent Kusaka Genzui in Edo from submitting to the han government in the first month of 1859 an anxious written request for Shōin's release.[25]

Subsequent events would partially vindicate both groups. Shōin was later shown to be correct in his assumption that the Bakufu's resistance to reform-oriented policies would be substantially loosened only by the resolute use of force, as it was by the group assassination of Ii Naosuke on 3/3/60 and by the wounding of Senior Councillor Andō Nobumasa on 1/15/62. The Edo students were correct that Chōshū men would have better opportunities if they waited. For the moment, however, Shōin's fate was sealed. When the smoke cleared in the twelfth month, he was a prisoner.

PERSISTENCE AND RESIGNATION

Shōin had taught his students to be patient and resolute. He taught them never to yield. In the months following his reimprisonment, he showed some of this same spirit of determination. From his cell in prison he devised another project, involving direct access to the daimyo and cooperation with the court. When this, too, failed, however, Shōin found that he was tired. Still, he found time to revise his tactical approach to Kyoto politics, and to forgive his momentary adversary Sufu Masanosuke.

By the second month of 1859, while still confined in Noyama prison, Shōin had begun to shape a new plan. Because circumstances had forced him to abandon his efforts to eliminate Manabe Akikatsu in Kyoto, his new strategy was more modest. Since 11/58 Shōin had advocated that the Mōri house avoid the period of *sankin kōtai* attendance scheduled to begin in March of 1859. Takachika still intended to go to Edo for this purpose, however, prompting Shōin to devise his "petition at the palanquin" plan (*Yōgasaku*).

Shōin's strategy was premised on the cooperation of Chōshū and the court, a concept that would later become a key to the politics of the 1860's. The plan provided that as the Chōshū daimyo Mōri Takachika passed through Fushimi, the court noble Ōhara Shigetomi and several of Shōin's students would slip past the guards and persuade him to enter Kyoto rather than continue on to Edo. There he could add the weight of Chōshū to court and activist resistance to Bakufu policies. Indeed, Takachika's entering Kyoto would itself be a dramatic official protest by Chōshū han against Bakufu policies. Besides that, even if the daimyo were not persuaded to make a detour, which was likely, the firm effort to make direct contact with him would have an impact on han policy. "Even if the plan fails, its influence on the daimyo will not be small," as Shōin put it.[26]

For the mission of approaching the daimyo, Shōin dispatched the student Nomura Wasaku to Kyoto on 2/24. Nomura carried a letter of explanation to Ōhara, and with Ōhara was to carry out the "petition at the palanquin" on 3/19. Shōin's efforts to divert Mōri Takachika into Kyoto as a loyalist sponsor were frustrated, however. Maebara Issei and three other students from the Hagi group doubted the propriety of the petition attempt, and informed the han government. Thus alerted, the han authorities thwarted the plan. Nomura was apprehended on 3/22 and sent back to Chōshū, where he was confined in Iwakura prison.[27]

Students in Edo who had opposed the Manabe assassination plan would not support the petition effort either, and this time they were joined by Maebara and others in Hagi. Shōin was most dissatisfied. On 3/29 he wrote to Kusaka Genzui in Hagi, criticizing him for not supporting the petition plan and breaking off relations with him. This intransigence was short-lived, however, and he received Kusaka and Shinagawa Yajirō as visitors at Noyama prison on 5/14.[28]

After his plans to petition the daimyo were also blocked, Shōin devoted some effort in the fourth month to revising his views of what a workable strategy for Kyoto politics might be: "Since last year I have exercised my power in suitable ways, but this nowhere succeeds and I am just sitting in prison. At present neither the Bakufu nor the several daimyo come to anything. Both are easily distracted. One can only hope for someone who will bring about a rising among ordinary, independent persons (*sōmō kukki*)." * The solution, he now felt, might lie in a greater reliance on unaffiliated activists, meaning students in the two capitals and other samurai or declassed elements who were politically conscious but not directly engaged in domainal service: "My trying to make a partner of the government was the error of a lifetime. In the future I would surely like to try again, relying on proposals that use ordinary, independent persons (*sōmō*)." [29] In the early 1860's Shōin's followers would rely to great advantage on this strategy of using "ordinary, independent persons" in their efforts to counter Bakufu influence.

It is sometimes supposed that in his last years Shōin relied on individual activists rather than on the han government because he was more interested in political style than in political results. The opposite was more nearly true. Shōin sought repeatedly to use the obvious instrumentality of the han government. When he got no sustained results, he turned, somewhat tardily, toward a theoretical reliance on the use of students and other activist elements in Kyoto.

Shōin's mood after the failure of his petition plan was marked by disappointment and acquiescence. In a letter of 5/13/59 to Takasugi Shinsaku, advising him to abandon plans to free his teacher from prison, Shōin interspersed observations like these: "Since the daimyo left for Edo I do not want to do anything, or even to be alive. . . . I want to sleep and do not do much reading and writing either. My desire to do research is also meager. I just want to have some pleasantness." [30]

Shōin also devoted a passage of his letter to the exoneration of

* *Yoshida Shōin zenshū*, ed. Yamaguchi ken kyōiku kai, 9: 326. The literal meaning of *sōmō* is "grassy field," in the sense of "grass roots" participants.

Sufu Masanosuke, the leader of the Justice faction: "You know that Sufu thinks well of me. You know that Sufu is a great personality, and you know how hard he works. If you look back on the affair of last year, there were errors on Sufu's part, on my part, and on the part of many persons who used their offices in between. . . . I really do not bear a grudge against Sufu."[31] Because there was no longer any political result at stake, Shōin could abandon his critical attitude toward Sufu. Shōin and Sufu had been on good terms prior to their collision in 11/58, and Sufu would actively assist the reformist efforts of Shōin's students in the 1860's. Shōin sensed that Sufu was a fundamental ally and wished to avoid any lasting antagonism building up between him and the Sonjuku.

Shōin had persevered in his political pursuits, even though confined in a cramped and drafty cell at Noyama prison. Repeated setbacks, however, had finally brought him to a state of emotional fatigue. He had lost interest even in scholarship, which previously had held a transcendent meaning for him. Weariness and failure had made Shōin, at least for a time, into an ordinary man, with elementary concerns and desires.

EXECUTION

Shōin was not to be allowed much time in Noyama prison to rebuild his morale. In the fourth and fifth months of 1859 the relentless scythe of the Ansei Purge was finally approaching Shōin himself. Again it would be the highly placed Chōshū conservative Nagai Uta who would play an active role in Shōin's downfall. Once again, as at the time of his imprisonment, Shōin's friends stood by him.

The drama leading to Shōin's death had already begun to unfold in the wings on 4/19/59. On that day the Bakufu, acting on reports of its Kyoto agent Nagano Shuzen, had ordered that Shōin be delivered to Edo for interrogation. The Bakufu's order was promoted within the Chōshū government by Nagai Uta, who was trying to initiate talks on the foreign problem between himself as Chōshū's representative on the one hand and the Bakufu on the

other. Nagai had earlier played a pivotal role in Shōin's reimprisonment by Chōshū on 12/25/58. He was trying to impress
the Bakufu with Chōshū's good faith.

On 4/21 Nagai left Edo for Hagi, in order personally to deliver
the mandate for Shōin's extradition and to oversee its execution.
Nagai carried a han order authorizing that Shōin be turned over
in secret. This procedure, said the order, was to be carried out
without informing anyone unnecessarily, even in the Hagi government. The purpose of this was to prevent public debate from
"boiling up" as it had when Shōin was removed to Noyama prison
the previous December.[32] This was an exercise in public deception. It was because Nagai already knew that much of the public
would oppose this maneuver that he concealed it from the public.

Secrecy was observed. Shōin's vocal relatives in the government,
Sugi Yūrinosuke, his father, and Tamaki Bunnoshin, his uncle,
were put under house arrest to stifle any reaction that might have
been led by them. There was no farewell party this time, but the
younger of Shōin's jailors, who had attended the Sonjuku, allowed
him to return to his home for a day to say goodbye to his family.
Then at dawn on 5/25 Shōin was placed in a prisoner's portable
cage and sent on his way to Edo. This departure was further
clouded by the fears of those closest to him that he would be
poisoned while en route by Nagai Uta.[33]

A month later Shōin reached Chōshū's compound in Edo, and
on 7/9/59 he was taken to the Bakufu's Demmachō prison for interrogation. He found the examining commissioner to be of tol-
erant disposition and told him more than was in his best interest.
The interrogation process was repeated on 9/5 and again on
10/5.[34]

The interrogators' recommendation to the Bakufu council on
10/16 asked only that Shōin be banished to a distant island, but
Chancellor Ii Naosuke personally intervened, as he often did in
Ansei cases, and changed the sentence to death. The announce-
ment of the penalty also described Shōin's offenses. Among the
crimes listed were his attempt to study abroad and his having

written "Words of a Madman," one of the memorials in which he had advocated social reconstruction.[35]

Most of Yoshida Shōin's outside contact during his last months was with Takasugi Shinsaku. The others of the Sonjuku inner circle had been recalled to Hagi to prevent their political involvement. Nagai Uta and the han government had taken special care to delay Takasugi's learning that Shōin had been extradited, fearing what he might do. When he did find out, Takasugi became a frequent visitor at Demmachō prison, bringing his mentor food and books. In October, Takasugi was called back to Hagi in his turn, through the influence of his father, who did not want him associating with political prisoners. Shōin was grateful and disappointed. He wrote to Takasugi on 10/7: "Your being in Edo at the time of my misfortune was an extremely happy circumstance. I am deeply appreciative of your kindness. Hearing suddenly of your return to the han, I could not help greatly regretting it."[36]

Shōin might also have enjoyed the company on the inside of Demmachō prison. The inmates at that time included some of the foremost activists of the realm—men like Rai Mikisaburō, son of the reformist historian Rai Sanyō, and Hashimoto Sanai, the talented scholar from Echizen. These young leaders and others were sentenced to death early in the tenth month.

Yoshida Shōin was sentenced on 10/17 and executed ten days later on 10/27. By the executioner's account, "Shōin's attitude at the moment of death was truly admirable." He seemed at peace with himself. Before taking his place at the block, he turned to the attendant who had guided him to the execution chamber and said, "Thank you for your trouble (*gokurōsama*)." At the moment of death, as in life, he was a "true gentleman."[37] The last words to come from his brush had been his "Record of a Halted Spirit" ("Ryūkonroku"), a political will for his family and students that he had completed on the eve of execution.

The teacher's last remains were received by four of his followers and buried next to those of Hashimoto Sanai at the Ekōin temple in a suburb called Kōzukahara. Two of the four, Kido

Kōin and Itō Hirobumi, would later become major architects of the new Japan. They left on their teacher's grave only a rough stone marker that read, "Shōin—Twenty-One Times a Valiant Samurai (*Mōshi*)." It was Itō, future author of the Meiji Constitution, who wrote to Kusaka and Takasugi in Hagi: "You must try to imagine the outrage and despair experienced by the four of us."[38]

Yoshida Shōin's conduct in 1858 and 1859 represented a high level of political engagement. He was acutely aware of political events and tried to respond to them in a way that would allow his dreams for the realm to come true. The unusual degree of Shōin's commitment has led many observers to mistake his imaginative hopes for irrationality and his transcendent determination for irresponsibility.

Although Shōin's attempts to sway national politics in 1858 and 1859 were not immediately successful, his activities provided a crucial organizational groundwork for the political undertakings of his followers in the 1860's. He closely monitored affairs in Kyoto in 1858, and when shogunal leadership seemed to be veering in a permanently conservative direction, he sought to develop a strategy that would prevent this. He sent his students out to Kyoto, Edo, and elsewhere and cultivated among them a vital network of communication, with one another and also with the reformers and activists of other domains. This network would provide essential information and also in later years would serve as a basis for widely coordinated and highly effective political action.

At the same time, Shōin was working out some of the other strategic solutions that would later bring success to the Chōshū movement. He anticipated the desirability of political cooperation between the court and Chōshū and between the court and young activists of many domains. These alliances would dominate the stage of national politics in the early 1860's. Shōin proposed in his memorials that Chōshū recruit a new military from among commoners and send part of this army to Kyoto to counter Bakufu influence there. He went further and actually drilled commoners with his own students in Western rifle formations. This new kind of military, too, would prove to be an invaluable resource for his followers later on.

In short, Shōin not only established the organizational cohesion of the Sonjuku group; he also thought out several elements of the basic strategy by which his followers would later prevail. Although his political efforts in the late 1850's failed and he himself met with a tragic death, the cadre he had nurtured and the methods he had developed would begin in the 1860's to bear fruit. Those early successes would be due in large measure to the resourcefulness of another man, a brilliant political observer and organizer who, like his predecessor, was prepared if necessary to give his life as well as his talent for the reformist cause.

CHAPTER FIVE

The Early Career of Kusaka Genzui
1859-1862

ALTHOUGH Kusaka Genzui is almost unknown in Western scholarship, he was the most gifted and versatile of the great Chōshū restorationists. Even though he would be required to step down from the political stage at an early moment, he was already distinguished for his political skill and sheer intelligence, as well as for his physical courage.

After Yoshida Shōin's death, leadership of the Sonjuku group, both spiritual and practical, fell to Kusaka as the most promising of his followers. The students did not disown Yoshida's memory, but rather, under Kusaka's guidance, they drew closer together to reaffirm the ideals that he had died for. The Sonjuku academy for public men survived its founder's passage, so that it might still fulfill the great hopes that he had placed in it.

Kusaka would develop a pattern of close cooperation with high-ranking Chōshū bureaucrats of the Justice faction, and was one of the first of Shōin's followers to move into the han bureaucracy. Cooperation with Justice officials would prove a key to the political effectiveness of the Sonjuku group in the years ahead. Approaching sympathetic elements in the government might seem to have represented a sharp break with Yoshida's expectations, but actually it did not. Kusaka's ties with highly placed reformist officials long antedated his teacher's death, and there had always been friendly exchange between Justice bureaucrats and the Sonjuku. The social origins of the bureaucrats Kusaka worked with were virtually identical with those of the Sonjuku leadership itself. The two groups were part of a shared ethos, and the only criterion that clearly differentiated them was age.

Kusaka Genzui's activities in Hagi and Kyoto did not represent a startling transition. They represented a startling continuity.

KUSAKA'S EARLY LIFE AND
POLITICAL EDUCATION

Kusaka Genzui, like Yoshida Shōin, was born into an environment in which vocational expectations were high and material comforts were few. Unlike his mentor, however, Kusaka became involved in the exhilarating street politics of the metropolis at an early age. He inherited the many contacts that Yoshida had acquired over the years and developed many more of his own. He became an accomplished practitioner of Kyoto politics before he was twenty, and it was above all in this role that he would serve the reformist movement in the years ahead.

Kusaka Genzui was born in Hagi in 1840, the second son of the han physician Kusaka Yoshimichi. Although Yoshimichi belonged to the seventh of Chōshū's seventeen samurai (shi) ranks, his family received only 25 koku of income, an amount not far removed from bare subsistence. Nonetheless, the scholarly accomplishments of the Kusaka household had been plentiful. Genzui's older brother Genki was an assiduous student of Western medicine, and his translations of Western books were widely known. In the course of his studies he had discovered the West's miraculous technique for preventing smallpox and had introduced smallpox vaccination in Chōshū. Genki's scholarship was one measure of the professional dedication that distinguished the domestic milieu into which Kusaka Genzui was born. Moreover, both Genzui's father and his brother Genki died in the early months of 1854, leaving Genzui at fourteen as the sole male representative of the Kusaka house, a situation that heightened further the vocational expectations to which he was heir.

Kusaka began his education at a neighborhood grammar school, where Takasugi Shinsaku also attended as a small child. He then studied privately under the Buddhist priest Gesshō, a friend of both Yoshida Shōin and Sufu Masanosuke. Gesshō recommended that Kusaka arrange to study at the Shōka Sonjuku, but the young physician chose instead to spend his early adolescent years studying with his peers at the Meirinkan.[1]

In the spring of 1856 Kusaka set out on a grand tour of Kyūshū, as Yoshida Shōin had done six years before. Early and frequent travel was the hallmark of the samurai of modest origins who was grooming himself for professional service. Such travel was usually rich in observation, often in a poetic mode, and permitted many friendly stops along the way. Travel for young men with Kusaka's acumen was also politically useful. It was a constant source of helpful contacts and information.[2]

In Kumamoto, Kusaka met Miyabe Teizō, who like Gesshō encouraged him to study with Yoshida Shōin in his own Hagi; so that when Kusaka returned to Chōshū in June, he finally sought admission to the Sonjuku. Among the exceptional young men who gathered at Yoshida's school, Kusaka soon came to be regarded as the most capable. After a year and a half at the academy, he applied to the Chōshū government for permission to study in Edo, an honor given only to the finest students in the han. This was granted in January 1858, and a going-away celebration was held at the Sonjuku. Forty-two of the students offered poems for the occasion, and the instructor made an address. These remarks revealed both the profound regard that Yoshida Shōin had for his departing pupil and the explicit hopes he placed upon him for the future of Japan.[3]

Kusaka Genzui's practical education in the ways of the metropolis was now about to begin. On 2/26/58 he set out from Hagi for Edo, the first of many Sonjuku students who would eventually do so. Yoshida had provided his protégé with as many introductions as he could. Kusaka carried papers for Kido Kōin and letters for two samurai of Matsushiro han urging them to use their good offices so that he might study with Yoshida's old teacher Sakuma Shōzan.[4] Yoshida provided other useful contacts and advice. Shortly after Kusaka's departure, the instructor sent this message ahead for him: "In Ōsaka visit Ōkubo Kaname. At Kyoto, visit Mito's

Ugai Kichizaemon, then Umeda Umpin and Yanagawa Seigan. Seigan knows many court nobles, too. It would also be entertaining to inquire after the [Bakufu's] municipal commissioners Asano and Kawaji, pretending to be a page. The officials of the Bakufu offer an appearance of great genius, as might be expected."[5] When he reached Edo on 4/7, Kusaka put in an appearance at Sakurada Hall in accordance with his traveling orders. Soon afterward, however, he set out again for Kyoto, where he would spend most of the rest of the year.

It was in the spring of 1858, just as Kusaka arrived in Kyoto, that the great questions of the Harris treaty and of shogunal succession first began to be debated among the Bakufu councils and the public. Kusaka plunged into the already increasingly turbulent politics of the imperial metropolis. He befriended Yanagawa Seigan and Umeda Umpin, the leaders of Kyoto activism for a decade, and formed as many ties as he could with anyone with whom he seemed to have political interests in common.[6]

Kusaka expressed his excitement at being in Kyoto in a letter he wrote to Yoshida Shōin in the fall of 1858, after hearing a rumor that the Chōshū government was about to order him back to Hagi: "I heard we might have to leave the capital and return home. . . . I have been hiding out at Umeda's since this morning. . . . For me there is no honor in returning home, and even if the Hagi officials order me to again and again, I will never return to the han. You may guess what my true feelings are. These days I am thinking about taking refuge in the Takada area of Yamato."[7] At this moment a rash of arrests was occurring, linked to the Ansei Purge, and Bakufu pressure in Kyoto and on the Chōshū government was increasing. Political intrigue was in the air, and Kusaka Genzui thrived on it.

Kusaka brought up another matter in his letter that revealed what was coming to be his keen sense of Kyoto politics. The contents of Yoshida's proposals had actually leaked to the public while en route to his students in Kyoto. Kusaka sharply criticized his mentor for allowing this to happen and painstakingly explained to him a procedure by which he could prevent it.[8] Kusaka would serve as the Sonjuku's increasingly resourceful agent in Kyoto for much of the next four years. When his value in that role became apparent, he would serve in the same capacity for the Chōshū government, at first unofficially and later officially. In 1863 he would be appointed by han order to the post of chargé for Kyoto affairs (*gakushūin goyō gakari*).[9]

After he was established in Kyoto, Kusaka became a contact for younger Sonjuku students when they arrived in the city. In July of 1858, Yoshida wrote Kusaka telling him of the six Sonjuku students and associates who were on their way, including Itō Hirobumi and Yamagata Aritomo. Kusaka was especially impressed by the sincerity and commitment of Yamagata, who had come to Kyoto with this group even though he was not himself a Sonjuku student. It was on the strength of Kusaka's subsequent recommendation that Yamagata would first be admitted to the school when he returned to Chōshū in September. The Sonjuku group thus acquired another prominent future leader of the new Japan.[10]

When Yoshida wrote to his students two months later trying to enlist them in his plan to assassinate Manabe Akikatsu, both Kusaka and Takasugi Shinsaku were unreservedly opposed. They and three other students outlined their opposition in a letter to their instructor on 12/11/58. Kusaka explained that Bakufu repression was too great and that action would be futile unless postponed and combined with a general swell of public resistance.[11]

Kusaka had a sense of what Bakufu police in the street meant, in a way that his long-confined mentor could not. His friend Umeda Umpin had been taken into custody only a few months before, and his regular association with Umeda was no secret. On that basis alone he had good reason to believe that he was under surveillance, and that if there were trouble with Chōshū men, he would be the first person Bakufu agents would seek out. Yoshida was simply not in a position to appreciate the delicate relationship that existed in 1858 between the Sonjuku students in Kyoto and the Ansei Purge. Still, Kusaka's rejection of his teacher's assassination plan was not a rejection of Yoshida or his goals. Just a few weeks after his critical letter to Yoshida of 12/11, he submitted another to the Chōshū government in Edo pleading for his instructor's release from Noyama prison.[12]

Because the Chōshū government also feared trouble for Kusaka from the Bakufu, an order was issued on 12/15/58 directing him to return to Hagi. Kusaka had long been expecting such an order, and did not want to go. He first went to Edo to protest, but finally gave in and set out for home on 2/15/59, arriving there a month later.[13]

When Kusaka returned to Chōshū in his nineteenth year, he already enjoyed a reputation as an unusually promising student, and this reputation had been enhanced by his selection for study in Edo. Far more important than this for Kusaka's future, however, were the many contacts he had made in the metropolis and his urban political experiences. During his year in the two capitals he had acquired a sense of practical politics that complemented the considerable theoretical knowledge he had earlier absorbed at the Shōka Sonjuku. Both his correspondence and his conduct revealed that he had achieved a certain feel for Kyoto politicking, and in the years ahead, the cause of Chōshū activism would have need of every iota of Kusaka's hard-won political acumen.

THE CONTINUATION OF THE SONJUKU

In the course of 1858 Kusaka had been the first of the Sonjuku students to come to grips with the political realities of the metropolis. In 1859 and 1860 he would be faced by another pathbreaking task: that of sustaining the integrity and spirit of the Sonjuku group at the time of its first encounter with death.

After his return to Hagi in the third month of 1859, life was quieter for Kusaka, and he may have missed the exhilaration of life in the capital. Nonetheless, his tactical dispute with Yoshida Shōin over the use of direct action in Kyoto grew more intense for a time. On 3/29 Yoshida broke off relations with him. These hard feelings among old friends were short-lived, however, and had largely evaporated within a few weeks. On 5/14, Kusaka and Shinagawa Yajirō made a social call on their reconciled mentor at Noyama prison. They even talked him into allowing one of the students to make a portrait of him for the Sonjuku. This was done none too soon. At almost the same time, Nagai Uta arrived in Hagi with his furtive extradition order, and Yoshida was spirited away to Edo the following week.[14]

When Yoshida was executed several months later, Kusaka and the others had to consider what this event would mean for the common purpose that had been cultivated at the Sonjuku, and indeed whether the school would continue to exist. It was Kusaka Genzui who at this juncture assumed leadership of the Sonjuku group. Yoshida while imprisoned in Edo had specifically instructed Kusaka in Hagi to look after the education of younger students like the Irie brothers, and Kusaka was widely recognized by persons within the Sonjuku and without as the school's most capable member.

The teacher himself had left clear instructions to his students as to how they should feel toward his death: "You all know what my purpose has been. Therefore I wish that you not grieve over my execution. Grieving over me is not as important as acceding to my ideas and goals and developing them further."[15] Whether because they were roused by entreaties like this from their mentor or because of loyalties and affection built up over the years, Kusaka's and the others' response to Yoshida's death was that which he requested. Kusaka wrote at this time to his new protégé Irie Sugizō: "To lament the teacher's sad life is profitless. The important thing is not to let the teacher's intentions falter. . . . Shinsaku is growing more and more and advances greatly in his insights and studies. . . . I will also send letters to Terajima, Ariyoshi, Maebara, Shinagawa, and the others to encourage them."[16] Takasugi Shinsaku and the other students also assumed this attitude of distilling grief into commitment.[17]

After Yoshida's death, Kusaka spent much of his time at the Sonjuku, and the other students continued to come as well to read their teacher's works and to share with each other their sorrow. They gathered together all of the letters that Yoshida had written, and by January of 1860, Kusaka was convening the students regularly to read, and even gave lectures himself beginning on 1/7/60. On 2/7, one hundred days after their mentor's execution, the students gathered in a larger number than usual to renew their commitment.[18]

These gestures surrounding Yoshida Shōin's death were not without a certain method. Both Yoshida and those who survived him had been quick to grasp the potential of the execution as a way of infusing meaning into the reformist cause. There was a transference of leadership and a kind of process of martyrdom and canonization that served to invigorate the Sonjuku movement. A kind of political scripture emerged in the form of Yoshida's assembled letters. Reaction to the teacher's execution was remarkable for the continuity it revealed in the life of the group. There was no collapse or swift transformation, but rather an evolving political sophistication that was not checked by death.

Yoshida Shōin was gone, but the "academy of the village under the pines," the chosen instrument of his spirit and political will, still lived. Under Kusaka's leadership, and propelled now by a deepened current of personal commitment, the Sonjuku was as strong as it had ever been. Thanks to the dedication of Kusaka and the others, the academy continued to thrive, and continued to be nourished by the example of its first teacher.

KUSAKA, SUFU, AND NAGAI

In the following two years, 1860 and 1861, Kusaka achieved some of the highest forms of academic recognition available in Chōshū and the realm. His politicking in the two capitals continued, but he also found time to develop personal ties with highly placed reformist officials of his own domain, especially Sufu Masanosuke. Close cooperation between street activists and the Chōshū government would have a decisive impact on national politics in 1862 and 1863, and some of the personal basis for that cooperation was laid by Kusaka and Sufu in the early 1860's.

In the second month of 1860, as one of the han's most promising students of Western learning, Kusaka was enrolled by the Chōshū government in the Bakufu's Naval Education School (Gunkan kyōkōsho) in Edo. Even during the heady political months of 1858, Kusaka had been able to sustain his scholarly pursuits. He had entered the school of Yoshina Kinryō and even studied briefly in the Bakufu's Bureau of Foreign Books (Bansho shirabesho). He had also been appointed a dormitory master at Chōshū's Bureau of Western Learning (Seiyō gakusho) in 1859. In accordance with his enrollment now in the naval school, Kusaka was required to journey to Edo once more.[19]

Kusaka arrived in Edo in May, just as the death of the head of state had engendered a new wave of political instability. Two months before his arrival, a platoon of transient Mito samurai had swept past Chancellor Ii Naosuke's sixty-man escort and killed him, as he approached the Sakurada gate of Edo Castle. The harsh policies of the Ansei Purge were then moderated, and loyalist reformers discovered that they had more latitude for action than ever before. Kusaka found himself, then, spending much of his time with Takechi Zuizan of Tosa, Tokiyama Naohachi of Edo, and Kobayama Sanen of Satsuma. With these activist leaders and others he discussed the possibility of achieving an alliance between the four han of Satsuma, Chōshū, Mito, and Tosa, as well as other policy options involving informal diplomacy or direct action.*

Sufu Masanosuke, already the most prominent member of the Justice faction in the Chōshū government, came up to Edo in the eighth month. Sufu was a modestly stipended Great Group samurai of 68 koku who had proven himself as a scholar in his earlier years and then risen through the ranks of the Chōshū bureaucracy to a position of influence in the government. Although Sufu had been obliged by the pressures of his office to play a brief part in re-

* Shōka sonjuku no ijin Kusaka Genzui, ed. Fukumoto Yoshisuke (Tokyo, 1934), p. 37. Kido Kōin, working in concert with Kusaka, was engaged in similar essays in interhan alliance during the course of 1861. For this purpose he cultivated ties with Mito's Nishimaru Tatewaki and Minobe Shinzō, and Satsuma's Kawaminami Jirōemon and Kobayama Sanen. He also strove successfully to put these men in touch with ranking Chōshū officials like Sufu and Shishido Kurōbei for more substantive talks. See Ōe Shigenobu, Kido Kōin (Tokyo, 1968), pp. 56–57.

turning Yoshida Shōin to Noyama prison in 1858, he subsequently proved himself a dependable ally of the Sonjuku group.*

In the latter months of 1860, Kusaka managed for the first time to arrange personal meetings between Sufu and activist leaders of other domains whom he and his slightly older Sonjuku colleague Kido Kōin had screened.[20] From 1861 to 1864 Kusaka, Sufu, and those who worked with them made a formidable combination at the forefront of the reformist movement in Chōshū. They were formidable because of the broad range of policy options they could orchestrate, from street violence in Kyoto to official acts by the Chōshū daimyo.

The policy issue that presented the strongest challenge to the new association of Kusaka and Sufu in 1861 was the proposed mediation of Nagai Uta between the Bakufu and the court. A descendant of the house of Mōri, Nagai came from a social background that was different from that of the Chōshū reformers. His family's hereditary income of 300 koku was much greater than that of most of the members of the Shōka Sonjuku. In his youth Nagai had had private tutors in abundance, and being from the older, upper reaches of the Great Group stratum, he was allowed to become a page and personally to assist the daimyo. Nagai avoided routine administrative work during the early stages of his career, performing instead the more prestigious task of educating the heir. He first came into political view in the early 1860's as Chōshū's envoy to the Bakufu, an activity that again involved prestige and protocol rather than daily toil. For service in this capacity he was raised to the exalted rank of middle elder (*churō*) in 1861. Nagai belonged to the favored group of "inner vassals" that Yoshida Shōin often bitterly criticized.[21]

Nagai was in Edo in 1858 and, in his post of direct inspector, was given the task of dealing with the Bakufu during the Ansei Purge. Being of conservative bent, he sought to keep relations with the Bakufu as mutually accommodating as possible. To this end Nagai played an active part in the fatal deliverance of Yoshida

* Compare Yoshida's letter of 5/13/59 to Takasugi Shinsaku quoted above: "You know that Sufu thinks well of me. . . ." (p. 87).

Shōin in 1859, so that the attitude of the surviving Sonjuku students toward him was never one of good feeling.

By 1861, Nagai's carefully nurtured association with the Bakufu was coming to fruition. In an attempt to serve as a mediator between the Bakufu and the newly emergent court, he composed a national program that was ostensibly a compromise between the interests of the court and those of the Bakufu. The content of Nagai's program represented a modification of the "open country" (*kaikoku*) ideas advocated earlier by Yoshida Shōin and other reformist thinkers in Chōshū. Yoshida in his "A Policy Route" of 1858 had advocated an aggressive policy of "crossing the seas and trading" (*kōkai tsūshi*), sending talent abroad, and adopting a militant stance at home, before signing the Harris treaty with the Americans. He had relied on loyalist rhetoric and had criticized the passive attitude of the Bakufu.[22] The blueprint for mediation that Nagai presented to the Chōshū government in the third month of 1861 emulated Yoshida's kaikoku language. Its title, "A Policy for Crossing the Seas" ("Kōkai enryaku saku"), echoed Yoshida's slogan, "Cross the seas and trade." The intent of that language was reversed, however. Nagai's kaikoku was not an aggressive policy alternative to the Bakufu's passive treaty with Harris. Rather Nagai portrayed "crossing the seas" as equivalent to measures already provided for in the treaty.

The han council referred Nagai's proposal to Sufu, who redrafted it to restore Yoshida Shōin's more rigorous emphases.* Sufu's version was offered up on 3/28/61 and accepted by the council.[23] When Nagai received approval of his mediation program in this modified form, he set out for Kyoto. He presented his proposals to the court noble Sanjō Sanetomi on 5/23, and since they seemed better for the court than other available options, they were approved by the emperor on 6/2.

The problem was that the policies Nagai offered to Sanjō resembled his own conciliatory position, not the strong mandate drafted by Sufu. Sanjō's contacts with reformist elements at all

* The respective contents of Sufu's draft and Nagai's are outlined in note 23, pp. 239–40.

levels were numerous, and it was not long before the contents of Nagai's mediation became known. Kusaka expressed his feelings on Nagai's position in a letter to Irie Sugizō on 6/22/61: "The 'cross the seas policy' was originally the view of our departed teacher Shōin. But these days it is a view that anyone can understand. It is a pleasing opinion especially to those whose chief aim is conciliation. . . . A policy that opens the way to navigation but does not send persons 10,000 miles beyond the seas will not do. . . . Advocating navigation in vain differs completely from the view of our teacher Shōin."* Nagai, unlike Shōin, had advocated opening the country without internal reforms. Kusaka criticized Nagai broadly in a memorial handed to the Chōshū daimyo by Sufu in September.[24]

Sufu was also displeased with Nagai for having altered the terms of the han's mandate. Therefore on 9/7/61 he and Kusaka went together to Kyoto to discuss the situation with the Chōshū heir, who was on his way to Edo. When they found that the heir had been delayed by illness, they decided to meet with Nagai himself, who was traveling in advance of the heir's party. They explained their position to him in detail, but Nagai was not moved and ordered both men back to Hagi. He had Sufu dismissed from his post and placed him under twenty days of house arrest as well. The two disappointed reformers set out for Hagi in mid-October.[25]

This experience gave Sufu an opportunity to get to know Kusaka well and left him favorably disposed toward the young Sonjuku leader. Sufu wrote to a friend in the government on 9/30/61 that "Kusaka Genzui's deportment matures from day to day. His conduct is impeccable, and although he is only twenty-two years of age, he has the discretion and frankness of an older man. He is a man of ability (*jinzai*) whom we should befriend, and we are fortunate to have him."[26] Kusaka Genzui's ability impressed Sufu Masanosuke as it had impressed Yoshida Shōin. Sufu was one of the most powerful men in Chōshū han and one who, like Shōin,

---

* Quoted in Ikeda Satoshi, *Takasugi Shinsaku to Kusaka Genzui* (Tokyo, 1966), p. 103. Explaining the difference between *kaikoku* and capitulation was a constant problem that Yoshida and his followers faced.

was deeply committed to the cause of reform. Although Kusaka's collaboration with Sufu was not destined to endure for many years, it would have important results.

THE AUMEISHA

It is tempting to regard Kusaka's association with Sufu Masanosuke in 1861 as an innovative development, a rejection by Kusaka of Yoshida Shōin and his extremist reformism in favor of a new patron with new approaches. Actually, Kusaka had known Sufu and other reformist bureaucrats for years before his teacher's death, in the context of a study group called the Aumeisha. A number of persons moved freely between the Sonjuku and Aumeisha environments, and it would never have occurred to Yoshida to oppose this. The two groups had been similar in purpose and character from the outset.

The Aumeisha, or "warbling-of-birds society," was a study group formed by Sufu and his friends in 1845 when they were still students at the Meirinkan. Even in later years the group continued to meet, however, and in fact grew, so that in 1857 it had to be moved from its meeting room in the Meirinkan complex to a larger site nearer the castle. In some respects the Aumeisha might be described as the Sonjuku of the 1840's. In both rank and income the membership of this group was similar to that of the Sonjuku. Among the eighteen regular members for whom income is known, stipends ranged from 21 koku to 173 koku, with only one exception (see Table 5). This income range is very close to that of the principal members of the Sonjuku for whom income is known (compare Table 3, p. 37).

The rationale for the existence of the Aumeisha was also similar to that of the Sonjuku. It was made up of "men who were not satisfied with their previous education at the Meirinkan" and who gathered "to argue together, and thereby investigate history, ancient and recent, and also the problems of current affairs." Moreover, the Aumeisha had risen quickly to political prominence, as the Sonjuku would afterward. The group included many talented men besides Sufu himself, and had been formed when all of them

TABLE 5

Aumeisha Members by Rank and Stipend

Name	Stipend in koku	Name	Stipend in koku
Yorigumi		*Ichidai enkintsuke*	
Kuchiba Tokusuke	520	Nakamura Kyūrō	47
Ōgumi		Nakamura Yurizō	21
Maeda Magoemon	173	*Hanshi*	
Yatsutani Fujibei	149	Okamoto Nariaki	unknown
Yamagata Hanzō	147	Sashiga Haruo	unknown
Yamada Matasuke	142	*Baishin*	
Naitō Marisuke	110	Takashima Ryōdai	47
Hōjō Genzō	109	Matsushima Gōzō	40
Hōjō Raibei	109	Nōmi Ryūan	unknown
Hatano Kingo	100	Tsuchiya Shōkai	unknown
Tanazaki Yahachirō	100		
Kurihara Ryōzō	73		
Sufu Masanosuke	68		
Kaneshige Jōzō	60		
Kamifusa Kendo	unknown		
Kunishige Masafumi	unknown		
Nakamura Bunuemon	unknown		

SOURCE: Umihara Tōru, *Meiji ishin to kyōiku* (Tokyo, 1972), p. 57.
NOTE: Kuchiba Tokusuke, the one exception to the range of stipends of 21–173 koku, was also an acquaintance of Yoshida Shōin's. He had two distinguishing characteristics, a weak constitution and a strong scholarly interest. He died of illness before the activist decade of the 1860's; so it is difficult to say whether he would have acted politically as a member of the Aumeisha or not. See Naramoto Tatsuya et al., eds., *Yoshida Shōin to sono monka* (Tokyo, 1973), p. 146, for a short biography of Kuchiba.

were at the beginning of their careers—Chōshū's most promising and brightest. Ten years later the Aumeisha's membership had come to dominate the Justice faction in the bureaucracy and, through it, the han government. In this sense, too, the Aumeisha was to the mid-1840's what the Sonjuku was to the late 1850's. The Sonjuku was also a group of promising young scholars who within a decade would rise to high positions in the Chōshū administration.

Aumeisha members were aware of the Sonjuku and welcomed Sonjuku students at their own meetings. They and others with an intelligent interest in political questions often attended. Although Yoshida Shōin could not go himself, because he was living in domiciliary confinement, Kusaka Genzui often did. On 6/5/56 his name was placed on the attendance roster of the meeting held that evening at Sufu's house. On 8/18/56 he attended again, as did Yoshida's older brother Sugi Umetarō, and the activist Buddhist priest Utsunomiya Mokurin, who was then visiting Hagi. On 8/24 Sugi's name was put on the roster without Kusaka's, but on 10/16 Kusaka's name appeared again. Sugi attended regularly in part because the Aumeisha library was a major source of books for the voracious literary appetites of Yoshida and his students. Each time Sugi came to an Aumeisha meeting he brought an imposing armful of volumes back and took a new armful with him when he left. In other words, much of Yoshida Shōin's extraordinary scholarship was being conducted with the Aumeisha's books. Another frequent name on the attendance register was Gesshō, a Buddhist priest, rural educator, and reformer, who enjoyed many close personal ties with both the Aumeisha and the Sonjuku.[27]

The active political cooperation of Sonjuku and Aumeisha leaders was new in the 1860's, but the proximity and mutual cordiality of those leaders was not new. There had long been friendly contact between the two leadership groups.

SAKAMOTO RYŌMA AND OTHERS

Even while Kusaka strengthened his ties with the Aumeisha, he continued to cultivate dozens of vital associations with sympathetic persons of other domains. This was essential if Chōshū ever hoped to wield influence in the arena of national politics. During his travels Kusaka had met frequently in Edo with samurai of Tosa, Mito, and elsewhere, as we have seen. While he remained in Hagi by han order in the winter of 1862, he continued this practice, as men of other regions came to see him.

Sakamoto Ryōma, the Tosa activist, visited Kusaka on 1/14/62 and stayed until 1/23. He brought letters from the influential Tosa activist Takechi Zuizan and took a reply to Takechi when he left. In his message Kusaka asserted that the various daimyo could not be relied on to take the initiative in dealing with the alien problem and suggested that the solution might have to lie with common "men of high purpose" (*shishi*) banding together without regard for han lines. Kusaka dispatched a letter in a similar vein to Kobayama Sanen of Satsuma on the same day. On 2/16 a Tosa man named Yoshimura Toratarō came with more papers from Takechi, and on 2/17 Kusaka was visited by a Kurume samurai named Mita Daisuke, who came with an introduction from Miyabe Teizō.[28] Kusaka also made short trips to Shimonoseki at this time to speak with Shiraishi Shōichirō and his guests. Shiraishi was a hosteler and shipper as well as a reformist sympathizer. Many of the samurai who passed through the inevitable transit point took lodgings with Shiraishi, and his hostel had become a favorite meeting place. On 3/14 Kusaka met with Saigo Takamori of Satsuma and Yoshimura Toratarō of Tosa, both of whom were lodging there.[29]

The Sonjuku group maintained close contact with Sakamoto, Takechi, Saigo, Kobayama, Miyabe, and scores of other leaders whose names are not usually associated with Chōshū activism. These many carefully nurtured ties gave the Chōshū men flexibility and in the near future would greatly enhance their opportunities to enter into mutually advantageous political combinations on a national scale.

THE FALL OF NAGAI

In the spring of 1862, Kusaka Genzui would again become politically active in Kyoto. His objective was to dissolve the conservative hold on Chōshū policy exercised by the new han elder Nagai Uta. Kusaka's opposition to Nagai sprang in part from his perception that removing Nagai was essential if domainal policy were to be guided in a decisively reformist direction. It also sprang from his awareness of the covert role that Nagai had played in the death of Yoshida Shōin. The Nagai affair illustrates the nature of the occasional split between Sonjuku and Aumeisha leaders over whether or not direct action, including violence, was an acceptable mode of political conduct. It demonstrates that although the two contingents disagreed over political methods in the early 1860's, they did not hold different goals.

By the end of the third month of 1862, the Chōshū government had given Kusaka another opportunity to participate directly in the politics of the two capitals. On 2/23 he was dispatched eastward by an order of the Justice official Ura Yukie, ostensibly as a soldier to join Chōshū forces in the Hyōgo coastal area. In reality this was an order allowing Kusaka to return to Kyoto. A handful of Sonjuku students went with him, and Kusaka's small party entered the ancient city on 4/11.[30]

Shimazu Hisamitsu of Satsuma had meanwhile displaced Nagai Uta in the favor of the court, and this change enabled Kusaka to turn once more to the task of weakening Nagai's influence on han policy. In the early months of 1862, Nagai had been acting as Chōshū's high diplomatic liaison with the court and the Bakufu. In this capacity he had continued to guide Chōshū's participation in national politics in a moderate direction. Kusaka had not been in a position to oppose Nagai effectively since Nagai, by means of a han order, had forced him to leave Kyoto in October of 1861; nonetheless, on 3/6/62 he had already submitted to the Chōshū government a paper outlining Nagai's offenses anew. Some of the bitterness felt by the Sonjuku toward Nagai was revealed in this document.[31]

On 4/19, eight days after his arrival in Kyoto, Kusaka followed up his statement of 3/6 with another, more lengthy paper that was more positive in terms of making alternative policy suggestions. In it he recommended that Chōshū apologize to the court for the conduct of Nagai, which was neither in accord with the feelings of the daimyo nor in accord with the mandate the han had given him. Kusaka repeated the stories of Yoshida Shōin's death and of Nagai's having slighted the illness of the heir at Hanaoka station in 5/61, and went on to accuse him of making unseemly concessions in his dealings with the conservative court noble Miura Shichibei. As for Nagai's punishment, Kusaka thought the han government, "having a special mercy," should require of him only personal suicide (*seppuku*) and should not sever his house and name. Chōshū could thus show its respect for the court and gain a foothold for a more progressive mediation.[32]

Even as Kusaka was presenting this second impeachment request, however, Nagai's influence in the Chōshū government was rapidly waning, for two reasons. One of these was that Nagai had alienated many Justice faction bureaucrats in the government.

Sufu, as we have seen, found not only that Nagai would not take his advice, but also that he would not listen to it graciously. Other officials, too, resented Nagai's having been promoted so rapidly and found him lacking in humility. It was this kind of antagonism that caused Justice faction official Shishido Kurōbei, while on vacation at Iwayama in 1861, to write to a friend apropos of Nagai: "As for me, I will not perform as one of the esteemed servants of the esteemed middle elder."[33]

A second reason for Nagai's fall was the failure of his program at court. Nagai had left Kyoto on 4/14 apparently successful in his offices, for he bore from the court an order calling the Chōshū daimyo to Kyoto for the last phase of policy mediation. Shimazu Hisamitsu entered Kyoto from Ōsaka on 4/16, however, and offered Sanjō Sanetomi better terms. Sanjō did not conceal the fact that the court would accept, leaving Nagai's embassy in the cold. This news reached Edo ahead of Nagai and provided the Justice faction with the ammunition they needed for a stand against the overbearing elder. Sufu had already been recalled from retirement and restored to the councils of the government, arriving in Edo on 4/11. The senior Sonjuku student Kido Kōin also had been given a post bearing on political policy for the first time. The maneuvering within the government took several months, but the final result was that on 6/18 the han dismissed Nagai and ordered him to be returned to domiciliary confinement in Hagi.

As Nagai's party passed through Kyoto on 7/1, Kusaka Genzui, still not satisfied, lay in wait with the intention of taking his life. Itō Hirobumi and Nomura Wasaku realized belatedly what Kusaka was up to, after drinking with him into the wee hours, and set out in hot pursuit to talk him out of it. When they found him, however, he rather talked them into it. This small episode is a measure of the extreme flexibility of the Sonjuku group. Each of its members was prepared to discuss a wide range of strategies and policies at all times.

Kusaka's attempt at direct action did not materialize, however, because Nagai, forewarned, was traveling incognito, separate from his party. Still, Nagai was not destined to escape by this simple stratagem from the resentment of reformist elements in the domain. The Justice faction also was not satisfied with his merely being dismissed, and so on 11/15/62 they secured a han order requiring Nagai to commit seppuku, which he did in the privacy of his own family compound on 2/6/63.[34]

There is no other case in the Bakumatsu period in which the Sonjuku group and the Aumeisha group joined forces to harass a political opponent in Chōshū to his death, and it is not entirely clear why they did so in the case of Nagai. The residual bad feeling over Nagai's less-than-honorable role in Yoshida Shōin's execution certainly was part of the reason. A further explanation may lie in Nagai's having denied to han bureaucrats of modestly stipended shi rank the opportunity to participate in the policymaking process, even though such participation had become their traditional prerogative. After becoming a middle elder in 1861, Nagai had guided Chōshū's national policy by his own lights, rather than guiding it in close consultation with senior Justice faction officials as did Masuda Danjō and the others of the han's three Justice elders. Masuda sought the Justice chief Sufu Masanosuke's wise counsel regularly, but when Sufu presumed to advise Nagai in 9/61, Nagi had him placed under house arrest. This, too, probably had something to do with Nagai's ultimate fall.

Meanwhile, Kusaka did not want his carefully laid ambush to count for nothing, and so on 7/4/62 announced to the Chōshū official Ura Yukie in Kyoto that he had unsuccessfully tried to assassinate the middle elder three days before. By this declaration, he hoped to pressure the Justice faction into dealing more severely with Nagai, an object that was probably achieved.

Although Kusaka's assassination attempt sprang from immediate political goals that were essentially the same as those of the Justice bureaucrats in the administration, the latter could not approve of his methods, just as they could not condone Yoshida's private expedition to Kyoto in 11/58. As a part of this pattern of ongoing friction over the use of personal action, Kusaka was sent back to

Hagi in 7/62 and put under house arrest, where he would remain for two months.[35]

In the past, this difference in predilection for methods between bureaucrats and Sonjuku activists has been taken as a sign that these two groups had different goals and differing political outlooks generally. Yet there is reason to believe that this was not the case and that reformist bureaucrats and Sonjuku students sought the same things for the same reasons. The differences between the two groups over methods sprang not from differing goals, but rather were related directly to office and indirectly to age. They were a natural outgrowth of the fact that from 1858 to 1863 the options of Sonjuku students and Aumeisha officials were substantially different. The officials could choose between official action or personal action, and generally chose the former. The Sonjuku students, lacking office, did not have this advantageous choice. Rather, they were forced to choose between personal action or no action at all, and they generally chose the former. Thus, although the two groups shared the same political aims, they were in the early 1860's sometimes at odds over this issue of the propriety of direct, personal action. After 1863, when the Sonjuku leaders were drawn into the offices of their fathers and patrons, these differences disappeared. In the meantime, however, this disagreement over methods brought several months of house arrest to Kusaka.

Kusaka Genzui had spent his earliest years poring over books at his home in Hagi. In the autumn of his twenty-second year, he found himself once more reading books at home. In the intervening decade, however, Kusaka had acquired a political education. He had studied at the Meirinkan, at the Sonjuku, and in Edo. He had been instructed by Yoshida in the ways of political community and of ideology. He had learned in the streets and sake shops of the two capitals how to meet and move other men.

Kusaka Genzui was the student for whom Yoshida Shōin's expectations, both as a scholar and as a political leader, were highest. In some respects, Kusaka was the quintessential alumnus of the

Sonjuku, well read and politically engaged. It is perhaps for this reason that Kusaka at the time of Yoshida's death not only maintained the political activities in the metropolis into which his teacher had earlier directed him but also took it upon himself to keep alive the activities and the spirit of the Sonjuku itself in Hagi.

Kusaka's responsiveness to Yoshida's hopes may have stemmed in part from the fact that his personal background was, like his teacher's, professional and academic to an unusual degree. He was born to a family of han physicians of 25 koku of income, and had studied at the Meirinkan and at the han's Naval Education School. At the Shōka Sonjuku he earned a reputation as being academically the most capable of the ambitious students who gathered there.

In the early 1860's, Kusaka, following his mentor's example and advice, maintained personal ties with scores of activist leaders from other domains, including Tosa's Sakamoto Ryōma and Satsuma's Kobayama Sanen. Such persons each represented a modest amount of influence, and part of the struggle of the 1860's would involve bringing enough of these men together to affect the political outcome at the national level. Kusaka also initiated a pattern of effective cooperation between the Sonjuku group of students and the older Aumeisha group of Chōshū bureaucrats. This pattern, too, would prove to be of vital importance for Chōshū's participation in national politics in the mid-1860's.

Kusaka Genzui's historical reputation does not rest primarily on his early efforts to maintain the unity of the Sonjuku, however, or on his forging of new working ties with the Aumeisha in 1861 and 1862. Rather his reputation derives from the events of the years that immediately followed. In the early 1860's Kusaka had been observant and enterprising as ideological strategies of reform gave way to diplomatic strategies. In 1863 and 1864 diplomacy would give way to warfare, and during those turbulent years of transition it would be Kusaka as much as anyone who would chart the increasingly hazardous course of Chōshū activism.

CHAPTER SIX

Kusaka and the Politics of Civil Violence
1862-1864

IN THE LATE 1850's, beginning with the Ansei Purge, the struggle between reformist and conservative elements had gone beyond the stage of public discussion. Opponents of reform, and then proponents, too, had begun resorting for the first time to physical coercion and violence to enhance their political leverage. Still, this coercion was always on a small scale and aimed at particular persons. In 1863 and 1864, however, the reformist struggle would pass gradually into yet another phase, that of large-scale violence and military confrontation. These were the most dynamic and mercurial years in the Chōshū activists' quest for social change. The shifting fortunes of these years made political action perilous and uncertain in the extreme.

Kusaka Genzui guided the Chōshū movement in this unstable time. He did not always lead successfully, but he always led with resourcefulness and courage. He constructed a pattern of political cooperation that thrust outward in two directions, toward reformist nobles in the court and toward reformist terrorists of many domains in the street. Moreover, he made this alliance work successfully to impel the political center of gravity in a sharply reformist direction. He was instrumental in the creation of a new form of military organization that not only would prove vital to the ultimate success of the Chōshū movement but would also have profoundly egalitarian social implications.

When the time came to cower before superior might, or to go forward without fear and accept the challenge of a larger and more anguished struggle, Kusaka firmly placed Chōshū on the latter course. His contributions to the strategy of the Chōshū movement in these years were a sine qua non for the activists' final triumph. Kusaka made a further contribution in the mid-1860's by defining more precisely the reformist movement's goals. In a series of papers he asked for an end to Bakufu authority and spelled out the need for a new and more orderly kind of government centered on the imperial court. These proposals, inspired by still earlier ones put forward by Yoshida Shōin, were extremely important, for they represented a basic theoretical arrival at the institutional foundations of the Meiji transformation. The Meiji Restoration was not a sober afterthought to the self-indulgent chaos of the 1860's. Rather, the major provisions of the Meiji settlement had been the object of urgent petitioning by the Chōshū activists for some years prior to the dramatic coup of 1868.

A FIRST DRAFT OF RESTORATION

Kusaka Genzui's writings of 1862 may have served as a kind of rough draft for some of the basic institutional reforms of the Meiji Restoration carried out six years later. These documents are thus extremely important for historians trying to locate the theoretical origins of the Meiji change. During his house arrest of July and August 1862, Kusaka prepared two memorials for the Chōshū daimyo, "Turning Back the Waves" ("Kairan jōgi") and "Foolish Words on Severing an Arm" ("Kaiwan chigen"),[1] in which he suggested that the Bakufu in its capacity as the government of the realm be replaced by a new government, a specialized bureaucracy, based on the court. Scholars have paid little attention to the institutional aspects of these two documents, since they dealt primarily with the importance of taking a firm stand against Westerners. Although Kusaka's principal object in these papers was to convince the reader emotionally of the necessity for new policies and practices, rather than to describe the practices, a careful reading nevertheless reveals the kinds of institutional change he had in mind.

In the earlier of these memorials, Kusaka urged that an office of political affairs (*goseijisho*) superseding the Bakufu's authority at the national level should be established in Kyoto, that imperial troops be gathered in the Kinai, and that the various daimyo, "the three hundred lords," be made to contribute part of their han product directly to the imperial establishment for the support of these new activities. That is, the new central government would draw its funds and military personnel from all geographic areas, a solution that Yoshida Shōin had already put forward four years earlier.[2]

In the second memorial, Kusaka elaborated on some of these measures. The right to govern the entire realm, he wrote, should be withdrawn from the Bakufu and restored to the Eight Ministries and Six Boards of the court bureaucracy. "The hundred civil and military bureaus" (*bumbu hyakkan*) should once more assume the real functions—revenue, public works, foreign affairs, and so on—that corresponded to their traditional spheres of responsibility. This should not be accomplished in haste, because "names are the guest of reality": that is, it would take some time and experimentation to implement the new system in such a way that it would actually operate. An imperial high court or chancery (*kirokujo*) should be established to resolve disputes in the realm.

Set above all this to make national policy would be a new bureau of political affairs, a *Chi-dajōkan* (literally "knowledgeable, supreme political bureau"). On extraordinary occasions in the past, Kusaka pointed out, such an institution had been established in the court. As on those occasions, the new bureau should not give special treatment to privileged persons or to "men with courtly titles" (*kammei*). Recommendations like this, along with Kusaka's insistence on many discrete bureaus and gradual implementation, leave little doubt that Kusaka had in mind a specialized merit bureaucracy as the more efficient structure that should supersede the Bakufu.[3]

In his memorials of 1862 Kusaka described, albeit roughly, the basic institutional arrangement of the Meiji government from 1868 to 1873. When the Restoration government of the Sonjuku leaders and their allies would take power from the Bakufu in 1868, they actually would replace it with a supreme political agency called the Dajōkan, which would supervise numerous bureaus modeled ostensibly on the traditional bureaucratic structure of the court. These agencies would be headed by court nobles like Sanjō Sanetomi and staffed by "men of ability," including the Sonjuku survivors, Kusaka's associates. That is, the government after 1868 followed Kusaka's formula of putting new wine into the old bottles. It revived the widely venerated ancient forms, even while establishing what was in substance a specialized merit bureaucracy, much as Kusaka had recommended.

For its first six years, despite the nominal abolition of the various han in 1871, the Meiji government would rely for its existence on troops from friendly han, and on funds drawn from the various han and Bakufu territories, a pattern not basically at variance with Kusaka's suggestion in 1862 of how this might work. The Meiji government would be able to transcend this dependence only after the establishment and implementation of the conscript military and the land tax, subsequent to 1873. The Dajōkan itself would be maintained as the highest organ of the new government until it was recast as a Western-style cabinet system in 1885.

The Dajōkan bureaucracy would be the vehicle of many other reforms carried out in the 1870's in education, the military, class structure, diplomacy, commercial regulation, local government, and the system of justice. Many of these other reforms were also foreshadowed in Yoshida Shōin's and Kusaka Genzui's writings, and even the reforms not described in their work usually represented a further application of the two main principles from which they had worked—the elevation of talent, and the more pragmatic use of institutional resources.

Although Kusaka Genzui's memorials of 1862 are far from being a detailed blueprint of the Meiji Restoration, they nevertheless constitute strong evidence that the Chōshū activists had a clear idea of what they wanted, and that what they wanted was something very much akin to the Meiji reforms that they later implemented.

THE TRIPLE ALLIANCE

In September 1862 the government ended Kusaka's promising career as a political essayist by releasing him from house arrest. Kusaka welcomed this opportunity to return to the metropolitan arena of political action and by November 2 had entered the capital of Edo once more.[4] Over the course of 1863, he would strive to create a powerful new framework of political coordination. He sought to develop sympathetic contacts with Sanjō Sanetomi and other reformist nobles in the imperial court on the one hand, and with activists of many domains in the street on the other. He tried to place himself at the center of a web of communication that linked the court, street activists, and the Chōshū government, to which he was already close. His object was the simultaneous exertion of political leverage from all three camps against the Bakufu.

There is a danger in regarding Kusaka as the sole driving force behind this effort, for countless other reformist leaders were also involved. Dozens of persons, men like Sanjō, Sufu, and Maki Izumi, had contacts in each sector of the tripartite web of court, activists, and the Chōshū bureaucracy. Nevertheless, Kusaka was a pivotal figure, and he exercised as much initiative as anyone in guiding the formation and activities of this broad network.

The street activists' contribution to the alliance politics of the early 1860's took the form of their visiting violent reprisal upon any court noble or Bakufu agent who favored or furthered conservative policies in the two capitals. This often meant assassination, as, for example, in the case of Shimada Sakon, who was a retainer of the conservative noble house of Kyūjō. In exchange for 10,000 ryō, Shimada had identified reformist activists for Bakufu agents during the Ansei Purge. This lucrative conduct had proven fatal to those so identified; so on 7/20/62 five activist samurai of Tosa and Satsuma interrupted Shimada's evening bath to take his life.[5]

Shimada's death was the first blow in the rising crescendo of street violence that culminated in late 1862 and early 1863. The heads of many victims, like Shimada, were displayed in public places with political messages attached, a gesture meant to increase the public impact of these actions. In the ensemble, such direct tactics were called Heaven's Revenge (*tenchū*), and as political conduct they were effective. Bakufu officials and conservative court nobles were intimidated into silence and passivity.

At the same time, sympathetic nobles in the court like Sanjō Sanetomi provided the reformist movement with radical imperial pronouncements. These tended to legitimize the position and activities of both street activists and the Chōshū government. Thanks to Kusaka and others, there grew up in 1863 a reciprocal relationship between reformist nobles in the court and young reformist samurai in the street. The more radical policy pronouncements by the court and other authorities became, the more legitimacy and protection there were for loyalist activists in the street. The safer the activists were, the more vigorously they could subdue the opponents of the radical nobles by violence.

Chōshū, too, participated in this schema, lending to the movement mediational services between court and Bakufu, its compound for use as a meeting place and refuge, and the legitimacy of support by an established political power. The court, Chōshū, and Heaven's Revenge worked in concert. Above all, Chōshū provided its partners in the triple association of 1863 with a stable system of communication that reached high and low, from the emperor's closest ministers to the humblest loyalist in the street. It was in this realm that Kusaka Genzui played a crucial role. He was Chōshū's foremost liaison with the floating terror. As Chōshū's representative, he condoned many of the political assassinations perpetrated by Heaven's Revenge, and also prevented some. The relationship of Chōshū to the terror was one of guidance rather than control, and although the Chōshū activists did not approve of all the terrorists' actions, they did try to orchestrate the terrorism so as to enhance its political impact.

Kusaka was raised out of his student status and given a post in the Chōshū bureaucracy for the first time on 4/22/63, and was also given a major promotion in rank that made him eligible for the highest administrative positions in the domain. Since his commission was as a chargé at the han's compound in Kyoto (*Kyōto-tei goyō gakari*), his official duties consisted of maintaining contacts with young samurai of various other han. For that reason he was given a special dispensation allowing him to keep his nonregulation long hair. Contact with the terror was the policy of the reformist bureaucrats who controlled the government, and Kusaka's being involved in it did not hinder his being recruited into the han bureaucracy at the normal age and in the normal way.[6]

In the spring of 1863, the close cooperation between Chōshū, the court, and activists in the street would begin to bear fruit. Already in the later months of 1862, Kusaka, Sufu, and other Chōshū leaders, working closely with the reformist court nobles Sanjō Sanetomi and Nakayama Tadayasu, had succeeded in replacing the Satsuma mediation between court and Bakufu with their own. By 1863, with Nagai Uta's influence neutralized, the Chōshū mediation represented an unequivocal commitment to remove the Western presence from Japanese territory. Given the relative strength of the feudal domains and of the European navies, there was little hope of achieving this in the short run if Western authorities were determined to oppose it, a fact that did not discourage the Chōshū leaders.

Immediate military victory was not their aim. Rather, the Chōshū activists wanted to achieve a definitive mandate for institutional reform. This was to be done by making a firm commitment to a task that would necessitate reform, that task being a competitive diplomatic and military performance vis-à-vis the West. If an early military clash exposed the inadequacies of current defense arrangements and jolted the realm into a sense of crisis, so much the better.[7]

On 4/20/63 the Bakufu reluctantly succumbed to the double pressure of anti-Western jōi pronouncements from the court and jōi violence in the streets, and announced that 5/10/63 was to be the date on which expulsion would begin (although the Bakufu itself had no plans for implementation).* This was a great victory for the reformist alliance. For the first time (and the last) the

* *Jōi*, literally, "expel the barbarian."

Bakufu was formally committed to a military engagement with the Westerners that would test its institutional capabilities against those of the extraordinary foreigner.

The Chōshū activists had accomplished in 1863 what only several years before had seemed impossible. They had in less than a year maneuvered the Bakufu into public acceptance of a struggle with the imperialist powers of the West, and so also into an implied acceptance of the institutional changes needed to implement that struggle. The Bakufu declaration, won at such a high cost in terms of social disorder, was a major triumph for the reformers. It remained for them to realize the potential that this opportunity offered. Above all, they had to make sure that it would not slip away, not become just one more empty utterance.

THE FORMATION OF THE KIHEITAI

One of the developments essential for the Chōshū movement's ultimate effectiveness was the founding on 6/6/63 of a new kind of military unit called the Kiheitai. This radical departure from customary arrangements was made possible by the Bakufu's expulsionist declaration of 4/20/63, but still would not have taken place without the vigilant persistence of Kusaka Genzui and other leaders. Although credit for the emergence of the Kiheitai is usually accorded to Takasugi Shinsaku, it was largely Kusaka who was responsible for the actions that led to the corps' formation. Years earlier Yoshida Shōin had described the need for such a commoner military. The Kiheitai and its sister units would later become the basis for Chōshū's crucial victories in 1866 and 1868.

Even before being named to his new bureaucratic post in April 1863, Kusaka Genzui had left Kyoto for Shimonoseki with a band of thirty men, many of whom were destined to become the nucleus of the new Kiheitai organization. To ensure that the Bakufu's declaration of 4/20 would not become a dead letter, Chōshū's leaders had resolved that they would themselves engage the foreigners militarily, thus putting the Bakufu's words beyond rescission. This engagement was to take the form of shelling Western ships as they passed through the Shimonoseki straits, and it was there that Kusaka and his band headed.

Many of Kusaka's followers were students who were not of full shi rank. His party included the Sonjuku students Yamagata Aritomo, Yoshida Toshimaro, and the Irie brothers. Kusaka and his comrades immediately petitioned the han government, which had been moved to the interior capital of Yamaguchi for greater safety, to let them serve as the vanguard in the coming engagement, but their petition was refused on the grounds that acceptance would impair the authority of Mōri Noto, who had already been appointed general commander (*sōbugyō*) for the region. Nor could they join Mōri's corps, because some of them were not of proper shi rank, a fact that would invite scorn and intramural discord. Kusaka's group was therefore dispatched separately to Shimonoseki under the rubric of reconnaissance of the enemy.

Kusaka's followers, thus rebuffed, billeted themselves in the Kōmyōji temple near Shimonoseki, where they continued to be very vocal in their criticism of existing military arrangements in the han. They soon came to be known as the "Kōmyōji party," and were joined by two other groups of Chōshū-led volunteers from Kyoto during the next weeks. By 5/5 there were some sixty activists at the Kōmyōji compound.[8]

Mori Noto's forces began shelling Western ships on schedule on 5/10 with an attack on the American ship *Pembroke*. A French craft became the target on 5/23, and an unsuspecting Dutch warship on 5/26. These vessels, though damaged, had fled; so it was with confidence that the Chōshū batteries opened fire on the American *Wyoming*, which entered the straits on 6/1. The *Wyoming*, however, had been sent to retaliate for the earlier attacks, and proceeded to level the battery at Kameyama and destroy three of Chōshū's own small Western-style ships. There was more disappointment for the Chōshū men on 6/5, when the French ships *Sémiramis* and *Tancrède* bombarded the remaining batteries into silence and landed 250 marines, who with little difficulty occupied for a time the battery at Maeda.

There was panic. Chōshū's conventional military arrangements had been tried and failed, while sixty youthful advocates of egalitarian Western forms of military organization watched critically from the Kōmyōji. This situation gave the government, in sympathetic Justice hands throughout, more than enough of a mandate to effect the Sonjuku group's long-standing desire for the establishment of new military forms in Chōshū. The government did not wish to appear to have simply yielded to the importunate demands of Kusaka's Kōmyōji faction, however, and so resorted to the expedient of calling on a third party, Takasugi Shinsaku. Takasugi was then living in retirement, having recently taken the tonsure to protest what he felt to be the government's indecisiveness. He was acceptable to the Kōmyōji faction, but was also from a respectable Great Group family.

Takasugi was summoned to Yamaguchi on 6/4, and was dispatched to Shimonoseki on 6/6 as an assistant to the general commander (*sōbugyō temoto-yaku*). His commission was to organize the competent volunteer elements who were already in the area into a new military unit under han authority. Takasugi chose as his base of operations the hostel of Shiraishi Shōichirō, who was then serving as the han's civilian quartermaster. There were fifteen men at the hostel when Takasugi arrived on the night of 6/6, and he promptly formed them into three five-man squads. By 6/10 Takasugi's Kiheitai, or "special military corps," numbered sixty men. That was too many for the hostel, and so on 6/14 Takasugi moved them to a nearby temple called Amidadera.[9]

Most of these sixty troops came from the Kōmyōji party, starting with the Sonjuku students Irie Sugizō and Akane Takendo. They were, in short, the highly motivated and politically conscious activists that Kusaka Genzui had brought from Kyoto six weeks before. Kusaka himself might have led them in a body into the new Kiheitai, were it not for the fact that he had already departed for Kyoto on 5/27. The day after the third successful bombardment on 5/26, he had set out for the capital, prematurely as it turned out, to encourage other han to take part in the expulsion campaign.[10]

Takasugi organized the new corps in the fashion of the Western-style rifle company. The unit was to be structured "in the Western manner, not in the Japanese manner," as he put it. Moreover, the Kiheitai was organized on a basis of real capacity, not rank, much as Yoshida Shōin had specified in his "Confidential Advice" petition of 1853. The unit's founders "did not single out han samurai (shi), rear vassals (baishin), or foot soldiers (keisotsu), but mingled all in the same manner." This meant that the corps ignored hereditary social standing altogether, a revolutionary practice with far-reaching implications.[11]

By 7/6 the Kiheitai could boast twenty five-man squads that drilled every day in the Western manner. On 7/16 the corps emulated another feature of the Western military and established a field hospital with five doctors. They also toiled at rebuilding the shore batteries, since Western raiders could return at any time.[12] That Takasugi and some of his comrades had studied Western infantry methods six years before at the Shōka Sonjuku no doubt contributed to the swiftness with which the corps were shaped along Western lines.

In the months after its establishment in 6/63, the Kiheitai would expand steadily, spinning off a number of similar corps, the ensemble being called simply "the various corps," or *shotai*. The highly motivated members of the early Kiheitai moved as officers into the new units, which were made up of sub-shi-level samurai, priests, sons of rural administrators, and assorted commoners. Some of these men joined the shotai out of political conviction, and some joined for the prestige, the adventure, or the livelihood that membership in these units purportedly brought.

All of these corps were supported by the Chōshū government, which supplied them with arms, provisions, and a small allowance in specie. The formation of Western-style rifle units had been a goal of the Justice faction in the administration at least since 1847, when the Justice official Yamada Uemon was put under house arrest for recommending it to the then conservative-controlled government under Tsuboi.[13] Yamada had been one of Yoshida Shōin's four supervisors during his early Meirinkan years, and Yoshida, too, had argued for the establishment of commoner military units in Chōshū in 1858. The Justice view of the desirability of rifle units was only heightened by the increasing possibility of Western naval intrusion in the 1850's, and officials were quite willing to arrange support for the Kiheitai and its sister units, once the Shimonoseki encounter had finally jolted a few of them into existence in 6/63.

Although the Kiheitai was organized on a basis of ability only, there was another special corps in Chōshū—the Sempōtai—that was organized solely on a basis of rank. The Sempōtai, or "vanguard corps," had existed in some form since 1853. Its members were predominantly of prestigious and lucrative Near Group rank, with incomes that were multiples of those of their Sonjuku counterparts. The Sempōtai, like the Kiheitai, was assigned a territory to defend at Shimonoseki after the French attack on 6/5.

The bitter and violent antagonism that came to characterize relations between the Sonjuku-led Kiheitai and the aristocratic Sempōtai is one of the more obvious indications that there was a grave horizontal rift in Chōshū society that was related to hereditary income and rank. The Sempōtai clashed repeatedly with the Kiheitai from the time of the latter's inception in 1863 until the Chōshū civil war in 1865. The first serious incident occurred on the night of 8/16, when a quarrel developed over the hazing by Sempōtai members of a new Kiheitai recruit named Miyashiro Hikosuke. The bad feeling generated by this incident actually threatened to become a full-scale military battle between the two corps. It was finally defused only by the anxious and repeated offices of Takasugi between the two parties and the heir Sadahiro, and by the sacrificial suicide of Miyashiro.[14]

Formation of the Kiheitai was not a historical accident. The Chōshū reformists not only had arranged for the Western military stimulus, but also had seen to it that potential corpsmen with the requisite knowledge of Western organizational forms were available on the scene at the critical moment. Despite the immediate military embarrassment and such problems as friction with aristocratic groups, the Chōshū activists derived an extremely important advantage from the Shimonoseki bombardments. They led in a direct way to the formation of the Kiheitai, an element that would be indispensable for Chōshū's ultimate triumph over the Bakufu.

TERROR IN EXILE

Even after obtaining Bakufu consent for the expulsion of Westerners on 4/20/63, loyalist activists of Chōshū and elsewhere continued to cultivate a broader commitment among all authorities to resisting foreign influence. By the eighth month of 1863, this effort involved a plan for a military campaign against Westerners led personally by the emperor. This ambitious prospectus caused the emperor to bolt into the welcoming arms of conservative elements. The loyalist reformers of Chōshū were thus shut out of the court, and the influence they had at last come to exercise over the affairs of the capital was lost. Loyalist domination of the metropolis had rested on a precarious triple alliance of court, Chōshū, and Heaven's Revenge. With one leg of the tripod gone, Chōshū's influence collapsed. This ultimate result was perhaps not too surprising.

It is what happened next that is astonishing, given the ingrained character and habits of Tokugawa society. Reformist loyalists from scores of different domains flocked to the one han of Chōshū for shelter and comradeship. They were joined there by reformist nobles from the court, men who still claimed to represent the true imperial will. The successful loyalist association of court, Heaven's Revenge, and Chōshū was thus preserved by the ingenious expedient of transplanting it all onto Chōshū soil. Chōshū had clearly come to represent something more than its own special interests. As never before, it had become the credible champion of imperial reformism for publicly aware persons of the entire realm.

In the fifth and sixth months of 1863, Kusaka Genzui made the arduous journey between Kyoto and Shimonoseki twice, in an effort to coordinate reformist efforts in the two locations. After the situation at Shimonoseki had stabilized in the sixth month, Kusaka reentered Kyoto on 6/21 probably expecting a protracted stay.[15] There, despite military reversals at Shimonoseki, Kusaka labored with other loyalist activists to further develop the expulsion policy. Their next project involved having the Emperor Kōmei personally lead a military campaign against resident foreigners, a campaign that was to be initiated by an imperial visit to one of the shrines in the nearby Yamato region to the south. Kusaka, Kido, Maki Izumi, and reformist nobles including Sanjō met at the Gakushūin on 8/15 to discuss the details of the imperial procession.*

Plans for the imperial visit were obstructed, however, by an unanticipated development. The Emperor Kōmei was weary of Heaven's Revenge. Nor did he favor a campaign against the belligerent Westerners led by himself. Therefore he arranged to put an end to Chōshū's dominance in Kyoto, and to rid himself of the radical nobles like Sanjō who were always hurrying around him. Through sympathetic courtiers Kōmei put himself in contact with the conservative han of Satsuma and Aizu. These authorities were more than willing to cooperate in removing Chōshū from the favor of the court.

In the predawn hours of 8/18/63, troops of the two han were moved into the imperial compound. These garrisoned each of the nine gates and sealed them. At the same time Kōmei handed down an edict that terminated his association with Chōshū, disowned the latter's vigorous expulsionist policies, and described as personae non gratae seven of the leading reformist nobles, with Sanjō heading the list. The seven were also to be denied all access to the compound.[16]

---

* The Gakushūin, or "study institute," had been established in Kyoto only in 1847, as an academy to serve court nobles interested in further education. In the court as in Chōshū, the reformist movement was associated with academies and schools of higher learning. The Gakushūin building came to serve as the headquarters of kuge reformism. Many contacts that informed court-Chōshū cooperation in the early 1860's were maintained at the Gakushūin. It was there that the reformist nobles Sanjō, Nakayama Tadayasu, Anegakōji Kintomo, and Iwakura Tomomi met regularly with reformist samurai from the various han. This arrangement was reflected in the institutional practices of Chōshū. Beginning in 1862, there existed in Chōshū a category of official called Gakushūin chargé (*Gakushūin-yō gakari*), whose job it was to deal with nobles at the Gakushūin in Kyoto. In 1862 there were 14 men holding this post, including Kido, Takasugi, Shishido Kurōbei, Maeda Magoemon, and Yamada Uemon. See *Nihonshi jiten*, ed. Takayanagi Mitsuhisa (Tokyo, 1972), p. 169; Suematsu Kenchō, *Bōchō kaitenshi* (Tokyo, 1967 [1921]), 1: 341.

Chōshū men, who had seemed to be achieving ever greater successes at the Kyoto court, were caught completely by surprise. Chōshū had several hundred troops in the city, but without legitimacy little could be done. Effective civil authority throughout the capital therefore reverted almost immediately to the Bakufu and to han such as Satsuma and Aizu that were sympathetic to court-Bakufu cooperation (*kōbu gattai*). The coup of 8/18/63 also had a jarring impact on internal affairs within Chōshū. It produced a mutual maneuvering in terms of threatened violence among both conservatives and reformists. With the new Kiheitai weighed in the balance, however, the reformist faction managed to retain their slender hold on the administration.[17]

Kyoto was now unsafe for the radical reformist elements that Chōshū's special relationship with the court had protected. These included the seven nobles themselves and also several hundred young samurai activists and jōi terrorists. Both groups withdrew from the capital and sought refuge in Chōshū. There they installed themselves near the Inland Sea coast at Mitajiri, and chose as their headquarters a teahouse called the Shōkenkaku. This term soon came to stand for the entire establishment of Kyoto loyalism-in-exile in Chōshū.

Word spread, and the men who had previously gone to Kyoto to join the movement there now came directly to Mitajiri. This was partly because Miyabe Teizō and others, with rousing statements by the seven nobles in their hands, traveled through the realm recruiting. Nakaoka Shintarō, for example, fled to Mitajiri when his own han of Tosa had become unsafe for loyalist reformers in 10/63. He was not alone. There were fifteen other men from Tosa in the Shōkenkaku already, and Nakaoka was elected to the Shōkenkaku's policy council. Envoys of the Shōkenkaku came and went constantly, maintaining contacts with the respective home regions of its members.

The Shōkenkaku men were mostly young samurai who had been studying in the capital or traveling before taking posts in their respective han, or who would never be given posts because of their views or because there were not enough posts to go around. Despite

their diverse origins, Shōkenkaku personnel observed a strict regimen, with lessons in "letters and arms" in the morning, practice
in martial arts in the afternoon, and after-dinner lectures on military writings. Different activities were specified for each day of the
month: military drill on the first, political discussions on the
fourth, hiking on the seventh, poetry and music on the ninth,
and so on.[18]

The Shōkenkaku activists, although energetic and ambitious,
lacked experience in institutional politics. The character of the
group is reflected in the leader most closely associated with it,
Maki Izumi (1813–64). Maki was born in Kurume han, from which
he received a modest stipend of 10 koku as a hereditary Shinto
priest. He studied hard as a youth, and is said to have shown sur-
passing ability at the han school, to which he was admitted as a
priest even though he was not a samurai and could not hold office.
He became an impassioned advocate of loyalist reformism, and
at the age of thirty-eight was imprisoned for having participated
in a political struggle aimed at han reform. In the eleventh year
of his imprisonment he escaped and made his way to Kyoto to join
the loyalist movement there. Though pardoned by Kurume han
the next year, he remained in Kyoto. By then he was fifty years
old, and had become a leader of floating activism in the capital,
by seniority and by manifest ability. Moreover, he had something
in common with his youthful followers. Like them he had never
held an office of responsibility and was divorced from participating
in the public affairs of his own han.[19] Like the Shōkenkaku membership in general, Maki was, despite his intelligence and years,
more energetic than he was experienced. Like them, he was removed from his own country. The Shōkenkaku were an army of
youths far from home, on their own and inexperienced.

The three elements of reformist nobles, loyalist samurai from
all han, and Chōshū bureaucrats seem to have been a colorful pot-
pourri, an unlikely alliance of convenience. Still, these groups
may not have been as much of a hodgepodge as they appeared. All
three may have represented the more idealistic members of those
professional echelons who had been prepared for elite service in the

various han (or court), but were excluded, because there were no posts, or because they advocated radical reform. That is, many of the young samurai in the Shōkenkaku may have stood in the same relation to their own domains that the Sonjuku group stood in with respect to Chōshū, with the exception that in Chōshū the government was wholly sympathetic. In Chōshū able young idealists became the loyal protégés of influential bureaucrats. In other domains, similarly promising youths became outlaws and exiles, and in the end, not surprisingly, they too gathered in Chōshū for shelter.

The presence in Chōshū of court nobles and militant young reformists from all over Japan was a clear signal that Chōshū had assumed leadership of the loyalist movement for the nation. Chōshū leaders had taken up this role only gradually during the late 1850's and early 1860's as the reformist hopes that had been placed on the Bakufu, Mito, Satsuma, and Tosa had faded. It was not so much that Chōshū reformers had sought to lead as it was that in their quest for reform there was ultimately no one to follow, and they were compelled to act alone. Nevertheless, hosting the terror-in-exile at Mitajiri would prove to be a delicate matter for Chōshū han, far more delicate than sponsoring the group's activities while in Kyoto.

REFORMISM AND LOYALISM

There were two kinds of restorationist active in these years. Although many of the elements at the Shōkenkaku probably shared quite similar backgrounds with their Sonjuku counterparts, it is also very likely that some of the young men there came out of a different background and were motivated by a different set of values. Many of the Shōkenkaku members described themselves as "loyalists" (*kinnō ha*), which often meant that they claimed a deep emotional devotion to the emperor, and were dedicated to attacking foreigners in Japan in the most simple and direct sense. There they parted company with the Chōshū reformers, for whom both loyalty to the emperor and the contest with the Western military represented only particular aspects of a highly complex and sophisticated view of polity and the role of institutions in society. The fabric of that understanding derived from concepts drawn from the Chinese classics (*keigaku*), and indeed it was the classics that made up the nucleus of their education. Most vital of all for the reformers was the notion of "the people's welfare" (*ammin*), which was for them the objective of all social action.

The education of loyalists, however, was often light on the classics, and focused instead on the martial arts (*bujitsu*), where esprit and the unity of thought and action were all-important. Like the reformers, many of the loyalists were dedicated students from Edo or Kyoto, but unlike them, they frequently were students whose lives were disciplined by fencing and the way of the sword rather than by reading and the way of the brush. In short, they came out of an educational preparation in which emotional commitment, rather than intellectual rigor, was most highly emphasized.

The Shōkenkaku as a group embraced not only resolute "reformers" but also many of these xenophobic "loyalists." The Chōshū activists cultivated ties with influential loyalists despite their differences, and recruited them regularly for their military and paramilitary activities. There was no doubt a strong sympathy between the Chōshū reformers and the loyalists, based on harmonious objectives and perhaps even on mutual admiration. The Chōshū operatives would be able to rely on many occasions on the incomparable spirit and daring of their loyalist rank and file. Indeed, without the immense reservoir of vitality that the loyalists represented, the Chōshū movement might not have been able to prevail.

Still, the loyalists caused the reformers endless amounts of trouble, because of their unpreparedness to consider broader strategic questions, and because of their untutored antipathy for Westerners and anyone who dealt with them. In the end, the loyalists' naiveté took a heavy toll on the reformers; Kusaka himself would flee for his life more than once from xenophobic loyalists, and the Chōshū activist Inoue Kaoru would be gravely wounded by them. Perhaps most tragic of all would be the deaths at their hands of the two senior reformist thinkers to whom the Sonjuku group had been closest throughout, Sakuma Shōzan and Yokoi Shōnan. Use of the loyalists as a political instrument was at best a double-edged affair.

It is impossible to say without close biographical scrutiny what proportion of the Shōkenkaku participants were motivated primarily by reformist ideas (*keigaku-ammin*), and which primarily by their loyalist attitudes (*bujitsu-kinnō*). It is a reasonable guess that every important leader of the period had a fair understanding of both of these constellations of values. Still, most leaders favored one configuration over the other. It is probable that leaders like Miyabe Teizō and Takechi Zuizan, with whom the Sonjuku activists had been in close contact, were motivated largely by the loyalist syndrome. It is likely that men like Sakuma Shōzan and Yokoi Shōnan were motivated almost exclusively by reformist values. For other figures, it is more difficult to say. The senior Shōkenkaku leader Maki Izumi, for example, seems to have been moved at times by reformism and at times by loyalism.

The Shōkenkaku was not an exclusive organization, and leaders of either type were welcome. As a consequence, the Shōkenkaku embraced many elements whose objectives were only loosely consonant with those of the Chōshū reformers. The Shōkenkaku were a group of great energy, and great impulsiveness, a blessing for the Chōshū movement, but one that was by no means unmixed.

WATCHFULNESS AND MOBILIZATION

Kusaka Genzui's services to the Chōshū movement in the early months of 1864 would have to do with the all-important timing of a Chōshū advance on Kyoto, and with restraint of Shōkenkaku militants. After the coup of 8/18/63, Chōshū was endowed with its own autonomous legitimacy and military force. Still, it was shut out of national councils in Kyoto. The obvious next step for the reformists in Chōshū was to move some of their pieces forward so as to reestablish their influence in the capital. The only real question remaining was that of how to move their loyalist troops back to Kyoto, and when.

The Chōshū han council, which was dominated by the Justice faction, had on 9/20/63 already agreed in principle that a force led by the heir would eventually go up to Kyoto. Nonetheless, Chōshū strategists of both the Aumeisha and Sonjuku generations sought to delay the advance to Kyoto until circumstances would be most favorable. Kusaka Genzui and others were stationed in the city accordingly to observe conditions.[20] The question of when to "march out" was greatly complicated by the presence of the Shōkenkaku on Chōshū soil. The Kyoto loyalists who composed its membership were extremely eager to return to the metropolis, and in some cases were doing so without the Chōshū government's consent. Both Kusaka Genzui and Takasugi Shinsaku were thus required in the early months of 1864 to devote considerable efforts to restraining the Shōkenkaku and preventing any premature actions that would discredit the movement.[21]

Restraint of the loyalists in exile at Mitajiri had become even more essential since the Shōkenkaku, renamed the Yūgekitai, had been designated as a unit of Chōshū's new Western-style military forces. Swollen by the influx of loyalist refugees, it was easily the largest of these new corps. Its official commander, from the Chōshū government's point of view, was Kijima Matabei, who had been released from his senior positions in the government for that assignment.[22]

In spite of intense pressure from the Yūgekitai, however, the Chōshū government avoided any hasty commitment of troops. In March, Kusaka Genzui journeyed from Kyoto to report to the administration personally on conditions in the capital. He advised that it certainly was not time to mobilize, and that prospects of using undercover contacts to obtain exoneration for Chōshū were improving. Kusaka then returned to Kyoto a few days later on 3/25.[23]

In April the outlook for a military return to Kyōto radically improved. After the anti-Chōshū coup of 8/18/63, authority in

Kyoto was shared by a council of great han and the Bakufu, the so-called Sanyo Council. Its members were quarreling already by March 1864, and in April its principal participants finally left Kyoto in protest against each other and the Bakufu, leaving the Bakufu's emissaries alone in the capital. The Bakufu, however, did not need the goodwill of the court if its authority were not contested by the great han; so the shogun also left Kyoto.

Kusaka Genzui was monitoring all this, and on 4/23 he wrote to the government in Yamaguchi that the time to march had come.[24] Kusaka knew how to bide his time, but he also knew an exceptional opportunity when he saw one. His sudden, deliberate, and eminently practical conversion to the "marching out" view precipitated an intramural debate that gripped the Chōshū government from top to bottom. Among the older officials of the Aumeisha generation who opposed marching were Sufu Masanosuke and Shishido Kurōbei, who was then director of the Chōshū compound at Ōsaka. In the Sonjuku generation, Kido Kōin in Kyoto and Takasugi Shinsaku in Hagi opposed. Still, the rest of the leadership of both generations was in favor, and so the die was cast.

The han council in Yamaguchi decided in the fifth month to dispatch several thousand men to Kyoto as soon as possible. The main Chōshū forces were divided into three contingents under the three progressive elders Fukuhara Echigo, Kunishi Shinano, and Masuda Danjō. The first of these moved out on 5/27, and all were under way by 7/6. The heir, Sadahiro, was to follow on 7/13 with a fourth contingent. Kusaka, who had returned to Yamaguchi on 5/28, conferred with his colleagues in the government and then joined the force under Kunishi. The other three forces were composed of regular han military and indigenous shotai. Kunishi's force, however, was the Yūgekitai, the Kyoto terror going home. If problems of coordination or discipline arose, it would be in the Yūgekitai; so it was to that company that Kusaka attached himself.[25]

By the second week of July, Chōshū's three forward contingents had taken up positions on the outskirts of Kyoto. Fukuhara Echigo's corps arrived first and camped at Fushimi. Kunishi Shinano billeted his Yūgekitai at the Tenryūji temple to the west of the city, and on 7/15 Masuda Danjō's forces stationed themselves at Otokoyama to the south.[26] By the middle of the seventh month, Chōshū's forces were poised on the outskirts of Kyoto. Less than a year after their demeaning exclusion from the imperial precincts, the Chōshū leaders had returned to the capital accompanied by an army.

These months marked the point at which Kusaka Genzui's contribution to the Chōshū movement was at its height. He had performed to perfection the role of political observation and analysis that was first thrust on him in 1858. The critical question of whether Chōshū's legions should rest or take up arms had been balanced on his seasoned judgment.

THE TRAGEDY AT OTOKOYAMA

Historians know that when the Chōshū forces finally engaged their antagonists in combat, things went badly. Less well known is the fateful war council that was held the night before in the elder Masuda's camp at Otokoyama. In a sense, the real climax, the real drama, and the real tragedy of Chōshū's march on Kyoto was played out here, and the rest was just a stormy denouement.

Bakufu officials were extremely apprehensive about Chōshū's loyalist troops being bivouacked on the outskirts of the city, and with sound reason. The Bakufu's highest representative in the capital, Hitotsubashi Yoshinobu, sent envoys to the Chōshū elder Fukuhara Echigo on 7/3, demanding the withdrawal of some of his troops. Fukuhara countered with an envoy to the court requesting that Chōshū's forces be allowed to enter the town. Meanwhile, Kusaka Genzui began canvassing the various han compounds in Kyoto, seeking to line up support for Chōshū's readmission to the court.

It was apparent by this time that if a peaceful compromise were to be reached between the Chōshū leaders and the Bakufu sympathizers who controlled the capital, prolonged and intricate negotiations might be needed. Hitotsubashi thus instructed Fuku-

hara on 7/15 that Chōshū's forces must be drawn back as far as
Ōsaka by 7/18 as a gesture of good faith while negotiations were
in progress. The Bakufu authorities were not unprepared to take
the offensive if Chōshū's forces were not withdrawn.

Many han
of conservative or moderate tendencies, beginning with Satsuma,
Aizu, Kuwana, and Tosa, had armed contingents in Kyoto that,
though united in little else, were united in their desire to hinder
the early reemergence of Chōshū's exclusive influence over the
court. Together the troops of these han outnumbered the men
Chōshū had at the capital on 7/15.[27]

The twenty or so Chōshū commanders held a war council at
Masuda's camp at Otokoyama on 7/17 to consider Hitotsubashi's
ultimatum. One of these twenty was Kijima Matabei, who would
have an especially important voice in the proceedings. Kijima had
been an official of the Justice faction and was a trusted senior
associate of Sufu's until his assignment as liaison to the Shōkenkaku. Sufu had always maintained a brilliant balance between
charismatic esprit and political calculation. Kijima did not. When
he took up his post as the military leader of the exiled loyalists of
the Yūgekitai, he fell under the spell of the euphoric commitment
that prevailed among them. His enthusiasm got the better of him,
and he became their spokesman.*

Kijima spoke first at the council, advocating preparations for
the army's immediate advance. When he took his seat, no one
spoke in affirmation. Angered, Kijima spoke again, urging his
comrades to remove the evil advisers from the side of the emperor. "What kind of thing was it to hesitate to attack," he chided.

It was Kusaka Genzui who stood up to reply, and he spoke in a
deliberate manner. He said that they had all come bearing shield

---

* Kijima's name may be found repeatedly in the lists of Chōshū's highest
officials in Suematsu, *Bōchō kaitenshi*, 1: 340, 471. Although Kijima was not
in the Aumeisha, he was a close colleague of Sufu's. In letters of 5/17/60,
8/24/60, and 3/27/63, Sufu discussed with Kijima such problems as procuring
funds for the heir's travels, preparations for Chōshū's first Western-style
cavalry squadron, the importance of Chōshū students' studying English, and
conservative currents in the government that could force Kijima's resignation.
See "Kijima Matabei-shū," Meiji Bunko Collection, Tokyo University, frames
55, 63, and 128 (microfilm).

and spear, and that all sought to be pure in their conduct toward the emperor. But, Kusaka said, the opportune time had not yet come. As for rinsing away the false charges that had been made against the house of Mōri on 8/18/63, and regaining access to the emperor, they should first "pile entreaty on entreaty." Since it was not their basic purpose to begin hostilities, they had all the more reason to wait in Ōsaka until the heir arrived with reinforcements, weigh their opportunities, and not take a stance of pressing on the imperial gates.

Kijima Matabei was not chastened by Kusaka's remarks. He responded that it was not for true retainers to ponder over advance or withdrawal while waiting for the heir. They should expel the evil near the emperor by a firm attack before the heir arrived. Kijima was speaking here for the Yūgekitai. From their point of view, the Chōshū government had been temporizing for almost a year, and if allowed to pull them back even from the threshold of the capital, the Chōshū authorities would go on temporizing forever. This was at odds with Kusaka's viewpoint, whereby temporizing was one of the essential tools of politics and diplomacy.

Kusaka replied. To advance then to the imperial gates without support, when preparations were still not complete, and with no plan for certain victory, was a very different thing from waiting for a military opportunity to mature, he said.

Kijima pointed at Kusaka and insulted him, calling him a coward. Then, in anger and high spirits, he said that if the others hesitated he would clear the evil from the side of the emperor with his own hands. He then abruptly walked out.

Kusaka might still have carried the council, but Maki Izumi stood up to second the feelings of Kijima. His remarks swayed other rear-echelon commanders to take Kijima's side, and the situation was beyond control. As twilight approached, the council dispersed, and Kusaka's aides returned with him to their camp at Yamazaki. He left the council "in a most dejected state." "He spoke not a word" as he walked along in the gathering darkness.[28]

The meeting at Otokoyama was the greatest failure of Kusaka Genzui's political career. It spelled disaster, and he knew it. Still,

Otokoyama represented the same medium that had brought him his greatest successes. His task in the Chōshū movement had always been to bind together many independent and highly emotional political participants, and to guide them in directions that would effectively serve the reformist cause. He and his comrades had been brilliantly successful at providing this kind of leadership in the early 1860's. They increased the influence of the reformist movement to a degree that even in 1861 had seemed impossible. These activities were exhilarating but hazardous, and Kusaka must have known from the start that some day fate might catch up with him.

THE FORBIDDEN GATE

The Meiji Restoration is sometimes characterized as a "peaceful revolution." Yet in the seventh month of 1864 there transpired a set of events leading to Restoration that were not peaceful. On the eighteenth day, the forces of conservatism and the forces of reform faced each other with sword and rifle. Many lives were lost, and Kyoto was ravaged by fire.

All Chōshū contingents were ordered to converge on the imperial palace at dawn on 7/18. Their object was to secure by force the sacred precincts and access to the emperor, both of which had been lost to Chōshū since the entry into the imperial compound of troops from Aizu and Satsuma on 8/18/63. Two of the Chōshū forces made little headway, however. Fukuhara Echigo led his contingent of Chōshū regulars out of Fushimi in the small hours of the morning, but clashed repeatedly with hostile troops before reaching the city. Fukuhara himself was wounded. His force was finally turned back by troops of Aizu and Hikone at Tamba bridge, and withdrew to Yamazaki. The contingent under Masuda at Otokoyama never set out for the palace, because by the time Masuda was done imploring divine aid at Hachimangu shrine, word had already reached him that the fighting was over.

Kunishi Shinano's force did far better. Kunishi's corps was based at Tenryūji temple, west of the city, and consisted primarily of the Yūgekitai under Kijima. The entire force marched before dawn, and when it reached Kitano, Kunishi divided it into two parts. There were two great parallel boulevards leading to the palace from the west, and each part drove down one of these boulevards. The elder Kunishi, leading the more northerly of these detachments, easily smashed through the Nakatachiuri Gate, which was defended only by samurai of Chikuzen. Several hundred yards to the south, Kijima's troops breached the Hamaguri Gate shortly after, but immediately found themselves in a pitched battle with troops from Aizu just within the gate. Kunishi's men, already inside the palace wall, rushed southward the short distance to the Hamaguri Gate to assist Kijima in the fighting.

The Aizu line faltered and fell back. Aizu was soon reinforced, however, by overwhelming numbers of Satsuma and Kuwana troops who had been guarding others of the nine palace gates. During the struggle Kijima Matabei himself, who had made himself an easy target by leading his troops on horseback, was shot from his horse and killed. With his force outnumbered, battered, and dwindling, Kunishi had little choice but to allow a retreat. It was this hard-fought clash at the Hamaguri Gate that gave the day its name: the Incident of the Forbidden Gate (*Kimmon no hen*).

There was a fourth Chōshū force outside Kyoto, which had been created earlier by detaching some of the Yūgekitai men, most of whom were serving under Kunishi and Kijima. This fourth force was commanded by Maki Izumi and advised by Kusaka Genzui. It had camped at Yamazaki, a village near Otokoyama about ten miles southwest of the city. This corps, too, marched toward the city before dawn in accordance with the war council's decision. Its troops reached the Sakaimachi Gate of the palace, but being a smaller band than that under Kunishi, they could not penetrate Fukui's defense. They therefore occupied Takatsukasa Hall, a mansion belonging to a family of court nobles. Amidst running exchanges of rifle fire they held it, against Fukui, Kuwana, Hikone, and later Satsuma and Aizu, who came to reinforce when Kunishi withdrew from the Hamaguri Gate. The activist band fought until the hall caught fire, forcing them to abandon their position and to retreat, this time from the city.

It was at Takatsukasa Hall that Kusaka Genzui made his last political decision. He was severely wounded in the gunfighting and took his own life rather than risk being captured or encumbering his companions. Terajima Chūzaburō, a younger Sonjuku member who was also wounded in one of the volleys that raked through the Takatsukasa, died with Kusaka. Two other Sonjuku alumni, Irie Sugizō and Ariyoshi Kumajirō, died at other points.

Maki Izumi, though wounded, escaped from the Takatsukasa and from the city. With a remnant of sixteen men he made a stand on Emperor Mountain (Tenōyama). When troops of Aizu and Kuwana tracked them down on 7/21, they fired a few shots, and then all sixteen, hopelessly outnumbered, committed seppuku. Twelve of the sixteen were from the three han of Kurume, Kumamoto, and Tosa, reflecting the origins of the Yūgekitai. There was not a Chōshū man among the sixteen.

Although the fighting was over by 7/19, secondary fires raged in the city until 7/21. Disorder was extreme. Ten mansions of noble families were reduced to ashes, and 28,000 other dwellings were destroyed. Refugees crowded the inns and highways leading from the city. Nomi Orie, director of the Chōshū compound, set fire to it himself, and sought asylum in one of the city's great Buddhist sanctuaries.[29]

Kido Kōin had been living at the Chōshū compound when the fighting broke out. After getting to the Sakaimachi Gate too late for the encounter there, he concealed himself under Nijō Bridge. Aizu troops would not think to look for him there, and he would be safe from the flames. When the fires waned, he managed to pass word of his whereabouts to a geisha of his acquaintance named Matsuko, who brought him nourishing stuffed ricecakes and other provisions.* After five days under the bridge, Kido fled to Izushi,

---

* This was not the last thing the fetching geisha ever did for Kido. When he emerged in the highest councils of the national government five years later, she married him.

a village in the interior northwest of Ōsaka, where he would remain incommunicado for several months.[30]

As Chōshū's various forces retreated from the capital, they were able to regroup only on the distant coast of Hyōgo. From there they made their disconsolate way back to Yamaguchi to report the events of the Forbidden Gate.[31] What had happened? Why had the expedition, which had seemed so promising, ended in disaster? The problem was that the Yūgekitai was not integrated in terms of effective command with the rest of Chōshū's troops. The Chōshū forces as a body, if skillfully played, could not have failed to be a powerful instrument of Chōshū's reformist policy. Yet, when they reached Kyoto, they did not operate as a body, but rather as two slightly antagonistic parts. From a tactical point of view, the war council of 7/17 should have resolved on the pullback advocated by Kusaka. This was unacceptable to the Yūgekitai leaders, however, who proceeded to cow the other members of the council into tacit assent for attack. Whatever they professed in council, however, the two non-Yūgekitai forces under Fukuhara and Masuda had but limited interest in a hasty offensive, and did not even reach the city on 7/18 to take part in the crucial gate fighting. This weakened the effect of the attack.

Kusaka had made an error, not about the political conditions in Kyoto, which were favorable, but about Chōshū's own forces. He had assumed that the often recalcitrant Yūgekitai would become more manageable once it were brought back to the vicinity of the capital. The opposite occurred.

CIVIL WAR

The Forbidden Gate marked the beginning of the third stage of the reformist struggle. Between 1853 and 1858, and to a lesser extent in the 1830's and 1840's, both the reformist movement and their conservative opposition had confined themselves to the use of polemical writing. The struggle, that is, was ideological. Beginning with Ii Naosuke's implementation of the Ansei Purge in 1858, a second phase of the struggle was inaugurated, a phase that involved the use by both sides of limited violence, violence directed against particular persons. That is, the Bakufu resorted to police repression, and the opposition countered with terror. Conservative elements responded to the terror with an escalation. They surrounded the palace with troops and imposed martial law on the capital. Reformers answered this challenge by mobilizing troops of their own, and the two sides met at the Hamaguri Gate in 1864.

The bitter encounter fought at the Forbidden Gate signaled the beginning of the third and final stage of the Restoration conflict. This third stage involved large-scale violence perpetrated by armed representatives of each side against those of the other—namely, warfare. While the basic goals of the Chōshū reformists remained clear and constant, their tactics evolved through three distinct phases: ideological delegitimation, terror, and civil war, a progression often found in revolutionary contexts elsewhere.

It was Kusaka Genzui who led the Chōshū movement in the years of transition from polemics to terror. It was Kusaka again who, when conservative elements surrounded the emperor with troops, guided the Chōshū movement into a response in kind. He encouraged the Chōshū leaders not to be afraid to take up arms when the times seemed to require it. When conservative musketeers finally killed Kusaka, it was too late. The band of dedicated reformers whom he led had already breached the forbidden gate of open warfare.

In spite of his career's early conclusion, Kusaka Genzui's years of political leadership brought great advances to the reformist movement in Chōshū. Kusaka extended the movement's stated institutional goals in his memorials of 1862. He played a key role in the development of the working alliance between Chōshū, loyalist nobles, and radical samurai in the street, which turned national policy in a reformist direction in 1863. He assisted in the formation of a new kind of military unit, the Kiheitai, and helped to shape Chōshū's firm policy of using its own military potential rather than merely acquiescing in the military movements of conservative authorities.

Still, in terms of their immediate impact, the policies of Kusaka that led to the Forbidden Gate had been a resounding failure. Chōshū was discredited and discouraged, and some of her best leaders had been removed from the scene. Even many of the Chōshū activists themselves judged the situation to be hopeless, and it would have been, had another figure not emerged from the ranks of the Sonjuku to lead the movement in a course of action that was as desperate as it was resolute.

CHAPTER SEVEN

The Early Career of Takasugi Shinsaku

TAKASUGI Shinsaku was a heavy drinker and a frequent visitor at the pleasure establishments of the Yoshiwara. He was the only member of the Sonjuku group who died young from complications that were not political. It is difficult to imagine a personality more different from the frugal and assiduous scholar Yoshida Shōin; yet each of these two men had his own kind of intensity, and a strong bond of mutual regard existed between them. This bond had been cultivated by Yoshida, perhaps in part because their personalities were complementary opposites, but also because he saw very early that the Sonjuku movement might one day have need of the aptitudes of an associate like Takasugi.

In popular stereotypes about Restoration figures Yoshida Shōin is sometimes regarded as a naive romantic, while Takasugi tends to be seen as a thoughtful strategist. In reality Yoshida was the thoughtful one, and Takasugi was the man of action who was able to indulge in bold strokes without thinking about it too much. His temperament was "frank and direct," to use his own words, and this directness would give him a unique mission within the Sonjuku movement.

Still, untypically brash as he was, Takasugi bore the unmistakable stamp of the cadet professional in Chōshū. The academies in which he was enrolled were among the finest in Japan. He distinguished himself at his studies and received educational appointments, as earlier Sonjuku leaders had. He traveled widely to enhance his wisdom and his awareness of public affairs. He established contact with other reformist scholars, notably Sakuma Shōzan and Yokoi Shōnan, as his fellow students had done. These characteristics, as they appear in Takasugi and the other reformist leaders, are extremely important for an analysis of the Restoration movement in Chōshū because they were intimately interlinked with the reformists' unusually broad public awareness and with their stated institutional goals. The professional ethos that these experiences represented seems to have shaped the Chōshū activists' political perceptions and guided them in their commitment to drastic reform. Takasugi shared in full measure the education and attitudes that were typical of the Sonjuku leadership.

EARLY EDUCATION

Takasugi followed the educational path to which most young samurai of his rank aspired. After distinguishing himself at the Meirinkan, he went on to study at Yoshida Shōin's school, where he again excelled. His credentials were such that he was later allowed to enroll in the Bakufu's nationally prestigious Shōheikō academy in Edo. He was critical, however, of the intellectual sterility of both the Meirinkan and the Shōheikō. The unusually assertive personality that would shape Takasugi's contribution to the reformist movement was often evident even in these early years.

Takasugi was born in 1839, the son of a modestly stipended samurai family. His father was Takasugi Kochūta, a Great Group samurai of 150 koku. Kochūta was a proud careerist of somewhat conservative leanings who held high posts in the Chōshū administration throughout the Bakumatsu years. Takasugi was his only son and heir, and his importance to his family may have influenced his temperament. He had a reputation for stubbornness that is borne out by a number of anecdotes remaining from his childhood. According to one of these, a New Year's Day guest once accidentally trod on Takasugi's kite as it rested on the ground, and broke it. Still a small boy, Takasugi angrily grabbed a handful of mud and threatened to throw it on the guest's crested kimono, a gift from the daimyo, unless he apologized in very abject terms. This demand was reluctantly met by the startled guest.[1]

Takasugi learned his letters at the neighborhood grammar school of Yoshimatsu Junzō, where Kusaka Genzui also attended. In those early days Takasugi was said to have excelled in fencing, whereas Kusaka was better at reading. At the age of fourteen, as befitted a Great Group samurai, Takasugi enrolled at the Meirin-kan. Although his interest in fencing did not diminish, he wanted to join the ranks of the scholarly elite who were chosen as boarding students. He was not good enough, however, and had to apply himself to his studies. He was finally selected for this honor in his fourth year at the academy.[2]

As often happened, this long exercise in formalized learning developed in Takasugi a thirst for education on the one hand and an attitude critical of the Meirinkan atmosphere on the other. To a friend, he wrote that it was a place for "frivolous socializing," and that he had never seen "the serious pursuit of reason there."[3]

Having reached this stage of awareness, Takasugi was ripe for recruitment by the Shōka Sonjuku. His name began to appear regularly on the Sonjuku rolls in 1857, shortly after he had been chosen as a boarding student at the Meirinkan. Takasugi's father did not approve of his going to Yoshida's school, but did not actively prevent him.

Takasugi's stubbornness did not win him many friends at the Sonjuku; rather it seems to have alienated everyone except the instructor. The student Watanabe Kōzō reported in later years that although Kusaka was much sought after as a companion, the students avoided Takasugi: "Because he was rough and rude, Takasugi had little popularity, while Kusaka had much."[4] One day Kido Kōin approached Yoshida Shōin and urged either that Takasugi's waywardness be curbed or that he be expelled from the Sonjuku. The instructor replied: "Up to now I have of course talked to Takasugi about his character, but have not tried to reform it. If you try to force a stubborn character to change, the person will just become incomplete, or rather, in later days, he will come to lose the intense willpower that is absolutely necessary for accomplishing great things. Takasugi is a man who in ten years will do much."[5] Yoshida may have sensed that someday resolute action might be required to fulfill his political purposes, and he may have foreseen a special role for Takasugi in this regard. "My keeping company with you," Yoshida wrote to him, "is not just for practice in reading, but so that you can realize great plans for the nation."[6]

When in 1858 the Sonjuku students began to be dispatched to Kyoto and Edo for study, Takasugi too wished to go. He received permission in July, and on the eighteenth of that month a farewell party was held at the Sonjuku. Yoshida offered an address, in which he said that Takasugi's intellectual growth had been remarkable since he came to the school (although not as remarkable as Kusaka's). He had special praise for Takasugi's quick, resourceful judgments, his "insight."[7]

Takasugi arrived in Edo in mid-August and promptly enrolled in the school of Ōhashi Totsuan. He did not like it, however, because the atmosphere was one of superficial rhetoric. "It is not enough to debate with bumpkins and bravados, even from Mito," he wrote.[8] Takasugi then switched in the eleventh month to the orthodox college of the Bakufu, the Shōheikō, but did not like that either, because the curriculum amounted to an empty ritual of formal learning. He would not find another school like the Sonjuku.[9]

Takasugi's educational progress was without flaw. He made the serious effort that was necessary to stand out at the Meirinkan and at the Sonjuku. He was able to distinguish himself even amidst the brightest and most diligent young men that Chōshū han had to offer. Like Yoshida and Kusaka, he was clearly a member of that portion of Chōshū's youth who were grooming themselves for a future of scholarly and administrative service. Like them, his perceptions and interests, including his commitment to structural reforms, were probably shaped in large measure by the dynamic educational milieu of which he was a part.

A VOW

Takasugi was still pursuing his education in Edo when the drama of Yoshida Shōin's extradition and death took place in 1859. Like the other Sonjuku members in the vicinity of the two capitals, he was not in favor of Yoshida's plans to eliminate Manabe Akikatsu in Kyoto, or of his "petition at the palanquin" proposal. Still, he was appalled at Yoshida's being turned over to the Bakufu, and went often to comfort him in prison. When Yoshida was finally executed, Takasugi vowed that he would never rest until he had destroyed the Tokugawa Bakufu. This vow itself is of historical importance.

Takasugi, though in Edo and Kyoto at the same time as Kusaka, was never drawn to the exhilarating world of street politics in the way that Kusaka and some of the other students were. The reason for this may have been that he lacked the patience and tact that some of the others had. There is some evidence that in these years his intolerant disposition made it difficult for him to remain on good terms even with his colleagues from Chōshū.

While in Edo, Takasugi lived at Sakurada Hall, one of Chōshū's compounds in the city. His roommate there was Nakatani Masa-suke, another student from the Sonjuku. Nakatani was a congenial fellow, and the whole Edo contingent of the Sonjuku group—Kusaka, Kido, Itō, Yamagata, Irie Sugizō, and Sugiyama Matsusuke—sometimes gathered in the room just to talk. Takasugi, however, regarded these sessions as an annoyance, and greeted those who came to them with conspicuous ill humor.[10]

Meanwhile, as Takasugi occupied himself with his studies and the nocturnal attractions of the city, Yoshida had been imprisoned, and politically active students in Edo like Kusaka were being ordered home. Because Takasugi was doing nothing of political significance, the Chōshū authorities saw no reason to send him home, and before too many months had passed, he found that he was the only member of the Sonjuku left in the capital—a distinction that became a source of embarrassment for him before the others.[11] After Yoshida Shōin was turned over to the authorities at the Bakufu's Demmachō prison in Edo in the seventh month of 1859, Takasugi often visited him there. Takasugi's father found out about this, however, and obtained a han order requiring him to leave Edo for Hagi on 10/17.

Only one man in a position of authority had ever believed in the tempestuous but gifted young Takasugi, and that man was Yoshida Shōin. When Yoshida was executed by the Tokugawa Bakufu on October 27, 1859, Takasugi's anguish manifested itself in a letter he sent to the Aumeisha chief Sufu Masanosuke on 11/16/59:

> Our teacher Shōin's head falling at the hands of the Bakufu is . . . a cause for deep shame. As for me as a disciple, my heart will never rest until I fell this antagonist. . . . While yearning for our instructor Shōin's shadow, morning and night, I have grieved deeply. . . . Practicing military arts in the morning and studying in the evening, tempering my mind and body, serving the spirit of my forebears, and accomplishing my own duty, all become merged in the task of destroying the enemy of our master, Shōin.[12]

Takasugi's dedication to his teacher's memory did not diminish in the weeks following his vow. On 11/27, ten days after his arrival in Hagi and a month after Yoshida's death, he and Kusaka arranged a Buddhist service for their departed teacher. Takasugi then attended the revived Sonjuku when it got under way several months later.

Takasugi's anguished vow to destroy the Bakufu and avenge Yoshida's death obviously represented a major event in his emotional life, but this vow has historiographical significance as well. It calls into question one of the basic tenets on which prevailing analyses of Chōshū activism are based, namely, that Takasugi rejected the ideals and methods of his teacher. Takasugi later would lead a number of daring military raids at the head of his Western-style rifle corps in 1865 and 1866, the object of which was always Bakufu or pro-Bakufu forces, often in overwhelming concentrations. These numbing collisions with Takasugi and his compatriots more or less assured the collapse of the Bakufu as a credible military power. Takasugi's vow at the time of Yoshida's execution suggests that these historically decisive assaults on Bakufu power were a direct legacy of his close association with Yoshida. Takasugi had first learned about Western military techniques from his teacher. Moreover, Takasugi's attacks often succeeded because they were not encumbered by too much emphasis on personal safety, and this calculated recklessness too had been an often-reiterated tenet of his mentor's. Takasugi's later military resourcefulness at the Bakufu's expense probably represented a direct affirmation of his loyalty to Yoshida, to his program, his principles, and his memory.

TRAVEL

Travel in Tokugawa Japan was considered a broadening experience, and it was one of the imperatives of education at the Shōka Sonjuku. Virtually all of the Sonjuku leaders journeyed within Japan to observe and record the ways of its various regions. In the early 1860's Takasugi chose to do this, and to pursue his education, rather than to join his more gregarious comrades in the politics of the street. As he traveled, he cultivated the same journalistic practices as Yoshida had. Like Kusaka and Yoshida, he routinely sought out the articulate older reformers Sakuma Shōzan and Yokoi Shōnan and felt an instant kinship with them.

In the second month of 1860, Takasugi entered Chōshū's Naval Instruction Bureau (*Gunkan kyōjū-sho*), which was directed by Matsushima Gōzō, a charter member of the Aumeisha. Like Kusaka and Kido, Matsushima was a han physician of low rank whose vocation had brought him a thorough exposure to Dutch learning. Matsushima planned to sail one of the han's schooners to Edo in April 1860 as a means of giving practical instruction in navigational skills. Takasugi applied as a crewman and was accepted. He embarked on the *Heishin-maru* on 4/5/60, but soon discovered that being an oceangoing sailor took more than savoring the salt spray for two weeks, and indeed required complex skills and hard work. He arrived in Edo wiser in the ways of navigation, and humbler.[13]

Kusaka and Kido met Takasugi in the capital and told him of

their current political tentatives. He was still not ready to participate, however, and instead applied to the han for permission to tour the Northeast, which was granted. Takasugi left Edo for this new adventure on 8/28/60, going northeast to Mito, northwest to Nikkō, and then west toward the Japan Sea. When he met with his teacher's teacher, Sakuma Shōzan, in Shirakawa on 9/22, the two talked until dawn. In Fukui on 10/1 Takasugi met with Yokoi Shōnan, whom Yoshida Shōin had first met on his travels ten years before in faraway Kumamoto. Except for a detour into Ōsaka, Takasugi traveled along the Japan Sea coast until he arrived back in Hagi some two months after his departure from Edo. Like Yoshida, he kept a daily record of his journey that was filled with astute observations about persons and places.[14]

He wrote to Kusaka on 11/19/60 telling him of the trip: "I conversed with Sakuma until dawn. I also talked to him about you, and it is certainly all right if you visit him next spring."[15] By visiting Sakuma, Yokoi, and other reformers, and reporting the content of those visits to his friends, Takasugi also helped to maintain the network of communication among reformist sympathizers that Yoshida, Kusaka, and many others had cultivated.

Once Takasugi was back in Hagi, the government sought to confer on him a status consistent with his recent scholarly achievements. He had been a dormitory master (shachō) at the Meirinkan briefly in March, before shipping on the Heishin-maru, and now on 12/10/60 he was made a lecturer (tokō) there. In subsequent months he devoted himself seriously to study, reading "A Military Discussion of Maritime Nations" ("Kaikoku heidan") by Hayashi Shihei, and the "Record of Traditional Learning" ("Ch'uan-hsi lu") of Wang Yang-ming, among other volumes. Then on 3/2/61 Takasugi was raised to the position of page-tutor to the heir, Sadahiro. Takasugi was the highest ranking of the Sonjuku students except for Nakatani Masasuke, and this promotion allowed the government to draw a Sonjuku man to the center of the castle without appearing to violate traditional barriers of rank.[16]

In the sixth month, Takasugi was ordered to travel to Edo as an escort (*bante*) to the daimyo's party, and thus arrived in the capital once more on 7/21/61. This was the period when Kusaka and Sufu were trying to construct a multi-han loyalist alliance of Chōshū, Satsuma, and Mito, and also to overthrow Nagai's mediation. Takasugi was still not prepared, however, to abandon his educational explorations. Traveling through much of the realm and having met some of the great reformists only gave him an appetite for more. He wanted to go abroad.

SHANGHAI

The same ethos of public inquisitiveness that impelled Sonjuku students to travel within Japan also propelled them beyond her borders. Not all of the Sonjuku leaders had traveled abroad, but most of them sought at some time or other to do so. The most famous effort to study in the West was Yoshida Shōin's carefully prepared attempt to go to America in 1854. In the late 1850's and early 1860's, other leaders wished to study abroad, but were hindered by their growing political duties. Kusaka had wished to visit the Amur River region in 1858, but was dissuaded by Yoshida on the grounds that events at home were too pressing. In 1861 Kido Kōin had sought to accompany a pending Bakufu mission to England and France. The Chōshū government decided against this, however, because Kido, too, had become a vital link in the han's networks of national politicking.*

Takasugi would finally be given an opportunity to journey abroad in 1862. The Bakufu planned to send a ship to Shanghai early in 1862 to investigate trading opportunities there, and requested that able men from the various han join the mission. Kido had submitted Takasugi's name, and the Bakufu orders came down with the necessary permission on 8/8/61. The Bakufu's *Sensai-maru* left Edo Bay on 1/3/62, with Takasugi on board.[17]

* *Yoshida Shōin zenshū*, ed. Yamaguchi ken kyōiku kai, 12 vols. (Tokyo, 1940), 9: 50–53; *Shōkiku Kido-kō den*, ed. Kido-kō denki hensanjo, 2 vols. (Tokyo, 1927), 1: 68. It was not until 1863 that the Chōshū government felt that it could risk dispatching men abroad on its own authority. In the fifth month of that year Chōshū sent to London a group of five persons that included the two younger Sonjuku members Itō Hirobumi and Inoue Kaoru. See *Itō Hirobumi den*, ed. Shumbō kō tsuishō kai, 3 vols. (Tokyo, 1940), 1: 105.

It is possible to look closely at Takasugi's Shanghai experience because of the journal he kept. His record of the trip leaves little doubt that he had a keen eye for significant detail. He noted the flourishing trade on the great Yangtze, the ways of the foreign consulates, and the sad living conditions of many ordinary Chinese. He observed firsthand the military efforts made by the British and Chinese against the Taiping rebels who were then approaching the city.[18]

Takasugi concluded from what he saw that China was virtually a European colony. On 5/21/62 he passed a toll bridge, built by the English when the Chinese authorities claimed they could not replace an older structure that had fallen. Chinese pedestrians had to pay a penny each time they crossed. In his diary Takasugi wrote: "One could say that the Chinese are being altogether taken advantage of by the foreigners. When an Englishman or a Frenchman walks down the street, the Chinese all scurry out of the way. Although Shanghai is on Chinese soil, is it not an English and French colony?"[19] Few of the Chinese who lived in Shanghai could see the ominous pattern that Takasugi discerned there almost immediately. The habits of thought and of public inquisitiveness that brought him to do this so effortlessly may go far in themselves to explain the difference between China's and Japan's nineteenth-century responses to the West. In Takasugi's case, these crucial intellectual habits had been nurtured at the Shōka Sonjuku.

When Takasugi finally returned to Hagi late in the seventh month, he immediately conveyed all he had learned to his Sonjuku colleagues. Many details of life in Shanghai found their way into Kusaka's two telling memorials of 8/62, in which he argued that drastic changes were needed to save Japan from a like fate. This was another case in which the habit of political reporting served the Sonjuku movement well.

TAKASUGI THE MONK

After returning home from Shanghai, Takasugi soon became once again frustrated at the lack of tangible results being achieved by Chōshū's role in the convoluted street politicking of the metropolis. The other Chōshū leaders realized, however, that there was a rhythm in the currents of public opinion that could not be hurried. Takasugi became impatient, and annoyed, and took the tonsure.

After several weeks in Hagi subsequent to his return from China, Takasugi had proceeded to Kyoto, where on 8/23 he formally reported to the daimyo on his China voyage. A few days later he was restored to an official status, this time as an attaché to the court nobles' academy, the Gakushūin (*Gakushūin-yō gakari*). This meant that his task would be to participate as a Chōshū representative in metropolitan politics, not an accustomed activity.[20]

Takasugi moved to Edo the following month, where Kusaka, only recently released from house arrest in Hagi, was trying to weaken Bakufu authority with acts of political street violence. None of this was to Takasugi's taste. It was shifting and uncertain and did not seem to have any solid results. In a letter to Kido Kōin, he complained that such pursuits as conversing with court nobles, petitioning Echizen han's Matsudaira Yoshinaga or the Bakufu's Hitotsubashi Yoshinobu, picking at small Bakufu envoys, and plotting with samurai of Mito and Satsuma were "futile activity." Takasugi recommended that Chōshū forget all this and embrace policies that would be more bold and direct.[21]

Kido did not respond favorably to this; so Takasugi related his complaints to Sufu. Sufu, the canny leader of the Justice faction, understood, as Kusaka and Kido did, that a foothold of legitimacy had to be eked out in the capitals before Chōshū could hope to do anything more audacious. He replied to Takasugi in this way: "It is as you say, but your discussion is too extreme. If ten years pass, the opportunity may come. Until then, it is important to weaken the influence of the Bakufu even if only by small degrees. . . . How would it be to work as a school official?"[22]

Being a school official was not what Takasugi had in mind. He wanted to work in a military capacity. Piqued by Sufu's answer, he announced to the government on 3/15/63 that if it were a question of waiting ten years for favorable circumstances, he wanted ten years of leisure in which to study and meditate. He shaved his head like a Buddhist monk to underline his argument, and changed his name to Tōgyō, which meant "going east," the point being that Takasugi intended to cultivate matters of the spirit. Takasugi was famous for his obstinacy, and the Chōshū government granted him a ten-year leave of absence from his official duties, as he had requested.[23]

The disgruntled activist left Kyoto on 3/26/63. He drank up his travel money twice before actually getting under way, and had to borrow, once from Sufu and once from the Chōshū compound in Ōsaka.[24] After he arrived in Hagi on 4/10, he lived quietly in the suburb of Matsumoto with the wife he had married at his father's behest early in 1860. This withdrawal from public life was very much in accord with Takasugi's nature. He would sooner remove himself altogether than participate in a compromise of doubtful sincerity.

TAKASUGI THE COMMANDER

The Chōshū leadership had little need for Takasugi's inflexible integrity in the fluid political milieu of the capital, but they would soon have need of it elsewhere. In the sixth month of 1863, he was finally assigned a mission in the Chōshū movement that suited his fancy and his temperament.

Chōshū had begun to bombard foreign ships at Shimonoseki on 5/10 in accord with court and Bakufu directives to expel Westerners from the realm, but on 6/5 the French warships *Sémiramis* and *Tancrède* had retaliated, while Kusaka Genzui's Kōmyōji party looked on. Kusaka himself had already returned to Kyoto to seek support for expulsion among other han, believing when he left that Chōshū's shore batteries had prevailed.

In order to appear to be dealing purposively with the situation, and probably to facilitate the formation of Kusaka's Kōmyōji party into Western-style rifle units under government auspices, the han government hastily restored Takasugi to an official capacity and dispatched him to Shimonoseki. There he was supposed to recommend and initiate effective military countermeasures against the foreign incursions. Arriving at Shimonoseki on 6/6, Takasugi had by 6/14 organized some sixty men from the Kōmyōji party and of other origins into a Western-style rifle company called the Kiheitai. He announced at the start that feudal rank would have no place in the corps, an institutional departure with overtones of major social change. The Kiheitai, like the Shōka Sonjuku, was to be based on principles of merit rather than precedent.[25]

Takasugi found a vocation in the Kiheitai rifle corps. Earlier in his life he had expressed a desire to become a military leader.* The Kiheitai did not float like Kyoto street politics, and leadership of it was more consonant with his direct temperament than participation in diplomatic activities in Kyoto. The gruff assertiveness that made him seem surly among his peers in Kyoto may have been an advantage to him in his new role as a military leader. Only after he had established a firm base in the Kiheitai did he engage for the first time in conduct akin to diplomacy. When in the eighth month of 1863 the Kiheitai was about to clash with the aristocratic Sempōtai, he went diligently back and forth using his diplomatic good offices between the heir and the parties in order to save the corps.[26]

In recognition of his services with the Kiheitai, Takasugi was raised to an office at the policymaking level of the han government (*seiyakumuchō*) on 9/15. At the same time he was awarded 160 koku on his own merit, independently of his father's income of 150 koku.[27] Early in the tenth month, he left the daily business of the Kiheitai to his trusted lieutenants in Ogōri and went to Yamaguchi to assume his new post.

RESTRAINT

After returning to the government, Takasugi was presented with another challenge that was appropriate to his inclinations. After

* In a letter to his father on 6/28/56, Takasugi set forth his wish to someday become a "vanguard commander" (*sempō taishō*). See *Tōgyō sensei ibun*, ed. Tōgyō gojūnensai kinenkai, 2 vols. (Shimonoseki, 1971 [1916]), "Shokan," p. 2; *Tōgyō Takasugi Shinsaku*, ed. Takasugi Tōgyō sensei hyakunensai hōsankai (Shimonoseki, 1966), p. 226.

the conservative coup of 8/18/63 in Kyoto, several hundred young loyalists, whose activities Chōshū had sponsored there, had come and camped at Mitajiri along with the seven radical court nobles under Sanjō Sanetomi. From the outset these youths felt a compulsion to heed the charismatic lure of the capital and return to Kyoto. The han government thus asked Takasugi to assist in the delicate task of dissuading them.

The specific problem the administration faced was that Kijima Matabei, the commander of the Shōkenkaku's Yūgekitai, was asking permission to lead his troops back to Kyoto, and threatening to go anyway if permission were not granted. On han orders, Takasugi went to Mitajiri on 1/24/64 to see Kijima. The two men heatedly debated the question of marching to Kyoto for several days, but the most Kijima would agree to was to confer personally with Kusaka, Kido, and Shishido Kurōbei in Kyoto before making up his mind about the Yūgekitai's marching unilaterally back to the imperial city.

At this juncture, Takasugi should technically have reported to Yamaguchi that his mission was a failure, and asked for further instructions. He decided instead to personally escort Kijima to Kyoto, where the government's battery of glib officials could surely wear him down, and the two men set out on 1/28. The tactic worked. Once in Kyoto, Kijima, no longer surrounded by his cheering legion, spoke one after another with Kusaka, Shishido, and Kido, who produced countless reasons why marching immediately on Kyoto would be undesirable, and finally talked Kijima out of it. In taking Kijima to Kyoto, however, Takasugi had not set a good example of martial discipline for the desertion-prone troops of the Yūgekitai, in that neither he nor Kijima had traveling orders.

The more basic problem of the Yūgekitai's desire to return to Kyoto regardless of the reason remained. Desertions of Yūgekitai men to Kyoto continued to be high in February and March, even though the government had tightened border inspections and authorized small contingents of loyalists to go to Kyoto as escorts to Chōshū officials. Moreover, desertion to Kyoto was beginning to spread from the Yūgekitai to the native Chōshū corps.[28] Takasugi's efforts to restrain the Yūgekitai were thus only a limited success. Moreover, his having hastily left the han with Kijima would have immediate repercussions that would serve to place him once more off the center stage of Chōshū politics.

"AT LAST, NOYAMA PRISON"

Takasugi Shinsaku's "frank and direct" temperament got him into difficulties with the authorities a number of times. Takasugi would soon find himself in Noyama prison for having impetuously left the han without authorization. The most significant aspect of Takasugi's prison experience of 1864 lay in the ongoing spiritual bond that this period of stress revealed between Takasugi and his departed teacher Yoshida Shōin. In his journal, in his poetry, and in his daily pursuits, he demonstrated his kinship with his inspirational instructor. A second personal tie, with Sufu Masanosuke, was also affirmed by Takasugi's imprisonment. The bonds of common social condition and of common political perceptions that had nourished the association of the Sonjuku group and the Aumeisha group in the 1850's continued to be strong in the 1860's.

Takasugi, as a representative of the Yamaguchi government, had set a bad example for the Yūgekitai when he took Kijima to Kyoto without waiting for the necessary papers. Therefore, when he returned to Yamaguchi with Kusaka on 3/29/64, he was ordered to enter Noyama prison for "fleeing the han" (dappan). In a sense, Takasugi was being punished for being unable to deal with Kijima's rashness, as Kusaka later would be.[29]

On the day of his imprisonment, and on many days thereafter, Takasugi recalled the destiny of his mentor Yoshida Shōin. Soon after entering the prison, he composed this verse:

> Longing for the teacher, who is far away,
> At last, Noyama prison.[30]

As had also been true of Yoshida, the rate at which Takasugi read increased when he entered prison. In the fourth and fifth months he kept a daily record of his broad readings, much as Yoshida had.[31]

At one point he was called upon to justify this ambitious activity before the other inmates. Noyama prison was regarded as the last step for terminal prisoners, and for a futureless person to devote himself to assiduous daily readings seemed a great waste of effort. Finally, one of the prisoners asked Takasugi why he bothered. He replied with the story of a teacher, called "Twenty-One Times a Valiant Samurai," who had taught him "the principle of thought and action." The teacher had foreseen his imprisonment and had counseled him in that case to "read books and refine the spirit," for "in ten years you will accomplish much." Although the teacher had "gone far away, I can still hear his words," Takasugi said. "So how could I fail to read and study?"

The inmate did not understand any of this. "If you are executed in prison, today's study will become as last night's dreams," he persisted. Takasugi smiled. "Why should a man who still lives speak of death," he said, and "inscribed the words of the teacher on the wall as an admonition" for himself.[32] The teacher was, of course, Yoshida Shōin. The extent to which Yoshida dominated Takasugi's thoughts during his imprisonment in 1864 reinforces the likelihood that his decisive conduct in the Chōshū civil war a few months later represented loyalty to Yoshida's politics, not a rejection of them.

Sufu Masanosuke, the leader of Chōshū's ruling Justice faction, also intruded upon Takasugi's quiet life at Noyama. One sultry summer day Sufu was drinking in the shade at the house of Tsuchiya Yanosuke. He felt frustrated because of the recent tilt of his colleagues toward a policy of marching han forces to Kyoto. While talking with Tsuchiya, Sufu recalled that Takasugi, the only member of the Sonjuku group in Hagi who still, like Sufu, opposed marching, was isolated in prison.

Suddenly Sufu strode out of the house, mounted his horse, and rode down to Noyama prison. Before the gates he reared up, waved his sword in the air, and shouted at the guards to open. The guards were startled at seeing a high official with drawn sword and quickly complied with his request. Sufu rode into the courtyard and shouted, "Shinsaku, where are you?" Hearing this greeting,

Takasugi thrust his head out of the bars to see what was going on. When Sufu caught sight of him, he said, "You have come to this because you have scorned your superiors, so while you are in prison, even if for three years, you must study and become an outstanding personality." So saying, he wheeled his mount around, and galloped away.[33]

Takasugi's spirits were buoyed by this. The next day he composed a verse in Sufu's honor:

> My friend still does not forget righteousness, and
> Yesterday he asked my name of the gatekeeper.[34]

Sufu, like Takasugi, had a flair for the gallant gesture.

The conservative Mundane Views faction made a great public clamor, however, over Sufu's having forced his way into Noyama prison, because they were eager to discredit him and his Justice colleagues. Drawing a sword in public for other than official reasons was a serious offense in Chōshū. The government finally was left with little choice but to mete out some punishment to Sufu, and he was placed under house arrest for fifty days on 6/14. Sufu was already so isolated by his own Justice faction's having ignored his leadership and chosen to march on Kyoto, that politically it mattered little if he were put under house arrest or not.[35]

Yoshida the visionary and Sufu the administrator did not make as incompatible a pair as it might at first seem as the objects of Takasugi's admiration while in prison. Both leaders had shown themselves to be sensitive to a broad range of political considerations. Yoshida had an intensely pragmatic side, as we have seen, and Sufu harbored deeply emotional policy commitments that sometimes took the form of direct action, such as his forcing his way into Noyama prison to see Takasugi in 1864. Sufu was a shrewd administrator, but he was not without feelings, and he sometimes allowed these to manifest themselves in emotionally charged gestures. Like Yoshida and the others, he was a practical man with a transcendent commitment.

Through his father's offices Takasugi was released from Noyama to house arrest in his family's custody on 6/21. Toward the end of the seventh month, news began to filter into Hagi of the debacle at the Forbidden Gate and of the deaths of four of the Sonjuku students, including Kusaka Genzui, the acknowledged leader of the Sonjuku group. Within a few weeks Takasugi would be swept up as never before in the current of public events.

TAKASUGI THE AMBASSADOR

Like the Sonjuku leaders before him, Takasugi was not to be insulated from public events for long by the house arrest imposed upon him in the sixth month. The news of the disaster that had occurred at the Forbidden Gate on 7/18 was already superseded toward the end of the seventh month by reports of the disaster that was about to occur at Shimonoseki. The four powers of Britain, America, France, and Holland had decided to chastise the Chōshū authorities for bombarding traffic in the Shimonoseki straits the year before. The powers were about to dispatch a large joint fleet to destroy the han's shore installations.

Takasugi Shinsaku would play a major role in the diplomatic efforts to minimize the damage done by the Four Nation Fleet. It was essential now that the Sonjuku leadership, in a weakened state and with the Bakufu antagonized, hold their laboriously created military forces out of any more needlessly destructive combat. Sonjuku ingenuity would serve the Chōshū movement well at this time, both through Takasugi's "frank and direct" temperament and through the reportorial and diplomatic skills of Itō Hirobumi.

Thanks to the journalistic imperatives cultivated at the Sonjuku, Chōshū men knew about the Four Nation expedition well in advance. Itō Hirobumi, Inoue Kaoru, and three other students had traveled to London for study the year before. Early in 1864, Itō read in the *Times* of the impending incursion by the Four Nation Fleet against the remote principality of Chōshū. He and Inoue hastened home. Because these two were more familiar than their associates with the English language and customs, they assumed a leading role in dealing with the British authorities behind the fleet action. They approached the English at Yokohama in June 1864 in a diplomatic effort to avert the proposed attack, but to little immediate avail.[36]

The Four Nation squadron drew up off the coast of Shimonoseki on 8/5. Fleet Admiral Küper had agreed to allow another round of negotiations with Inoue Kaoru before opening hostilities, but Inoue was delayed in reaching the fleet by his discovery that shotai elements on the shore, in a state of great excitement, were about to fire on the Western ships from the Chōshū side. It took several hours for Inoue to settle them down, and before he could contact Küper, the fleet had opened fire.[37]

The artillery duel went on for more than a day between the warships and Chōshū's coastal batteries. On 8/6 two thousand marines were landed to occupy the emplacements, and Chōshū forces were pushed back at almost all points. The shotai fared poorly in these clashes because they did not have the benefit of their best generalship. Itō, Inoue, and the others, knowing the powers' aims to be limited, were not even trying to orchestrate a victory and rather had been devoting all of their efforts to minimizing hostilities and combat loss.

After two days of skirmishing and bombardment, the English felt they had sufficiently demonstrated the firmness of their intentions. When Itō Hirobumi rowed out to the fleet on 8/8 to offer a renewal of peace negotiations, Ernest Satow, the young English diplomat representing the powers, cordially accepted the proposal. The rest of the Chōshū mission came out to the fleet on the same day.[38]

The head of this peace mission was Takasugi Shinsaku, who was presented to the English as the Chōshū elder Shishido Gyōba. Takasugi had become the adopted son of the elder Shishido Bizen for the occasion. Several ranking retainers accompanied the party; Itō Hirobumi and Inoue Kaoru served as its working interpreters.[39] Takasugi comported himself toward the English with all the hauteur befitting a plenipotentiary of high rank. He wore a crested kimono of light blue and yellow, and on his head a black *eboshi*, the mark of court nobility. Within this stiff ceremonial garb could be glimpsed a fine tunic of white silk. Satow described the Chōshū envoy as being "proud as Lucifer."[40] Once again, Takasugi's boundless confidence proved a resource for the Chōshū movement.

In the first session of 8/8, the two sides sounded each other out and slated the next session for 8/10. Takasugi got word on 8/9, however, that exponents of literal expulsionism were seeking to assassinate himself and Itō, prompting the two men to go into hiding. For the session of 8/10, the distinctive Shishido was replaced by the older but less compelling Mori Tōta, and Itō of course was also absent. The English were not disposed to accept this arrangement; so the talks were suspended and were rescheduled for 8/14. Inoue Kaoru reported this situation to the government, securing a promise from it to protect the two refugees. He then relayed this promise to Takasugi and Itō in hiding. In view of the difficulties posed by English intransigence, they agreed to take part in the talks again on 8/14 in spite of the danger.[41]

The third negotiating session, which was held on 8/14 with the two activists again present, proved conclusive, and a mutually satisfactory treaty was drawn up and signed. This instrument provided that Chōshū would no longer fire on vessels in the straits, that foreign ships would be allowed to land and purchase provisions, and that the Shimonoseki batteries would not be rebuilt. A compromise was reached on the issue of whether or not the costs of the Four Nation expedition would be paid by Chōshū. The treaty specified that the sum would be paid, but left ambiguous the point of whether Chōshū or the Bakufu would pay it.

Having achieved both a treaty and a working relationship with the Chōshū government, the mission of the Four Nation Fleet was accomplished. It steamed off on 8/20.[42] The Sonjuku leaders had thus overcome the danger of major and pointless military losses to the Westerners by mid-August 1864. No sooner had this difficulty been resolved, however, than they found themselves about to be buffeted from another direction.

THE FIRST BAKUFU EXPEDITION

In the latter months of 1864, the reformist leadership in Chōshū would have to impose upon themselves a severe restraint in the name of political pragmatism. They were compelled to stand by as many of their beloved elder associates were condemned to death. This sad result was warranted by the presence of tens of thousands of Bakufu troops poised on Chōshū's borders. It is very much to the Chōshū leaders' credit that they passed this painful test. They were able to endure this limited sacrifice in such a way as to avoid the likelihood of permanent defeat had Bakufu forces been provoked into entering Chōshū.

The Tokugawa Bakufu had in the incident of the Forbidden Gate a clear, publicly credible grievance against the Mōri domain. It took only several weeks for Bakufu policymaking officials to lay plans for an expedition to chastise Mōri han for its overzealous reformism. Thirty-five daimyo sent troops, totaling perhaps fifty thousand men. This diverse but massive army had taken up its positions on the perimeters of Chōshū by November 1864. Its object was to destroy Chōshū's reformist leadership and to compel that han, and by example others, to assume once more a durably subordinate attitude to Bakufu authority.*

The immensity of this impending assault placed Chōshū's Justice faction leaders under duress, both political and personal. Defeated at the Forbidden Gate, then distressed by the near disaster of the Four Power incursion, they were not in a buoyant mood anyway when word came in the later part of August of the Bakufu expedition that was being planned and of the massive form it would take. No one had had reason to anticipate that the Bakufu's reaction would be so enormous and so resolute.

The Justice faction leaders faced a hard choice. They could fight to the finish. Only the shotai troops, with an enrollment of under a thousand, could be counted on to do this. Fighting meant almost

---

* *Ishinshi*, ed. Ishin shiryō hensan jimukyoku, 6 vols. (Tokyo, 1941), 4: 148–54. It should be noted that the drama of the Mito civil war was unfolding in the North at about the same time.

certain defeat, along with aggravated reprisals against the belligerent Chōshū leaders responsible, and much general bloodshed. The other option, which the Justice leaders ultimately chose to act upon, was quietly to surrender their authority in the han government to the rival conservative party, the Mundane Views faction, allowing that party to take whatever measures necessary to appease the Bakufu and obtain peace. They knew those measures would include the execution of reformist leaders. Although the personal sacrifices would be very high, they chose as always to subordinate military policy not to their private feelings, but to their larger political goals.

The three progressive elders and the four Justice faction officials who had been most closely associated with the Kyoto expedition had already been removed from office in the eighth month and placed under house arrest. These seven men were Masuda Danjō, Kunishi Shinano, Fukuhara Echigo, Shishido Kurōbei, Sakuma Sahei, Takeuchi Masabei, and Nakamura Kyūrō. The detainment of these men removed much of the upper echelon of the Justice faction leadership from public life.

The most prominent leader remaining was Sufu Masanosuke. Though Sufu had opposed the Kyoto expedition, he had for many years been the foremost leader of the reformist party in the administration, and was squarely identified with its policies. Thus it was to Sufu, who had had nothing to do with the Kyoto expedition, that the decision of how to deal with the Bakufu's armies fell. As always, he assumed this task with ingenuity and determination. He was able to resolve immediately on the course of surrendering authority to the Mundane Views faction rather than fighting. By not resorting to armed strife, he could save many more Justice faction lives. In effect he had decided to concede the lives of some of the Aumeisha group in order to preserve the lives of the younger leaders of the Sonjuku group, and thereby to preserve the viability of the Justice faction. Only in this way could he assure the survival of the reformist movement in Chōshū.

Sufu went to the Chōshū branch han of Iwakuni on 8/3 and asked its conservative daimyo, Kikkawa Tsunemoto, to serve as envoy to the Bakufu's punitive expedition. Sufu suggested to him that Chōshū could avoid any more embarrassment than was necessary by the official sacrifice of the three progressive elders who had been at the head of the ill-fated Kyoto expedition the month before. Kikkawa agreed that the lives of the three progressive elders and a penitent attitude should be sufficient to appease the expedition authorities. Kikkawa arrived in Yamaguchi on 9/8 to advocate and assume his embassy.

Having prepared Kikkawa's mission, and thereby collaborated in the deaths of three men with whom he had worked on intimate terms all his life, Sufu took his own life on 9/25. One of his close friends who knew of his intention to commit suicide challenged it, saying that Sufu's presence was needed for the well-being of the realm. To this Sufu replied: "To think I am the only wise man [in Chōshū] is a great error. If those who go before exhaust the responsibility [for their errors] by dying, those who come after will surely rally, and strive to fulfill their hopes." [43]

Sufu's death was a signal for the remaining Justice faction administrators to relinquish their already waning authority to their Mundane Views counterparts. Within a few days the conservative faction was in complete control, and demonstrated as much by moving the seat of government, in Yamaguchi since 1863, back to the traditional capital of Hagi on 10/3. [44] The Mundane Views faction viewed the misfortunes of their Justice faction rivals at this time as the predictable consequence of their adherence to unprecedented and overambitious policies. They believed that their own sudden accession to power at last demonstrated the basic validity of their conservative perceptions. They felt, and with some justification, that the dangerous new ideas that circulated in the Justice faction had brought the han to the brink of a major disaster.

They decided to use this opportunity to decisively weaken the Justice faction's influence over the long term, by exterminating that faction's senior leadership. (This was a possibility of which Sufu had been aware, and to try to counter it he had had Kikkawa agree to drawing the line at the three elders before himself retiring from the scene.) In the tenth month Maeda Magoemon, Mōri Tōta, Matsushima Gōzō, and other Justice faction leaders were imprisoned, as a preliminary to their execution by the Mundane Views faction a few months later. Kido Kōin escaped the purge by remaining incommunicado in the interior northwest of Ōsaka. Younger Sonjuku leaders like Nomura Wasaku and Itō Hirobumi escaped by living quietly with units of the shotai in the inaccessible country districts where those units were stationed.

Takasugi Shinsaku fled to Hakata on 10/29, and when that became unsafe, fled again on 11/11 to the mountains of Chikuzen. There he resided with one Nomura Bōtō at her mountain retreat, the Hirao-sansō. Nomura was an elderly widow and poetess who had taken Buddhist orders when her samurai husband died, and was a loyalist sympathizer, as her husband had been. At Sister Nomura's Takasugi passed his days in agreeable simplicity, exchanging verses with his hostess, and with the other young refugees who had sought a haven there.[45]

In Chōshū the tempo of adverse developments did not diminish. The Hagi government issued an order for the shotai's dissolution on 10/21. This prompted the shotai—the Kiheitai, the Hachimantai, the Yūgekitai, and others—which had earlier gathered at Yamaguchi to protest Hagi policies, to relocate themselves in Chōfu, the westernmost of Chōshū's branch han, and they arrived there on 11/17. On Chōfu territory they could continue to enjoy official sanction for their existence despite the dissolution order of 10/21, because the Chōfu daimyo Mōri Sakyōnosuke and his government were still actively sympathetic toward the reformist movement.[46]

Kikkawa Tsunemoto, the conservative daimyo of the eastern branch han of Iwakuni and the Hagi envoy to the Bakufu army, had meanwhile begun negotiations with Bakufu representatives on 10/20. By 11/3 the two sides had agreed that the deaths of the three progressive elders, along with the recent change of government, the delivery of Sanjō Sanetomi and the other radical lords, the razing of Yamaguchi castle, and ample professions of penitence, would be sufficient evidence of Chōshū's having resumed a properly submissive attitude toward its feudal master the Bakufu. If these measures were realized, the Bakufu would halt its punitive invasion scheduled for 11/18.

In Chōshū the three elders, Masuda, Kunishi, and Fukuhara, were ordered to commit seppuku on 11/11, and the four Justice officials who served as their staff officers, Shishido Kurōbei, Sakuma Sahei, Takeuchi Masabei, and Nakamura Kyūrō, were executed at Noyama prison the next day. The heads of the three elders were delivered immediately to Bakufu representatives in Hiroshima. The massive Bakufu force, however, remained in place, to ensure that its other conditions would be satisfactorily met.[47]

Meanwhile, the Sonjuku leaders, though several of them headed units of the shotai, bowed to political reality as their senior associates were executed, and refrained from acting. Although these dark weeks in the eleventh month of 1864 proved the mettle of the reformist leaders' unflinching pragmatism, they represented the nadir of the movement's fortunes in Chōshū. The Chōshū leaders had lost at the Forbidden Gate, and now had to drink the bitter cup that the Bakufu offered.

Yet the pendulum of their political destiny was already poised for a long swing in the opposite direction, thanks to a series of events involving Takasugi Shinsaku that they could hardly have foreseen. Never again would the Chōshū leaders face so demeaning a discrepancy between the dictates of their higher political duty and those of their immediate personal feelings.

Takasugi Shinsaku came out of the same social and educational milieu as the earlier Sonjuku leaders. He distinguished himself academically at the Meirinkan and elsewhere. He shared the propensity of his predecessors for travel, and like them manifested highly developed journalistic tendencies. Being personally close to Yoshida Shōin, Takasugi was deeply wounded by the Bakufu's execution of his mentor in 1859, and this may have deepened his devotion to the reformist cause. Although Takasugi was not active as Kusaka and Kido were in trying to manage the political flux of the early 1860's, the reason for this seems to have lain in his gruff temperament rather than in any lack of commitment to the movement.

Takasugi's disposition did not lend itself to dwelling in the ambiguous and collusive world of Kyoto street politics. At the same time his spontaneity and directness made him exceptionally fit, among his Sonjuku associates, for the tasks of a military field commander, and it was above all in that capacity that he would serve the cause of reformist activism in Chōshū.

Prior to 1864, the Chōshū movement had seldom needed a man whose distinctive qualifications were defiant self-confidence and an instinct for decisive action. In the latter months of 1864, however, the reformist movement was on the brink of exhaustion, defeated and pursued. It was at just this moment of hopelessness that Takasugi stepped forward, to assume the responsibilities of leadership and to make himself the guarantor of the movement's future.

CHAPTER EIGHT

Takasugi and Civil War
1864-1867

TAKASUGI Shinsaku has come to be regarded as a significant historical figure because of his performance between 1864 and 1867 in a series of daring military campaigns. In the end, these hard-fought campaigns exhausted the martial resources of the once-mighty Tokugawa Bakufu and assured the national triumph of the Chōshū reformers' hopes.

While Takasugi languished in confinement in the seventh month of 1864, Kusaka Genzui, foremost leader of the younger Chōshū reformers, had been killed in a volley of rifle fire at the Forbidden Gate in Kyoto. Kusaka was not the only one who fell in this conflict, and some observers wondered if Chōshū's reformist commitment had not itself proven a casualty. Kusaka's march to Kyoto had been a catastrophe, and his resourceful judgment, on which many in the movement had relied, was now irretrievably lost.

The Forbidden Gate left the Chōshū movement in a state of hopelessness and despair. It marked the definitive transition of the reformist struggle into a phase of large-scale violence. Yoshida Shōin had led the Sonjuku in the 1850's when the contest was still primarily discursive and polemical. In the early 1860's, Kusaka Genzui's resourcefulness had kept the Chōshū movement viable as the political competition gradually came to involve repression and terror, and then major military encounter. Under Kusaka, the struggle passed out of its second stage, terror, and into the third stage, that of the massive use of military force. Moreover, in this latest phase of remorseless violence, Chōshū was losing. After at last accepting the most dreadful challenge of all, Chōshū was being overwhelmed by it. Defeat would mean the end of life for some and the end of hope for all.

It was at this trying moment that Takasugi Shinsaku stepped forward. Kido Kōin had disappeared, Kusaka had been killed, and the seasoned leaders of the Aumeisha faced execution. Takasugi, who had earlier held himself aloof from Chōshū politics, now emerged as a fresh reservoir of courage for the reformist movement.

The Sonjuku membership as a whole also responded to this new challenge of the mid-1860's, and the group assumed many new responsibilities during the years of Takasugi's leadership. The several dozen students who had read the classics together in the mid-1850's became administrators, diplomats, and soldiers in the next decade. When the times required it, they proved worthy of the positions given them despite their youth, and this was fortunate because their predecessors were destined to suffer an early departure from the political stage.

When push came to shove in the mid-1860's, Chōshū's young reformist leaders also found that they could rely on their loyal irregular troops, the shotai. A perusal of the shotai troops' origins provides a clue as to why they stood behind the Sonjuku leaders so steadfastly. Most of the shotai's members came from service backgrounds that were similar to those of the Sonjuku leaders themselves. They too were men of ability who had held only a marginal place in Bakuhan society.

The participants in the Chōshū civil war of 1865 aligned themselves along class lines. Scions of the great samurai houses supported the conservative regime to the violent and bitter end. Samurai of modest or negligible stipend, often from service backgrounds, led the armed opposition. It is even possible to assign precise income boundaries to the leadership groups involved in the conflict. This unexpected feature of the civil war may provide some important insights into the character and causes of the Meiji Restoration.

TAKASUGI'S REBELLION

Takasugi Shinsaku's biographers have sometimes described him as a pragmatic strategist in order to contrast him with his teacher Yoshida Shōin, whom they portray as an idealistic extremist. Although Takasugi was a pragmatic strategist, it is also true that he sometimes indulged in military actions that entailed such desperate risks that his Sonjuku companions were reluctant to have anything to do with them. He was, moreover, highly regarded by his comrades for this propensity to engage in extremely bold actions. Takasugi's singular courage served the Chōshū movement well on a number of occasions, and the eve of the Chōshū civil war was one of them. His solitary preparedness to act in the twelfth month of 1864 not only saved the many shotai corps from irreversible dissolution, but also placed them in a strong position tactically and psychologically for the decisive military confrontation that was about to take place between reformist and conservative forces in Chōshū.

Still, despite Takasugi's activities, the reformist movement suffered a severe loss in the last month of 1864 when seven additional Justice leaders were executed by the conservative regime in Hagi. With the execution of the seven leaders of Chōshū's ill-fated Kyoto expedition the month before and Sufu's suicide, this made a death toll of fifteen of the reformers' most capable older leaders. The Aumeisha and Sonjuku generations had been close in thought and action throughout the 1860's, and in the end it was the tragic sacrifice of Aumeisha officials that brought the wavering Sonjuku leaders to overcome their fears at the crucial moment and stand their ground short of complete capitulation.

Takasugi had been living prudently in exile when he heard of the deaths of his older friends, Sufu and the others. This appalling news jolted him into the realization that discreet conduct was no longer prudent. Prudence now demanded that he abandon himself to desperate action. When control of the Chōshū government had passed into conservative hands in the tenth month, Takasugi had fled to Chikuzen, where he dwelled in comfort and safety at the mountain retreat of Nomura Bōtō. Sometime late in November, Takasugi received word of the execution in Hagi of the three elders and four Justice officials who had led the Kyoto expedition. He brooded over this for several days. Perhaps he recalled what Yoshida had taught him about life and death, or the misery of the poor people of Shanghai, or Sufu Masanosuke's hearty visit to Noyama prison. In any case, he made up his mind to set aside his personal safety altogether. He would return immediately to Chōshū and raise the banner of rebellion. On 11/25 he bade farewell to the widow Nomura in verse, and set out alone on the road back to Chōshū.[1]

By the time Takasugi arrived at the joint shotai headquarters in Chōfu, he had already decided that an immediate rising by the corps against the conservative authorities in Hagi was essential. On 12/13 Yamagata Aritomo arranged a council at Shūzenji temple so that the various commanders could consider the idea. Akane Takendo, the recently returned shotai envoy to Hagi, spoke first, advocating conciliation between the Justice faction and the now dominant Mundane Views faction. Takasugi replied to this indignantly, saying that the two factions were so fundamentally different that there could be no conciliation between them. An officer of the Mitatetai, Yamada Ichinojō, then said that in order to make their cause clear they should wait until the problem of the five loyalist nobles was solved. (The Bakufu had demanded that they leave Chōshū, but the exact terms were not yet decided.) Fukuda Kyohei and other participants began to discuss the theoretical ramifications of this position.

Takasugi began to drink sake at his seat in the council. The shotai chiefs talked emptily, and the council drifted toward acquiescing in policies of conciliation that would lead step-by-step to the dissolution of the shotai, policies that were being firmly advocated by Akane. Takasugi, by now impatient with the whole proceeding, spoke with the directness for which he was famous:

Akane is just a farmer from Ōshima, while I am a samurai, a hereditary retainer to the house of Mōri. If you, captains of the shotai, accept Akane's views and produce none of your own, nothing more can be hoped of you. I will speed to Hagi and advise the daimyo personally. If he will not listen, I will commit seppuku to change his mind. If I am felled by the Mundane Views party on the way to Hagi, that is the fate of heaven. Samurai show one mile of loyalty if they go one mile, and two if they go two. We cannot sit about at our ease for even one more hour.[2]

This speech was followed by a long, uneasy silence. Takasugi's unrestrained efforts to sway the shotai council ended in failure.

One reason for the shotai leaders' reluctance to embrace Takasugi's call to arms was that the Bakufu's massive army was still poised on Chōshū's borders, and though its commander had called off the attack scheduled for 11/18, it could conceivably still intervene in Chōshū's affairs, should civil strife be initiated by the reformist faction. Another reason for the shotai leaders' reluctance may have been that most of them had been raised to respect Chōshū's public institutions, and they were uncomfortable with the idea of a civil war directed against a duly vested government.

Takasugi, however, was preoccupied with another calculation. The shotai leaders, paralyzed by their own fears, were being led down the road to dissolution by the conservative Mundane Views faction without the conservatives' even having to exert themselves. If the shotai were disbanded now, the Sonjuku group's influence would be completely lost. Dissolution would mean the end of the reform movement in Chōshū for which so many had already perished. Having made this appraisal, Takasugi was impatient of all others, particularly those that pled considerations of personal safety. He began canvassing his friends privately to see who would join him in a military campaign led by himself against the conservative government in Hagi.

By 12/15 the hopeful rebel had recruited eighty men. Half of these were the small Rikishitai corps, then under Itō Hirobumi. Most of the rest came from the Yūgekitai, whose members were not from Chōshū. The non-Chōshū men may have found it easier to rebel against the Hagi government than did their Chōshū brethren. The rashness of samurai in exile that had caused the

Chōshū leadership so much trouble at the Forbidden Gate proved to be more useful now, five months later.* After taking leave of the five radical nobles under Sanjō at Kōzanji, Takasugi with his band of eighty men and one cannon set out on the road for Shimonoseki. His plan was to occupy by force a branch office of the han's trading depot (*shinchi kaisho*) there, and to appropriate its store of funds and provisions. Taka-sugi's band reached Shimonoseki early in the morning of 12/16/64. When they presented themselves at the han's trading depot, the commissioner there, one Negoro Kazusa, had already been notified of the impending raid by the Chōfu daimyo. After brief negotia-tions Negoro agreed to make such moneys and stores as the in-truders requested freely available to them on loan.

Takasugi billeted his men at a temple called Ryōenji, then em-barked the next day with eighteen of them in a small boat for Mitajiri. There, after discussing the matter with the supervisor of the han naval bureau, Satō Yosaemon, they commandeered Chōshū's three Western-style warships, and sailed them back to Shimonoseki.[3]

When news reached the shotai in Chōfu of the ease with which Takasugi had worked his two coups at Shimonoseki and Mitajiri, the apprehensions that had immobilized them were overcome. It is also possible that the shotai had had in the meantime some intelligence that the Bakufu forces were unlikely to intervene in civil strife in Chōshū. In any case, the various corps at Chōfu gathered their equipment and started out. On the next day, 12/18, they could already be seen trudging along the narrow trails across the mountains to Hagi. To provide loyalist legitimacy for this

---

* After defeat at the Forbidden Gate, most of the exiled Shōkenkaku samurai returned to Chōshū with their units, much chastened, and divested of their more reckless leaders. One of their units, for example, was Maki Izumi's Chūyū-tai. After the Kimmon no hen, it returned to Chōshū, and Nakaoka Shintarō of Tosa became its new commander. Its members came from Echigo, Kurume, Tosa, Higo, and Chikuzen, there being not one Chōshū man among them. The Chūyūtai remained a discrete unit until half of it merged with the Yūgekitai and half with Takasugi's band on 12/18. These loyalists in exile continued to throw in their lot with Chōshū's Justice faction because the latter was virtually the only official authority that would tolerate their beliefs. See Hirao Michio, *Nakaoka Shintarō* (Tokyo, 1971), pp. 109 and 120.

force, the reformist noble Sanjō Sanetomi marched with it, as did his colleague Shijō Takauta. The shotai leaders, of whom Yama-gata Aritomo was foremost, chose as their temporary field head-quarters the village of Isa, which lies in a mountain pass halfway between Chōfu and Hagi (see the map on p. 176).* This was a good strategic choice. It meant that the shotai, and not the Hagi armies, would control the fertile coastal lowlands to the south.

By the end of 12/64 Takasugi with his fleet and small army at Shimonoseki blocked Hagi's access to the south by sea, while Yamagata's shotai at Isa controlled the Kōtō River valley, which was the main access route to the south by land. The rebels were thus secure very early in the better half of Chōshū as their terri-torial base.

Meanwhile, the huge Bakufu encampment on Chōshū's bound-aries, probably unaware of what the shotai's modest mobilization really meant, was at last about to disperse. Given the agreed-upon execution in Chōshū of the three Justice elders and four staff officials, the Bakufu's representatives were satisfied that all of the demands it had made on the house of Mōri either had been met or were about to be. This perception was based in part on the rea-sonable but inaccurate judgment of Bakufu agents that the im-minent clash between the shotai and the Mundane Views faction could only weaken Chōshū further. On 12/27 the long-awaited order for the dissolution of the Bakufu expedition was issued by its commander Tokugawa Yoshikatsu, and the individual han con-tingents began without delay to return to their own han.[4]

The conservative government in Hagi was going ahead at this time with its deadly purge of Justice faction officials. It executed on 12/19 seven of the Justice leaders who had been detained during the preceding two months: Maeda Magoemon, Narazaki Yahachi-rō, Watanabe Naizō, Yamada Matasuke, Mori Tōta, Yamato Kuninosuke, and Matsushima Gōzō. Along with Sufu's suicide and the execution of the three elders and four staff officials on

---

* *Tōgyō Takasugi Shinsaku*, ed. Takasugi Tōgyō sensei hyakunensai hōsan-kai (Shimonoseki, 1966), pp. 134–35. Sanjō and Shijō left the forces at Isa when they and the others of the remaining five nobles were compelled by Bakufu pressures to move to Chikuzen on 1/14/66.

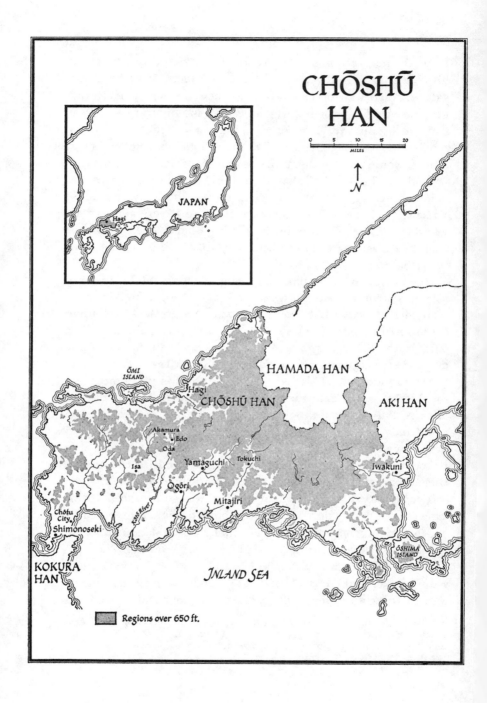

CHŌSHŪ
HAN

0 5 10 15 20
MILES

↑
N

JAPAN

Hagi

ŌMI
ISLAND

Hagi

HAMADA HAN

CHŌSHŪ HAN

AKI HAN

Akamura
Edo
Oda
Isa
Yamaguchi
Tokuchi
Iwakuni

Ogōri

Mitajiri

Kotō River

Chōfu
City
Shimonoseki

ŌSHIMA
ISLAND

KOKURA
HAN

INLAND SEA

Regions over 650 ft.

11/11, this was by 12/19 a total of fifteen senior officials of the Justice faction, six of them from the original Aumeisha group, who had been eliminated. With a few exceptions like Yamada Uemon and Kaneshige Jōzō, the entire top echelon of the Justice faction was now gone. Thereafter the less-experienced Sonjuku group would be on their own in the councils of Chōshū.⁵

Takasugi, still at Shimonoseki, heard of the deaths of the seven additional Justice officials on 12/19 about ten days after the event. Takasugi was outraged. As a show of his aggravation, his band, which had grown considerably since its earlier successes, attacked the han's trading depot again on 1/2/65. This time they expelled the officials in charge altogether and confiscated both funds and goods outright. Takasugi posted a public notice in front of the depot that read in part, "We will not have [the same] sky in common with the party of viciousness."⁶ He was tired of this regime that seemed devoted to annihilating his friends.

Takasugi's armed campaign to dislodge the incumbent Chōshū administration already faced a severe practical challenge at this time, however, which bravado alone could not dispel. This challenge had to do with military finances. The funds Takasugi had seized at Shimonoseki were by no means adequate to meet the needs of his band and those of Yamagata's larger force in the interior. Previously, the shotai had been maintained by the han government. The Kiheitai, for example, was given arms, provisions, and one-half ryō per person per month in personal allowances. Now, however, the shotai faced the necessity of being self-supporting. One of the sources of income to which Takasugi turned was that of soliciting contributions from concerned merchants like Yoshitomi Tōbei and Shiraishi Shōichirō, the Shimonoseki hosteler, whose hearts were in public life despite their being legally excluded from it, and who had proved themselves trustworthy in long personal association with the Justice faction. Though some moneys were forthcoming from this avenue, they amounted to only a fraction of the rebel army's operating expenses.

It was by the device of quasi-governmental taxation that the shotai would acquire the bulk of their funds. Earlier, taxes had passed from the villages to the government to the shotai. When civil strife broke out between the shotai and the conservative Hagi government in December, the shotai leaders soon hit on the obvious solution of collecting taxes themselves in the areas they controlled. As a consequence of their having positioned their troops in a strategically advantageous location, these areas included the broad ribbon of coastal plains on the Inland Sea, where two-thirds of Chōshū's cultivated land and also two-thirds of its population were to be found. The Hagi government sought to discourage rebel tax collection by an order issued on 12/16 that forbade villagers to give food, money, or any other aid to the shotai. In areas not controlled by Hagi, this order was ineffective.

Early in the first month of 1865 the Sonjuku members Nomura Wasaku and Shinagawa Yajirō, accompanied by fifty troops detached from the Mitatetai, left the force at Isa with the purpose of securing a more generous source of men and supplies in the south. On 1/7 they occupied the office of the han administrative deputy (*daikan*) at Ogōri and preempted his function of regional tax-gathering. Nomura went a step further the next day and summoned twenty-eight local administrators at the sub-daikan and village level (*ōjōya* and *shōya*). He requested their active assistance in restoring the reformist Justice faction government in Hagi.

The Ogōri shōya were pleased to pledge their full support to the shotai and were known thereafter as the Shōya League. These administrators were themselves service samurai of rural residence who, even more than the daikan who were immediately above them in the han hierarchy, were excluded by custom, not inability, from full participation in public life. They shared the class grievances of the Sonjuku men, and also had had much personal contact with officials of the Justice faction, men like Tamaki Bunnoshin and Sufu, who early in their careers had been dispatched to these rural districts.

Within the next week Nomura's small force, which like Takasugi's grew as it went, occupied also the deputy's office in Yamaguchi. Rural officials, though not all as active as the Shōya League in Ogōri, were generally sympathetic. It soon became clear that Nomura's activities in the southern lowlands would provide food and funds to the shotai in more than sufficient quantity.[7]

By the end of the twelfth month, Takasugi's most urgent objectives had been accomplished. The shotai commanders had brushed aside manipulative directives from the Hagi government urging dispersal, and had taken to arms. They had assumed tactically advantageous positions at Shimonoseki and in the interior, and they had organized a territorial base adequate for independent military operations. They were ready.

THE CHŌSHŪ CIVIL WAR

The Chōshū activists employed a variety of methods in coping with their conservative antagonists between 1858 and 1868. They found themselves progressing ineluctably from polemics to street violence to fully developed military operations. Thus, the technique by which they finally subdued the conservative opposition in Chōshū, to achieve for the first time an unconditional dominance of the administrative apparatus, was superiority in combat. In several bitter encounters for control of Chōshū's all-important highland interior, they repeatedly outmaneuvered and outfought the regular han forces sent against them.

The men who led the shotai into battle were former Sonjuku students, Takasugi, Yamagata, Itō, and Shinagawa, the Sonjuku militant. The shotai commanders were the same men who six years before had sat at the feet of Yoshida Shōin as he explained "the principle of thought and action," the importance of loyalty to Heaven, and the need for institutional reconstruction of the realm. No fewer than thirty of the shotai commanders were Sonjuku alumni.[8] The men were the same, and the rationale was the same. But the terrain had changed. There are many perils and opportunities for error for the young scholar making his way for the first time through the texts of Mencius or the Five Classics. Yet such perils could not compare with those that the still young Sonjuku members would face in their embattled journey from the remote mountain village of Isa to the capital of Hagi in the winter of 1865.

The reformist troops camped at Isa would not have long to wait for a military engagement. On 12/28/64, the day after the Bakufu's expeditionary forces were ordered to disband, the Mundane Views government in Hagi had commissioned a large force of han regulars for the final suppression of the rebellious shotai. The vanguard of this force, including the aristocratic Sempōtai, was placed under the command of one Awaya Tatewaki. Awaya moved his troops forward without delay in order to obstruct any further advance of the shotai toward the capital. His men bivouacked at the village of Edo, which lay in the mountainous interior only ten miles northwest of the provisional shotai headquarters at Isa.[9]

From Edo, a Mundane Views envoy carried a brusque order to the shotai camp demanding that the shotai dissolve and offer up their arms. Yamagata Aritomo replied for the shotai side, since Takasugi was at Shimonoseki. He wished to obey the government's duly promulgated order, he said, but the deep convictions of his loyalist troops would make them difficult to convince. Therefore, he wanted a period of grace, and asked that the government inform him as soon as possible how long a period would be allowed. This plea was shrewd though insincere. As expected, the Mundane Views officials fell to debating among themselves whether to give the shotai more time.

While his adversaries deliberated, Yamagata struck. On 1/6/65 shotai troops advanced secretly to Edo, fell on the vanguard army under Awaya Tatewaki, and had completely routed it by the next day. This victory brought the insurrectionists ten miles closer to Hagi. Shotai strategists, however, judged that the area around Edo village was not defensible. The whole force thus withdrew two miles to the south, and the shotai set up a new line of defense near the village of Oda.

At this new Oda perimeter the most important encounter of the civil war would be fought. The Kiheitai under Fukuda Ryōsuke took the right wing. In the center were the Hachimantai under Akagawa Reizō and the Ochōtai under Hori Shingorō. The

Nanentai under Sasaki Danya constituted the left wing. On 1/10/65 the shotai were attacked in these positions by the main body of the Hagi army. This attack was repulsed, but there was another on 1/12 and another on 1/14. On the fourteenth, the Hagi force launched a concentrated assault on the Hachimantai, and pushed it back out of its position. The Mitatetai rushed up, however, to join their beleaguered comrades of the Hachimantai, and the line held, at a place called Nomimizu. Unable to dislodge the shotai from their positions, the Hagi army, weary and demoralized, began to withdraw. Seeing that the enemy's vigor had diminished, the Kiheitai, using a byroad, attacked the retreating force at Kawakamiguchi. The conservative army broke into a disorderly retreat and fled to Akamura, four miles to the north.

On 1/15, Takasugi arrived from Shimonoseki to join in the Oda fighting. He led a fresh force and felt it was urgent that the enemy be swept away completely. The next stage of the conflict was entrusted to him. He mounted a coordinated assault on Akamura from two directions, using the Kiheitai, the Mitatetai, and his own Yūgekigun. This time the Mundane Views army quickly gave way and retreated on 1/16 to the outskirts of Hagi, leaving the shotai in uncontested control of the interior mountain passes and thus of most of the han, including the provident south.[10]

The shotai paused in their northward drive on 1/18 and 1/19 to hold a war council. All the commanders gathered to discuss their strategy for the next weeks. Chief among them were Takasugi Shinsaku, Nomura Wasaku, Itō Hirobumi, Yamagata Aritomo, and Shinagawa Yajirō. This council was a reunion of the Shōka Sonjuku. The principles and the program of the Sonjuku had not changed, but its methods had. Whereas the Sonjuku's struggle in the 1850's had been a struggle of ideas, each student now appeared in his capacity as the captain of a rifle company. The war of the brush had given way to warfare plain and simple.

The pragmatism that characterized military decision-making among the activists was evident in this council. Takasugi argued that the shotai should immediately advance on the enemy headquarters near Hagi, so that the shotai might consummate their victory with one more swift stroke and not lose their momentum. Yamagata Aritomo countered that this would entail a long march through the mountains. He urged instead that since the shotai had suffered many casualties, they should first proceed to Yamaguchi. There they could further secure their base of operations, which would enable them to march on Hagi from three directions, rested and well supplied. These two proposals were debated among the chiefs. Takasugi, like the others, finally concurred in Yamagata's. Most of the shotai marched down to Yamaguchi on 1/20, and on 1/21 the new shotai headquarters was established, not inappropriately, at the Yamaguchi Meirinkan.

By this time the political tide in Hagi had gradually turned in favor of the Justice faction. The reformist faction had enjoyed a solid margin of public support over their conservative rivals continuously since 5/57.[11] Nonetheless, when the Bakufu's massive military expedition began to take shape in 9/64, the entire han public, including the Justice leaders from Sufu down, immediately recognized the desirability of assuming as unassertive a stance as possible on the issue of controversial reforms. The Mundane Views faction thus came into power within a few weeks. Subsequently, however, the Bakufu's forces had been disbanded, and the Mundane Views' army had been sent reeling back from Oda on 1/14/65. The desires of the han public therefore returned to the status quo ante, and pressure mounted within Hagi for the restoration of a Justice government. On 1/16 a group of sixty Justice sympathizers led by Kaneshige Jōzō presented themselves at the castle and petitioned for the reappointment of a reformist government and the end of hostilities. They then removed themselves to Kōkōji temple to await an official response. News soon came of the Hagi army's flight from Akamura, and the numbers of the Kōkōji petitioners, known by then as the Peace Council (*chinsei kaigi*), soon grew to two hundred.

While the daimyo wavered, the shotai provided a gesture to aid him in his decision. On 1/28/65, Itō Hirobumi sailed the *Kigai-maru* into Hagi harbor and fired a blank broadside at the town, in order to demonstrate the complete vulnerability of the Mundane Views regime. This provided the leverage the daimyo needed to reestablish Justice influence. The initial changes in appointment were made that same day, 1/28, and the process of switching the government from Mundane Views hands to Justice hands was complete by 2/11.

Several incidents of conservative violence marred this interval, especially on the part of the Kiheitai's aristocratic opposite number, the Sempōtai. Nonetheless, with the detainment of the Mundane Views leader Mukunashi in March, the Justice position was secure, and the Sonjuku commanders of the shotai were able to resume once more their roles in the central government, leaving the daily tasks of the shotai's military administration to their lieutenants.[12] It is very much to the credit of Chōshū's public traditions that after the military point had been made in January, the transfer of power was achieved in the almost complete absence of further violence.[13]

Still, Takasugi had been right when he had said that the positions of the Mundane Views faction and of the Justice reformers were fundamentally different and irreconcilable. In the end the differences that divided the two parties had had to be resolved by open conflict and by a military victory for the Justice side that definitively removed the Mundane Views representatives from public life. The historical significance of this event is difficult to overestimate. It would give the Chōshū reformers an unprecedented opportunity to reshape the han's administrative institutions and efficiently to mobilize all of the han's resources for the reformers' ultimate military struggle with the Bakufu.

In some respects, however, the considerable historical significance of the Chōshū civil war is rivaled by its historiographical significance. When Chōshū conservatives and reformers squared off for their final uncompromising showdown in 1865, the leaders of the respective sides came from distinctly different social backgrounds. This fact may provide an essential key to the historian's question of who was fighting in the Chōshū civil war, and for what.

REBELS AND REACTIONARIES

The social differences that characterized opposing leadership cadres in the Chōshū civil war strongly suggest that the upheaval of Chōshū reformism derived from a social motive. Rebellion in Chōshū was associated with certain social groups and strata, the common denominator of which was affiliation with some kind of service profession. The insurgent forces were led by the Sonjuku group, whose origins we have already examined. Moreover, their followers, the rebel rank and file, were themselves service samurai, schoolmasters, Buddhist priests, physicians, and younger sons of rural administrators. These men who took up arms against a legally constituted government were elements of an insurgent intelligentsia.

The social background of militant conservative leaders in Chōshū contrasted sharply with that of their reformist counterparts. The conservative leaders derived predominantly from those strata of Chōshū society that Yoshida Shōin had referred to unflatteringly as "noble," and that Kusaka Genzui had called "rich notables." They came from the lavishly privileged aristocratic tier of Chōshū's samurai hierarchy. The hereditary stipends of the conservative activists were more than twelve times those of the Sonjuku leaders.

The Sonjuku group served as the main body of commanders and staff of the insurgent shotai. Sonjuku members had been nourished, as we have seen, on the values of literacy, intelligence, and action, by their mentor Yoshida Shōin. They were scholars and physicians who came predominantly from those echelons of high rank and low stipend where vocational involvement was keenest.[14]

The broader membership of the Sonjuku's rifle-bearing shotai also encompassed a large proportion of persons drawn from professional service backgrounds. Figures on the composition of three representative shotai units, the Kiheitai, the Yōchōtai, and the Second Kiheitai, appear in Tables 6–8.[15] The two small social

TABLE 6

Social Composition of the Kiheitai

Class	No. of men	Percent
Samurai:		
Shi	39	6.3%
Miscellaneous other	233	37.4
Shinto priests	18	2.9
Buddhist priests	7	1.1
Townsmen	25	4.0
Farmers:		
Shōya	77	12.4
Hyakushō	160	25.7
Unclear	63	10.2
TOTAL	622	100.0%

SOURCE: Tōgyō Takasugi Shinsaku, ed. Takasugi Tōgyō sensei hyakunensai hōsankai (Shimonoseki, 1966), pp. 442–44.
NOTE: Figures are based on membership rolls from 6/63 to 6/68.

TABLE 7

Social Composition of the Yōchōtai

Class	No. of men	Percent
Samurai	34	25%
Priests	21	15
Farmers[a]	78	57
Unclear	4	3
TOTAL	137	100%

SOURCE: Tanaka Akira, Meiji ishin seijishi kenkyū (Tokyo, 1965), p. 129.
[a]Probably about one-third of the farmers were shōya.

TABLE 8

Social Composition of the Second Kiheitai

Class	No. of men	Percent
Samurai	75	33%
Priests	7	3
Physicians	1	1
Farmers[a]	123	54
Unclear	21	9
TOTAL	227	100%

SOURCE: Tanaka Akira, Meiji ishin seijishi kenkyū (Tokyo, 1965), p. 129.
[a]Probably about one-third of the farmers were shōya.

categories of samurai of modest rank and priests accounted for just under half of the typical shotai unit's membership; 25 to 40 percent were usually samurai of modest shi rank or lower; and 3 to 15 percent were Buddhist or Shinto priests. These groups of samurai of modest rank and priests tended to be educated and vocationally disciplined, but were anchored in compulsorily minor service roles, so that they also may have resented the traditional system whereby all sectors were kept resource-poor for the sake of a lavishly endowed few.

About half (50 to 60 percent) of a typical shotai unit consisted of groups that in Tokugawa society were classified as commoners. Over 90 percent of the Chōshū population fell in this category. One would expect to find a greater need for the prestige and livelihood available in the shotai among the commoner strata than in the modestly stipended samurai and priest strata. In spite of this, the commoner strata are underrepresented in the shotai given their overwhelming numerical dominance in the population.[16]

Although it is reasonable to assume that some of these commoners had no vocational service ties, there is at the same time compelling evidence that many of them did have such ties. An entire stratum of underfranchised service official is submerged in the commoner category, namely, the stratum of village administrator (*shōya*). Village headmen in Chōshū had the status of very low-ranking samurai. They had the right to wear two swords and to use surnames. They were highly educated, both in techniques of administration and in the Chinese classics; they had to be. Despite their low status, they sustained one of the most essential administrative tasks in the han. The village administrator, once chosen by his community, was the han's representative in the village and the people's envoy to the han. He absorbed shocks going both ways, and if he was not able, he did not last. Still, he was absolutely immobile. Though in some cases he might enjoy considerable influence in his own village through landholdings, even then he had much less regional power, and far less influence at the center, than even the daikan of modest rank who was set over him. The educated, noninheriting younger sons of shōya families must have felt this predicament most keenly, since they were not heir even to the modest position of their fathers.

In the case of the Kiheitai, almost a third of those listed as commoners were actually the young sons of village administrators.[17] This slender service category, like that of priests, was vastly overrepresented. It is not unreasonable to assume that in the other corps also, up to a third of those listed as "farmers" (or about 20 percent of the total muster of each corps) were in reality members of the shōya service category. In that case, the three small service categories of samurai, priests, and village chiefs (about 10 percent of the overall population) would have accounted for about 60 percent of all shotai membership (40 percent samurai or priests, plus 20 percent shōya), while all other commoners (about 90 percent of the population) would account for only 40 percent of membership. In other words, although there definitely were commoners in the shotai, a samurai, priest, or shōya was 13.5 times as likely as a commoner to belong.

There is another striking feature of the shotai that suggests they represented Chōshū's service classes, and that may also be a key to the way in which corpsmen were recruited. It has long been known that many of the shotai's commanders were drawn from the ranks of Yoshida Shōin's Sonjuku. Recent research suggests that many of the remaining shotai officers, and perhaps the great majority of the troops as well, were drawn from small but vigorous academies similar to the Sonjuku that were scattered throughout Chōshū.

The male population of Tokugawa Japan had a literacy rate of close to 40 percent. This was achieved through a network of schools in town and country. In Chōshū there were five han schools: the Meirinkan, and one for each of the four branch han. There were eighteen major private academies (*juku*) scattered throughout the han, often in regional town centers. Besides these there were several hundred lesser academies and private elementary schools (*terakoya*). Many of these were located in rural areas, and although they enrolled many shōya and farmer students, almost all were founded and taught by a samurai or priest.[18]

There were an inordinate number of schoolmasters from such establishments in the shotai. Among the 227 members of the Second Kiheitai, no fewer than 12, or 5 percent of the whole corps, were headmasters of either regional private academies or village grammar schools (see Table 9). If each of these had brought 19 of his students into the Second Kiheitai with him, that would account for the entire membership of the corps. Moreover, the homes of the ordinary troopers, when plotted on a map, actually do cluster around the locations of the twelve academies.[19] The Mitatetai and Hōkokutai also are known to have had similarly close ties to particular schoolmasters and particular schools.[20]

One of the schools besides the Sonjuku that furnished many officers to the shotai was the Jishūkan, an academy run by the reformist Buddhist priest Gesshō. Although excluded by birth from administrative office, Gesshō's ability was nevertheless widely recognized. He was a close personal friend of both the Tempō reformer Murata Seifu and Yoshida Shōin. He was the childhood teacher of Kusaka Genzui and was warmly welcomed by Sufu, Maeda, and the other Justice faction leaders at meetings of the Aumeisha society. His own well-known academy was located in the prosperous rural district around Yanai, opposite Ōshima Island. Although Gesshō himself was of the earlier generation and had passed away in 1858, twelve of his twenty-three known students at the Jishūkan became officers in the shotai. Among those twelve men, six had already established themselves as headmasters of their own rural schools before entering the corps.[21]

There evidently existed in Chōshū a rich network of personal associations among educators that were centered on the circles of scholar-administrators like the Aumeisha and Sonjuku in the capital, but also reached broadly into the countryside. Close ties between the Sonjuku and regional schools had been cultivated even in Yoshida Shōin's day. In March and April of 1858 a dozen students of the Sonjuku had been exchanged amidst great good feeling with a similar number of students of the Ikueikan, the official school of Kiyomatsu branch han. In August of that year, Yoshida had brought in twenty-six youths from a farm village

TABLE 9

School Headmasters in the Second Kiheitai

Name	Class	Village	Year school was established
Akira Yūtarō	Rear vassal	Azuki	
Akutagawa Masato	Rear vassal	Ihoshō	1848
Hatano Setsuzō	Physician	Heda	1848
Kawaya Sanenobu	Shinto priest	Yobisaka	1853
Mikuni Kanryō (student of Gesshō)	Buddhist priest	Komatsu	
Mori Kakuto	Shinto priest	Jinryō	
Oshū Tetsunen	Buddhist priest	Kuga	
Ōta Ukyō	Shinto priest	Himae	1844
Shimamoto Taganosuke	Shinto priest	Shisa	1856
Shiomi Kiyotomo	Shinto priest	Muroseki	
Tamura Tandō (student of Gesshō)	Buddhist priest	Mikana	1853
Yanazaki Kenjūrō	Rear vassal	Kuga	

SOURCE: Umihara Tōru, *Meiji ishin to kyōiku* (Tokyo, 1972), p. 239.

called Heta and actually drilled them with his own students in Western rifle formations.[22] There were probably many other personal contacts between Yoshida's group and rural educators.

In sum, not only do the majority of the shotai troops seem to have been drawn from Chōshū's slender echelons of marginally franchised professional servants, but many of the rest of the corpsmen seem to have been their students and protégés. Former students of the Sonjuku and other schools led the shotai, but a heavy proportion of the rank and file, too, exhibited those traits that distinguished the Sonjuku leaders, namely, a high degree of literacy coupled with minimal social enfranchisement.

A drastically different social background characterized the most active elements on the conservative side in the Chōshū civil war. The nearest conservative counterpart of the militant activists of the Sonjuku was a special military unit called the Sempōtai. The Sempōtai, like the Kiheitai, had initially been formed by the Chōshū government in response to the foreign threat. Unlike the Kiheitai, it was organized exclusively on a basis of hereditary rank, not ability. The Sempōtai had been involved in incidents of violent antagonism toward the Kiheitai from the earliest months of the latter's existence. The Sempōtai had threatened civil violence in the Mundane Views faction's brief bid for power after the anti-Chōshū court coup of 8/18/63. The Sempōtai were in the vanguard of the Hagi armies that marched into the mountains to quell the shotai in January 1865. Members of the Sempōtai murdered three spokesmen of the Peace Council on 2/11 in order to spread rumors that the shotai had done it and thereby to discredit the rebels in the eyes of the Peace Council.[23] In short, the Sempōtai were consistent, enterprising, and violent supporters of the conservative Mundane Views faction, their only such supporters.

The income range of the Sempōtai leaders was 223 to 1,332 koku (Table 10). They were of Near Group (*yorigumi*) and Great Group (*ōgumi*) rank. Their mean income was 652 koku.[24] The starkly contrasting figures for the shotai leadership—the core members of the Shōka Sonjuku—show an average income of only 50 koku, less than one-twelfth of the Sempōtai leaders' average of 652 koku (see Table 3, p. 37). Clearly, these two groups, which took opposite sides in the Chōshū civil war, the Sonjuku and the Sempōtai, were characterized by wholly different ranges of income and rank.

Rank and income are known for another leadership group involved in the Chōshū civil war, namely, the moderate pro-Sonjuku Peace Council. These figures, too, are instructive. The income range of Peace Council leaders fell between that of the Sonjuku and that of the Sempōtai, being 23 to 363 koku, with a mean of 171 koku (Table 11).[25] Their mean income was thus about one-fourth that of the Sempōtai leaders. The Peace Council, who were much closer to the Sonjuku than to the Sempōtai politically, were also much closer to the Sonjuku than to the Sempōtai in terms of rank and income.

The patterns of social composition of participants in the Chōshū civil war actually make it possible to associate precise income boundaries with political attitudes in Chōshū. Persons who received less than 200 koku tended to support the reformist movement. Persons with incomes over 400 koku tended to oppose the reformist movement. Persons whose incomes fell between 200 and 400 koku tended to be divided between these two camps.

TABLE 10

Sempōtai Leaders by Rank and Stipend

Name	Stipend in koku
Yorigumi	
Naitō Magotarō	1,332
Watanabe Himonosuke	1,154
Wachi Tatewaki	845
Hino Zusho	576
Asonuma Sotojirō	481
Yamada Toranosuke	314
Ōgumi	
Sugiyama Taihei	280
Rika Sōsuke	223

SOURCE: Umetani Noboru, "Meiji ishinshi ni okeru Chōshū," in Sakata, ed., *Meiji ishinshi no mondaiten*, p. 340.
NOTE: The range of income is 223–1,332 koku; the mean is 652 koku.

TABLE 11

Leaders of the Peace Council (Chinsei kaigi) by Rank and Stipend

Name	Stipend in koku	Name	Stipend in koku
Ōgumi		*Ōgumi* (cont.)	
Sakurai Mikizō	363	Harada Chūzō	124
Akagawa Yūzō	350	Kawakita Hajime	111
Katsura Masakuma	300	Egi Seijirō	90
Reizei Gorō	300	Iida Kiichijirō	89
Kagawa Hansuke	200	Miura Shojirō	80
Izahaya Sakujirō	186	*Mukyūdōri*	
Kōno Kōtarō	162	Sugi Umetarō	26
Sugi Magoshichirō	156	Machida Umenoshin	23

SOURCE: See Table 10 above.
NOTE: The range of income is 23–363 koku; the mean is 171 koku.

It should be kept in mind while analyzing these data that one of the first official acts of the Chōshū reformers after 1868 would be to discontinue the stipends in Chōshū of all retainers who received over 100 koku. In the 1870's these same leaders would go on to dissolve all hereditary class privilege throughout Japan. At the same time, they would provide unparalleled opportunities at all levels for schoolmasters, administrators, and many other service categories. The universal education law of 1872, for example, would create tens of thousands of new positions for rural educators.

The potential historiographical significance of the Chōshū civil war is immense. Taken in conjunction with other aspects of the Sonjuku experience, the drastic social differences that characterized rebel and conservative elements point almost indisputably to a social motive for action. When Chōshū's rural schoolmasters risked their own and their students' lives beside the Sonjuku activists at Oda, it was no secret that they fought on the side of those who favored radical social change.

THE POSTWAR GOVERNMENT IN CHŌSHŪ

The military paroxysm of the Chōshū civil war was followed by the Justice faction's unchallenged dominance over the Chōshū government, and a real opportunity to implement reforms that it had never before enjoyed. The Justice faction had held a precarious plurality of power in the government most of the time since 1853. Their power in those years, however, had always been highly conditional. If they pushed any of their policies with too much vigor, so as to alienate influential conservative retainers or their protégés, they risked losing power to their more moderate rivals, the Mundane Views faction. The institutional terms by which the Justice faction had held power dictated perpetual compromise.

After the January victories, however, the Justice faction no longer labored under this constraint. Their clear military superiority, added to their superiority in the realm of public opinion, which had been established for some time, now made them immune from rumblings of discontent among conservative retainers. For the first time they had secured a degree of influence that would allow them not only to serve as caretakers of the status quo but also to effect major institutional changes that could ameliorate the social environment of life in the han. If there had been any doubt earlier of the Justice faction's interest in major institutional reform, these doubts were dispelled within a few weeks of the faction's assuming its new unconditional powers in 1865.

The men who entered the government at this unique moment, however, were not the same men who had patiently led the Justice faction through the troubled years of the preceding decade. The new leaders were younger men. They had been associated with more radical political methods in the early 1860's, and they were affiliated with the Sonjuku rather than the Aumeisha generation of leaders. It is tempting to interpret this marked change in leadership as an indication of new policy commitments or of exceptional genius among the younger leaders. In view of the intimate cooperation of the Aumeisha and Sonjuku groups throughout the 1860's, however, it is unlikely that there was any divergence of basic policy objectives between them, and even where political methods were concerned, there was little difference between the two groups by the mid-1860's. Nor can this abrupt accession to office by the younger leaders be attributed simply to their superior abilities. They were extraordinarily capable, but so were Sufu and the other Aumeisha leaders whom they now replaced.

The sudden accession to high office of Sonjuku leaders in 1865 was mediated not by genius but by tragedy. When the ragtag guerrillas of Oda marched jubilantly into Hagi in the second month, it should have been Sufu and Maeda who were borne to the castle in triumph on their shoulders. But, in a political gesture of unaccustomed harshness, the short-lived conservative government had executed not only the seven reformist leaders whose lives the Bakufu had demanded, but also seven others, most of them men still in their forties and at the peak of their careers. With the closely related suicide of Sufu, this meant that fifteen of the most experienced and resourceful of the Aumeisha's members would never again take their places in the councils of Chōshū. The purges of November and December had all but annihilated the Aumeisha, leaving the younger Sonjuku leaders with little choice but to assume the posts of their fallen comrades. As in the case of Yoshida Shōin's death years before, this change in leadership represented not so much political discontinuity as it did an almost startling perseverance.

Despite this sudden and unfortunate turnover in the leadership of the faction, control of the Chōshū government was securely in Justice hands by the fourth month of 1865. The reformist attitude that had been the perennial stance of the Justice faction would be very much in evidence in the following months. The reformers addressed themselves especially to two areas, the army and the administration.

The greatest reform worked by the reconstituted government was military, and foreshadowed major social change. The shotai had been organized along the lines of Western rifle companies since 1863. Now in 1865 the government reorganized the entire regular han military along Western lines, in an overtly functional way, regardless of rank. To minimize personal friction between high and low, units were formed by stratum. The highest stratum of samurai were all placed in one rifle unit, the next highest stratum in another rifle unit, and so on. Equivalence was then assumed between the units.

In this way social rank was in effect wiped out in the han's military arrangements. At the same time friction among ranks was avoided by segregating the respective rank groups. Because carrying a firearm rather than two swords had always been the mark of a foot soldier (*sotsu*), the placement of men from all samurai houses of even the highest rank into rifle companies had profoundly egalitarian implications, which could serve as a precedent in other sectors of han life.[26]

These military reforms were supervised by Ōmura Masujirō (1824–69). Ōmura, although not a member of the Sonjuku group, had had contacts with it through Kido Kōin since 1860. His vocational biography, too, was such as to make him highly compatible with Sonjuku personnel. The son of a rural physician, he had begun preparing for his inherited profession at an early age. At twenty-two he had gone to Ōsaka to continue his studies in the school of Ōgata Kōan, and later studied also in Nagasaki. Probably as a consequence of these experiences, he found his native village had become too small for him when he returned there to practice medicine at the age of twenty-six. In exchange for the samurai rank he was not born to, he accepted an offer from the Date house of Uwajima to serve that han as an expert on Western studies in 1853. Ōmura's native domain of Chōshū hired him back from the Date in 1860, also giving him samurai rank. His association with Kido Kōin of the Sonjuku group began the same year, when he submitted to the Bakufu jointly with Kido a petition for the development of Takeshima island, one of Yoshida Shōin's favorite projects. Ōmura served Chōshū in various capacities between 1860 and 1865, during which time he became one of the most trusted members of the Justice faction.[27]

In addition to their sweeping reorganization of the Chōshū army, the reformers made certain changes in the educational system and in the Chōshū administration. Considerations of social rank were now largely eliminated from Chōshū's academy, the Meirinkan, and even commoners were now for the first time freely admitted to the school. At the same time, men of talent who lacked qualifying rank were admitted in larger numbers to the government.[28]

The newly installed Justice leadership also made an effort to streamline operations by dividing the government into two branches, a civil administration branch (*minsei*) and a political affairs branch (*kokusei*). This pattern represented a rationalization of what had been the more gangling and complex feudal structure of the Chōshū government, which provided for one full hierarchy permanently resident in the han (*kokusōfu*), and another full hierarchy (*kōsōfu*) that accompanied the daimyo when he traveled to Edo to fulfill his sankin kōtai duties. The reforms preserved the duality of the government but strengthened and clarified the division of labor that had been evolving between the two branches, eliminating much overlapping authority and also a number of posts.[29]

In this newly structured Justice government that had emerged by the fifth month of 1865, members of the Sonjuku group filled most of the vital policymaking positions in the han for the first time. As of 5/10/65, there were beneath the two progressive elders twenty-one key administrative posts held by sixteen men. Four of Yoshida Shōin's teachers held four of them. This meant that six members of the Sonjuku group held over half of the policy positions in the government, including the three pivotal posts of ad-

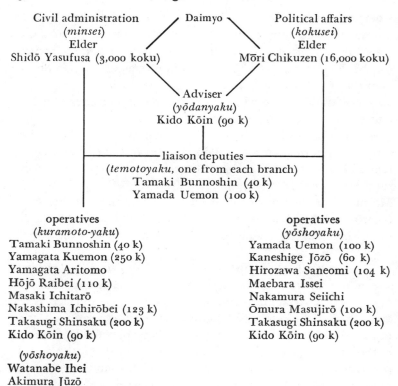

Figure 3. The top echelon of the Chōshū government as of 5/10/65. SOURCE: Shibahara Takuji, *Meiji ishin no kenryoku kiban* (Tokyo, 1965), p. 284. These data were compiled by Shibahara from Suematsu Kenchō, *Bōchō kaitenshi*, 2 vols. (Tokyo, 1967 [1921]), 2: 810–11, and Tanaka Akira, *Meiji ishin seijishi kenkyū* (Tokyo, 1965), pp. 187–89.

viser (*yōdanyaku*) and liaison deputies (*temotoyaku*) (see Figure 3).[30]

The most powerful post in the han, adviser, was held by the senior Sonjuku alumnus Kido Kōin, who had worked in a leadership capacity with the Sonjuku group through the 1860's. Kido had been missing since the catastrophe of the Forbidden Gate, and seven whole months had passed between that event and the conclusion of the Chōshū civil war. Kido's colleagues were pleasantly surprised when his geisha associate Matsuko arrived in

Chōshū seeking protection in February 1865, and informed them that Kido was living safely in a small village northwest of Ōsaka. Kido was hastily summoned by letter and assumed his duties in the government almost immediately upon his return to the han in the fourth month.[31]

The adviser had two liaison deputies, one from the daily administration branch of the government and one from the political affairs branch. The man from the daily administration branch was Tamaki Bunnoshin, Yoshida Shōin's uncle and the educator who had trained him. In 1858 Tamaki had resigned from office to protest his protégé's fatal reimprisonment. Tamaki's own son, Tamaki Hikosuke, had just been killed while serving as a shotai officer in the bitter fighting around Oda in 1/65. Tamaki had paid a high price for his right to serve in a reformist regime.[32]

The liaison deputy for the political affairs branch of the government was Yamada Uemon, an Aumeisha survivor, who had been one of Yoshida Shōin's supervisors at the Meirinkan, and is said to have been the first to apprise the youthful Yoshida of the Western threat. Yamada was the same Justice official who had been imprisoned briefly in the late 1840's for having even then openly advocated the formation of Western-style rifle units.

Beneath the liaison deputies, the civil and political governments counted in their ranks numerous other Sonjuku leaders, including Takasugi Shinsaku, Yamagata Aritomo, and Maebara Issei. Takasugi held two positions. As han officials, Yoshida Shōin's students implemented in 1865 some of the reforms that their mentor had repeatedly advocated in the 1850's. In the years to come they would implement still more.

TAKASUGI BETWEEN THE WARS

The Bakumatsu years were rich in exhilarating opportunities, but also fraught with danger and uncertainty. The ebb and flow of events in these years had a breathtaking dynamism, and some temperaments more than others partook of both the opportunities and the dangers to the fullest. That Takasugi Shinsaku was such a personality is nowhere more evident than in his incessant activity between the Chōshū civil war of 1865 and the Four-Sided War of 1866. This activity reveals a man who constantly provoked adventure, and who was rarely affected by either shame or fear. These were precisely the characteristics that made Takasugi an ideal leader for the reformist movement in Chōshū at its moments of crisis in 1865 and 1866.

Takasugi petitioned the han council in March 1865 that he be allowed to study in England. The Justice faction's peaceful dominance of the government had been reestablished in February, so that his services were not especially needed, and despite his influential position in the new government, he was bored. The council promptly granted his request, and on 3/26 the order came down for him and Itō Hirobumi to proceed to "Yokohama" to study English. (Technically, study in "England" was still against the law.)

The two had gotten no farther than Nagasaki, however, when an English trader of their long acquaintance, Thomas Glover, persuaded them that Shimonoseki should be opened as a port, as a means of obtaining Western arms. The two returned to Chōshū to implement this, but had to flee for their lives when jōi extremists of the Shimonoseki area, fearing loss of their district to foreigners, tried to assassinate them.[33] Making the best of a bad situation, Takasugi decided to go touring. He took along as his companion a Shimonoseki geisha named Ōno, whose indenturedness he redeemed with his travel allowance of 1,000 ryō.* Traveling comfortably as a rich merchant and his wife, the two went to Ōsaka. When Bakufu agents made it unsafe for them there, they went on a long excursion in Shikoku as well-to-do pilgrims. It was only some time after the ire of the Shimonoseki partisans had subsided that Takasugi was able to return to Chōshū and resume his role in public affairs.[34]

In September 1865, Takasugi was reappointed on the political affairs side of the government, and served in that capacity for a number of months. In the spring of 1866, Takasugi and Itō were

---

* *Tōgyō Takasugi Shinsaku*, pp. 291–92. After Takasugi's death, Ōno became a Buddhist nun.

given 1,500 ryō and dispatched to Kagoshima to conclude the purchase from Satsuma of the ship *Union*. They had gotten no further than Nagasaki, however, when Satsuma authorities alerted Takasugi that anti-Chōshū extremists would try to assassinate them in Kagoshima, and agreed to take the responsibility of Takasugi's mission on themselves. Takasugi then sent Itō back to Yamaguchi to report, and to request funds so that they could visit Shanghai.

While still in Nagasaki, Takasugi heard that negotiations between Chōshū and the Bakufu at Hiroshima were deteriorating. Judging that war was imminent, he gave up his plans to go abroad. Instead he purchased the steamship *Otento-maru* sometime late in April from Thomas Glover, who turned it over to him, sailors and all, for only his promise of payment. With this prize Takasugi sailed back to Shimonoseki. The officials at the han finance bureau, however, were not impressed with the necessity of purchasing the *Otento*, and adamantly refused to pay the price of 39,205 ryō. Moreover, they expected Takasugi to repay the 1,500 ryō he had received for the uncompleted mission to Kagoshima. Unfortunately, most of that 1,500 ryō had already been invested by Takasugi in the watering places of Nagasaki. Being quite annoyed, he notified the finance officials that if they did not pay for the much-needed *Otento*, he would go down with the ship off the Hagi coast. Inoue Kaoru finally intervened with the government on Takasugi's behalf. He argued that the slightly wayward activist had been of such great value to Chōshū during the civil war that even the outlay of thousands of ryō was admissible. In the end the bureau gave in, paid the price of the *Otento*, and also permitted nonrepayment of the 1,500 ryō.[35]

Fortunately for Takasugi, the great war with the Bakufu was almost at hand by the time the fuss over the *Otento-maru* died down. In its clear anticipation that fighting was about to begin, the han government restored Takasugi to the vocation with which he was most comfortable. He was made a naval chargé (*kaigun-yō gakari*) on 5/27/66, then raised to the post of general fleet commander (*kaigun sōtoku*) on 6/6. This was none too soon.[36]

It is difficult to imagine any of the other Sonjuku leaders purchasing a geisha with the han's money or buying a ship on his own credit. Most of the group's other members were more self-effacing. Takasugi, however, was completely undauntable. His activities between the wars made clear as much as any other body of data the range of temperaments that existed within the Sonjuku group. This breadth of personality within the movement had aided the activists' cause in diverse and unexpected ways in the past, and would continue to do so in the future. When the Bakufu's massive legions gathered on Chōshū's frontiers in 1866, Takasugi's flamboyant temerity would prove once more to be an invaluable asset to the reformist movement in Chōshū.

THE FOUR-SIDED WAR

Over the course of the 1860's, dedicated reformers in Chōshū found it necessary for their movement's survival to engage in terrorism, in guerrilla warfare, and finally in the fielding of regular armies. There is a natural tendency to regard the earlier terrorist activities and the later military activities as representing different political impulses. This was not the case where Chōshū was concerned, however. The energetic and resourceful leaders who mobilized Chōshū's regular forces in 1866 were the same men who had worked of necessity with terrorists in 1863. They orchestrated both activities with the same broader political objectives in mind. Only the fallen no longer participated.

Just as the Chōshū activists' involvement in terrorist activities had taken place in the context of a brutal police repression, their going to war in 1866 was a response to a major military initiative by conservative forces. Seeing that the reorganization of the army and the administration that had been implemented by the Chōshū reformers in 1865 represented an unequivocal abandonment of the traditional social order, the Bakufu took steps to send large numbers of troops once more to western Japan for the purpose of chastising the still insubordinate Mōri domain. Tens of thousands of troops, including both samurai and Western-style infantrymen, followed their lords westward to engage the Chōshū rebels. As a consequence of this massive expedition, the Bakufu's second in two years, there took place on Chōshū's borders in the sixth month of 1866 what was perhaps the most decisive military encounter of the Bakumatsu period.

The hostilities of 1866 had not come suddenly. Both sides knew for many months before the event that a large military encounter was almost unavoidable. By October 1865, Chōshū authorities had already judged war to be imminent and had dispatched deputies to each district to undertake preparations. After long negotiations, Kido Kōin concluded an alliance of convenience with Satsuma han in January 1866, which provided that Satsuma would come to Chōshū's aid if the fighting turned against Chōshū. The services of Tosa's Nakaoka Shintarō, who had been in the Shōkenkaku at Mitajiri, and of his Tosa colleague Sakamoto Ryōma, were essential for the Satsuma-Chōshū negotiations. The Satchō alliance was one more important consequence of the hundreds of lateral ties with samurai of other han that had been cultivated by Chōshū men since the early 1860's.[37]

Contacts with Satsuma were also used by Chōshū to expedite the purchase in 5/65 and 7/65 of eleven thousand rifles of recent Western make, some of them surplus from the just-concluded American Civil War. This allowed Chōshū to equip with Western arms the military forces that had recently been reorganized along Western lines. This figure of eleven thousand was probably close to the number of troops Chōshū was actually prepared to mobilize as front-line forces.[38]

On the Bakufu side, the decision to launch another expedition to subjugate a still unrepentant Chōshū was taken as early as 4/19/65. Indeed, the nucleus of the expedition left Edo and arrived at Ōsaka on 5/22. There it stalled for over a year, while disagreements arose first between the Bakufu and court, and then between the Bakufu and its many client han, over what demands to impose on Chōshū. A compromise was reached on the issue by 1/19/66, when the Bakufu announced that it would be required of Chōshū that the Mōri daimyo and heir step down in favor of the lord's grandson, and that the han's domains be reduced by 100,000 koku of territory. The demands would also entail restoration of the conservative Mundane Views faction to power and a reversal of reforms, much as the Bakufu had demanded during its earlier expedition of 1864.

Although the Justice faction leadership in Chōshū had no intention of acquiescing to the Bakufu's demands, negotiations were undertaken nevertheless between the Bakufu's representatives and Chōshū's at Hiroshima on 1/22/66. Chōshū participated in these talks as a demonstration of good faith to third parties but also to delay the Tokugawa invasion force as long as possible. The demands of 1/19/66 were fed into the talks in February. Thanks to various dilatory maneuvers on the part of Chōshū, the shogunate's expectations were not cast in the form of an ultimatum until 5/9, the deadline for compliance being 5/29. That day came and went without a response from Chōshū, obliging the Bakufu to make good on its threats and advance, which it finally did on 6/7.[39]

Meanwhile the Bakufu had sent large expeditionary forces to the Hamada and Aki domains in western Honshū and also to Kokura han in northern Kyūshū. The object was to invade Chōshū simultaneously on each of these fronts and also by sea. The campaign against Chōshū did not generate much enthusiasm among Tokugawa vassals, but in the circumstances they felt constrained to provide substantial numbers of troops nevertheless. There were some forty thousand men actually participating in the second Bakufu expedition. Chōshū's rifle-bearing soldiers were outnumbered by about four to one overall.

The Four-Sided War began on 6/7/66 when a Bakufu fleet of five steamships leading fourteen ships of Japanese type bombarded and occupied Ōshima island, forcing the Chōshū troops there to withdraw across the straits to Tōzaki (see the map on p. 176). When this was reported to Takasugi as the han's general fleet commander, he hastened to the scene with only his modest flagship, the *Heiin-maru*. He discussed the situation with Hayashi Hanshichi, the chief of the Second Kiheitai at Tōzaki, and told him that help could not be sent from any of the other fronts. Therefore the Second Kiheitai and the Ōshima militia, which had fled the island, would have to deal with the Bakufu forces there on their own. Nor could ships be spared, though Takasugi would do what he could for them with the *Heiin-maru* before returning to Shimonoseki.

On the night of 6/12 Takasugi moved the *Heiin-maru* up to the Bakufu fleet, which was anchored off the village of Kuga. There he sailed back and forth among the ships, bombarding them at close range, while the Chōshū men at Tōzaki looked on. The Bakufu's mariners, taken by surprise, were completely unable to respond. The Chōshū forces on shore took heart from this. Though Takasugi had to return to Shimonoseki, the leaders at Tōzaki of the Second Kiheitai, the Kōbutai, and the Ōshima militia, scorning the Bakufu fleet, crossed the straits to Ōshima in small boats on 6/15, and within two days had recaptured the island. Here was another occasion on which Takasugi's daring temperament and not very much else had helped secure a victory for the Chōshū movement.[40]

Takasugi's services were meanwhile needed on the Kokura-Shimonoseki front. The Bakufu's general commander in Kokura was the Tokugawa vassal Ogasawara Nagamichi. Ogasawara established his headquarters at Kaizenji temple on 6/3, and there gathered forces from several of the great han of Kyūshū in the hope of dislodging the Chōshū reformers from power with a military thrust from the south. Takasugi wrote a poem for him on 6/16:

> Both our armies fling away
> The papers of conciliation
> And grasp the iron whip.[41]

The days when Chōshū's reformers believed they could rely on the writing brush alone to achieve social justice were gone.

The Chōshū commanders felt that it would be advantageous for the fighting to be confined to the Kokura side of the straits; so before dawn on 6/17, Takasugi launched an amphibious assault across the narrow waters that divided the two domains. The Chōshū fleet of four vessels, led by Takasugi's *Heiin-maru*, set out first and shelled Kokura's shore battery at Tanoura. The fourth vessel in this group was the *Otsuchū-maru*, manned by a crew from Tosa under Sakamoto Ryōma. Covered by Takasugi's ships, the Kiheitai, the Hokokutai, and other elements crossed the straits in small boats. They overcame resistance on the beach and were able to advance several miles inland before Takasugi ordered a full withdrawal in mid-afternoon, fearful that the Bakufu side would discover how few Chōshū's numbers were. In his report to the han government on this day of fighting, Takasugi put Chōshū's dead and wounded at fourteen. Ogasawara, he reported, had eight thousand men and thirty cannon of Western make. The Kiheitai by contrast numbered only four hundred men, and Takasugi's whole force on the Kokura front was something under a thousand.[42]

Takasugi led a second assault on 7/3, similar to that of 6/17, except that the Chōshū fleet turned their guns on a Bakufu squadron that had anchored off Kokura in the meantime rather than on the Tanoura battery. The landing forces seized and burned the town of Osato, forcing Ogasawara to abandon his nearby headquarters at Kaizenji and establish a new one at Shimmachi. The forces of Kokura han were also pushed out of their headquarters at the Seitaiin.

After these successes, Takasugi once again withdrew the bulk of Chōshū's forces to their own side of the straits. The Chōshū men had secured a broad strip of the Kokura coast before leaving, however, and had forced Ogasawara to adopt a new strategy. This was to withdraw from the coast and construct instead a heavily fortified line of defense around Kokura castle. Several inland batteries were hastily built for this purpose on the high ground at Emmyōji and Akasaka.[43]

In the meantime Takasugi was sick in bed at the Shiraishi house in Shimonoseki. He was seriously ill. His neighbors brought sweets to cheer him up, and the Kiheitai sent him a plump carp for good luck. He spent 7/22 as an invalid quietly playing chess. He seemed to be growing stronger, however, and by 7/26 felt well enough to take an active part in the war council held at Shiraishi's.[44]

Chōshū's third major assault, again under Takasugi's direction, was mounted on 7/27. Chōshū's forces found no hostile presence around Osato and advanced further inland to probe the heavily defended perimeter that Ogasawara had established around Kokura castle. There were pitched battles at Hatchōgoshi and at Otaniguchi, which Chōshū lost, because the opposing forces were covered by the Emmyōji and other batteries. Nevertheless, at Torigoshi and other points the Bakufu's line of defense gave way, and its troops fell back within the castle itself.

Takasugi, with telescope in hand and messengers coming and going, supervised all this, deciding what corps were needed where and dispatching them. Yamagata Aritomo was one of his field captains, and Itō Hirobumi served as his personal envoy, rushing to this corps and that. After a day of fighting, Takasugi pulled his forces back to the coast so that the Chōshū leaders could decide what to do next. The obvious course was to storm Kokura castle, a move that, with some two hundred dead and wounded already, none of the Chōshū commanders relished.

Takasugi called the leaders together at Shimonoseki to consider how they should go about accomplishing this necessary but unwelcome task. On 8/1, however, while the commanders were still gathered in council, a column of black smoke appeared on the Kokura side of the straits. When Takasugi and Yamagata went to investigate, they found that the Bakufu forces had burned Kokura castle and fled. The troops of the various Kyūshū han had gone home. Ogasawara Nagamichi had left aboard a Bakufu warship, while the samurai of Kokura had withdrawn into the hills to carry on guerrilla warfare.

Chōshū men were now able to march unhindered into Kokura castle itself. The fires set in the castle were put out so that military stores there could be captured intact. Statements were issued to the fleeing people of Kokura assuring them they would not be abused by Chōshū forces, and a permanent military headquarters was established at Osato to prevent looting and to carry on other administrative functions. A truce was reached with Kokura guerrillas on 10/8/66, and a formal peace treaty between the two han was signed on 12/28.[45]

During this same interval Chōshū had also been fighting on two land fronts, the Hamada han front to the northeast and the Aki han front to the southeast. The Ōshima front, of course, with Takasugi's help, had been liquidated earlier. The results were substantially the same in Hamada and Aki as they had been on the Kokura front. The Aki front, under Ōmura Masujirō, was active from 6/13 until 8/7, yielding a de facto Chōshū victory by the latter date, without Bakufu forces having reached Chōshū. On the Hamada front, under Inoue Kaoru, hostilities began on 6/17 and had become a Chōshū victory by 7/15. The Bakufu officially declared an end to its expedition on 12/25/66, using as a pretext the death of Emperor Kōmei.[46]

The triumph of Chōshū's Western-style military units in 1866 dissolved the centuries-old public belief in the Tokugawa Bakufu's military supremacy. The Bakufu would never again be able to dictate the course of public affairs as it had earlier. Indeed, the Bakufu, which in the eyes of many had forfeited its moral authority by meekly acquiescing to the demands of Westerners in the 1850's, now also lost its authority in the realm of physical coercion. The Bakufu's days were numbered. A year of diplomatic maneuvering, a coup, and one more blow administered by Chōshū and Satsuma corpsmen at Toba-Fushimi, would seal its fate.

Chōshū's victory was owed in large measure to the inspired leadership of devoted reformist commanders like Takasugi Shinsaku. Takasugi had earned the gratitude and admiration of an entire population, though he would not be left much time to enjoy it. His days, too, were numbered.

THE DEATH OF TAKASUGI

By the time the excitement over Kokura's surrender of 8/1 had died down, Takasugi was very ill. On 9/4 he began coughing blood and was confined to bed. He had tuberculosis, and had had it for some time. In October he was relieved of his official duties and took up a life of retirement to recover his health. The daimyo gave him a house so that he might convalesce more comfortably, and raised his stipend to encourage him to get well. Sympathetic corpsmen and officials came to see him and left gifts to bring him luck. Takasugi's old friends of the Sonjuku, too, often came to visit, as did his relatives and the loyalist poetess Nomura Bōtō. He presented an open verse to her:

Trying to endure a world of dreariness and tedium. . . .

She, who knew him, replied:

What allows us to savor life is the richness of the human spirit.[47]

Takasugi often called his colleagues Itō, Yamagata, and Inoue over to him saying, "Because we have come this far, what happens from now on is of crucial importance, so give it your best effort, your very best."[48]

Takasugi died in peace and among friends on 4/14/67.

In several vital respects the final stages of the Chōshū reformers' struggle against the Bakufu resembled the initial ones. In the end as in the beginning and throughout, their efforts were marked by determination and methodical defiance. Like their mentor Yoshida Shōin, the Sonjuku leaders even at the end were prepared to stand against all odds for the course they believed was right. Like him, they manifested a learned disrespect for the directives of an authority whose antiquated policies had become antisocial. Like him, the reformers harbored a vision of a better world, and took every step necessary to keep their quest for it alive, even though many, like him, lost their own lives along the way.

The final victory of the Chōshū activists over conservative resistance, both within Chōshū and at the national level, was achieved by overcoming that resistance with superior forces in the field. The two conflicts in which this was done were the Chōshū civil war in the early months of 1865 and the Four-Sided War of 1866. Takasugi Shinsaku performed a vital leadership role during both of these campaigns.

Military operations were carried out in each instance with broader political objectives in mind. Chōshū's shotai rifle corps were available for the politically decisive struggles of 1865 and 1866 only because Aumeisha and Sonjuku leaders had twice held them out of combat situations in 1864 that could have destroyed or seriously weakened them. Political considerations were similarly paramount when the reformist armies prevailed.

Military success in the Chōshū civil war, achieved on 1/16/65, was followed within a few weeks by the installation of a Sonjuku government. This was followed in turn by a program of major reform in the bureaucracy and in the han military, and by policies defiant of the Bakufu. After the favorable outcome of the Four-Sided War also, the Chōshū men would translate their victory into national power through their diplomatic ties with other han and the court. This power, too, soon expressed itself in an even wider pattern of institutional reconstruction.

The social contours of the Chōshū civil war provide a clue to the activists' motives. The most enterprising leadership groups on each side were drawn from distinctly different echelons of Chōshū society, the rebel Sonjuku leaders from the samurai hierarchy's lower rungs and the reactionary Sempōtai leaders from its upper rungs. Moreover, most of the rebel army's rank and file not only tended to be of modest origins, like the Sonjuku men, but also like them had service experience in their backgrounds, being priests, schoolmasters, or rural administrators. This tendency, taken with other evidence, points to the likelihood that intelligentsia elements were themselves the main social force behind the drive for Restoration.

The reformist movement in Chōshū lost none of its momentum after the sweeping victories over Bakufu forces in the Four-Sided War. Takasugi Shinsaku's last inspired contribution to the movement marked the beginning of a new leverage in national affairs for Chōshū's reformers, a leverage that before too many months had passed would allow them to join with others in the task of restructuring the Japanese nation.

CHAPTER NINE

Idealism and Revolution

THANKS TO A series of diplomatic victories in 1867, Takasugi's comrades were soon able to force the dissolution of the once-mighty Tokugawa Bakufu. Making gains now with breathtaking speed, they were able to establish themselves as the leaders of a new national government in Tokyo within a year after Takasugi's death. During this period they worked as political equals with reformist statesmen from Satsuma in the framework of the Satsuma-Chōshū alliance, and welcomed into the new government reformist sympathizers from Tosa, Hizen, and elsewhere.

In the decade between 1868 and 1878, the newly constituted imperial government under the Chōshū leaders and their colleagues implemented national reforms at a rapid pace. A central administrative bureaucracy recruited solely on a basis of merit was established immediately. A national university was created in 1869, as if in belated response to Yoshida Shōin's repeated petitioning for one ten years before. An ambitious public educational system was founded in 1872 that would soon open tens of thousands of primary and secondary schools throughout the country. All of the gratuitous privileges of the samurai class were phased out in the 1870's, and official discrimination based on the old classes was completely abolished. Hundreds of semiautonomous feudal domains were legally reconstituted as homogeneous prefectures, and a solid fiscal basis for the new government was achieved by imposing a uniform tax on land. The new tax eliminated and displaced the heavy domainal dues on land that had been the main material foundation of the old aristocratic system. A modern army and navy patterned after Western models and open to talent were equipped and readied for service by 1876. Timely and imaginative reforms were carried out in the judiciary, foreign relations, banking, communications, and many other fields as well.

These sweeping changes altered the essential quality of public life. They brought a vitality and rationality that enlivened all spheres of public action. There soon followed unprecedented growth in crop yields, commerce, and industry. There arose a vigorous press and a healthy general clamor for democracy. Philosophy, literature, and the arts, nourished by foreign as well as native inspiration, flourished as never before. Famine was unknown, and modern medical knowledge spread across the land. In the end the reforms would rescue tens of millions of ordinary Japanese from ignorance, disease, and want. Their momentous impact makes the search for their origins a matter of utmost historiographical importance.

Let us return to the analytical propositions with which this study began. For purposes of argument we theorized, first, that the Restoration was carried out by Japan's highly educated and dynamic service intelligentsia; second, that the Restoration leaders were motivated by interests implicit in their unique social condition; third, that these leaders sustained a prolonged political insurgency, which began with the elaboration of iconoclastic ideologies, then progressed through successive phases of terror and civil war; and, fourth, that the Meiji reforms represented the social objectives of the insurgent classes, and followed closely programs that their theorists had developed in the 1850's and before.

These four propositions address several simple queries about the Restoration upheaval: who carried it out, why, how they succeeded, and where their program came from. We can now come to grips with these issues more comprehensively in light of the careers of the Chōshū activists explored in Chapters 2 through 8.

(The matter of how the reformers succeeded, by reliance on a three-stage insurgency, will not be separately discussed here, however, because it has been treated already at many points in preceding chapters.)

CLASS INTERESTS AND IDEAL INTERESTS

Among these queries, the question of why the Restorationists acted is of pivotal importance; so it will be advantageous to consider this complex issue of motives before approaching the others. The Meiji Restoration was a social rebellion carried out by Japan's disciplined and highly educated service intelligentsia, against aristocratic oppression and outmoded social forms. The Restorationists were motivated to act politically, first, because of material deprivations suffered by their class, and, second, because of their idealistic commitment to the welfare of the whole political community. Both of these motivating interests were deeply rooted in their social condition as members of the Tokugawa service intelligentsia.

A brief examination of class conditions affecting the service intelligentsia will make the nature of the class motive clearer. John Hall in his thoughtful study of the Ikeda houseband has described two kinds of samurai, the stably hereditary upper feudatories, which he called "legitimizing families," and the less securely tenured officeholders, which he called "service families."[1] In this distinction lies the key to the social identity of the Restoration insurgency.

In the steeply hierarchical Bakuhan world there coexisted two entirely different classes of samurai, an aristocratic class and a class of professional service personnel. Although the social contours of these two groups have not been exhaustively studied, contemporary observers were highly conscious of the division Hall describes. Yoshida Shōin spoke of it in terms of "inner" and "outer" vassals. Fukuzawa Yūkichi, later a famous popularizer of Western culture, spoke of the two classes more simply as "upper samurai" and "lower samurai."[2]

In manners, custom, dress, wealth, and influence, the "upper samurai" was as thoroughly different from the "lower samurai" as the latter was from the common artisan. He represented a different life-style, a different ethos, and, in short, a different social milieu altogether. The "inner vassal" rode a horse; the "outer vassal" walked. When a member of this privileged class happened to pass, his humbler counterparts were obliged to fling themselves down into the mud in obeisance. The inner vassal wore silks and a courtly *eboshi* on his head. He was likely to be steeped in the aesthetic sensitivities associated with the imperial court in Kyoto. He actually was a courtier at the lesser court of his own daimyo, and often had personal ties in the Great Interior of his lord. He was leisured, and cultivated the elegant tastes appropriate to his station in his appreciation of paintings, tea vessels, poetry, chess, and courtly fashion in dress and facial cosmetics.

The upper samurai lived in a large mansion or compound with many servants, and might win the right to have a sedan-chair landing built into his hallway. As a matter of pride, he would never venture out at night without servants carrying lanterns, nor would he ever be seen carrying anything in his own hands except some sign of his leisure, such as a sword or fishing pole. Nor were these measures extravagances for him, because he enjoyed an income many times that of lesser samurai.

The upper samurai had access to the highest offices in the domain as a matter of birth, regardless of his often inferior qualifications. (It was this fact more than any other that capable lower samurai found to be excruciatingly unfair and essentially antisocial.) He had other advantages in law that the lower samurai did not. He often had the right to hunt boar and to fish on domainal land. He could have audience with the daimyo in person, and might have been employed as a tutor to the daimyo's heir or as a page in the Great Interior, besides holding high office himself. Because of this, han law tended to operate in favor of the upper samurai to the disadvantage of the lower whenever matters came to a dispute between the two.[3]

The life and manners of the ordinary service samurai were in stark contrast to those of his highborn fellow clansmen. Although a "lower samurai" might win marginal or symbolic advancement within the numerous ranks of his own class, "he would no more hope to enter the ranks of the upper samurai than would a four-legged beast hope to fly like a bird." There was no intermarriage between the upper and lower strata of samurai, leading one contemporary commentator to describe the two groups as constituting "two different races of people."[4]

The lower samurai kept a modest household, and might have a small family if his income were high enough. He faced a constant struggle to live within his income, and his wife and children would sometimes weave or do handicrafts to make this possible. Instead of colorful silk, he wore conservative cottons of a dark hue. He never wore courtly dress or an eboshi, and rather it was the sharp creases of the starched *kataginu* on his shoulders that distinguished him in a crowd. He had little leisure for the elegant pastimes of the courtier. But he did have a thorough education in the Chinese classics, the histories, Sung philosophy, and the martial arts. He aspired not to courtly accomplishments but to the stern loyalty to family and lord that were expected of the "true gentleman" (*kunshi*). Beyond that, an administrative samurai, even in the lower ranks, had a detailed knowledge of public affairs, in his own and other domains. He understood the sophisticated theories of social organization that had been advanced by Ogyū Sorai and others since the eighteenth century. He had to; it was he who made the society work.

The service samurai's hold on office was precarious. Winning office and promotion depended on superior competitive performance at the domainal academy and thereafter on satisfactory service on a day-to-day basis. If he were one of the fortunate few selected, he would begin his career not as a page in the Great Interior of the castle, but rather in an administrative office in the remotest rural districts of the domain. He would not have personal access to the daimyo, though after decades of service he might sit in council meetings where the daimyo himself would be present. "Outer vassals" of this type were not wealthy courtiers with great households and silk kimonos. They were earnest technocrats, who disdained massive material rewards and served the domain because of their loyalty to it.

There were two classes of samurai. One existed to work; the other existed to enjoy its leisure. In this social peculiarity lay the genesis of the Restoration upheaval. Although intergenerational acquisition of the meager perquisites of the service strata depended on a high level of discipline and performance, the greatest benefits the han had to bestow—fabulous wealth, high public honors, cultivated leisure, and the rest—were nevertheless reserved for an entirely different group, an anachronistic and socially useless feudal remnant. In short, the service strata provided all of the enormous mental and technical effort, bore the psychological and physical burdens, that were needed to make the han society function, while all of the more exhilarating consolations the han had to offer were nonetheless reserved for another group, the idle highborn. Some had all the pain, others all the gain.

The Restoration movement in Chōshū was an uncompromising attempt by members of the stern and highly literate service element to overthrow the leisured and lavishly endowed aristocratic element, and to use the enormous social energies thus made available to radically ameliorate both their own lot and that of the broader society. Many kinds of data can be adduced to show the likelihood that class interest guided the Chōshū activists. They frequently and explicitly denounced in their writings the privileges of "nobles," "inner vassals," and the "highborn," and pressed instead for fair treatment for "men of talent." A number of these statements have been discussed above in Chapter 3. A class-based motivational pattern is suggested by the fact that virtually the entire Chōshū movement derived from the distinctive, competitively educated strata of Chōshū society, whereas, with a few fascinating exceptions, the movement's antagonists came from the ranks of the leisured highborn. (The social origins of the Chōshū activists will be reviewed in detail below.)

The reformist program developed by the restorationists in the 1850's also points to class motives. One of the two fundamental principles informing that program was the substitution of ability for birth as the exclusive criterion for elite preferment, as we have seen.

Although perceptions of material (and political) class interest of the kind suggested above bred a powerful longing for social reconstruction among the service classes, they were also motivated to act by a set of ideal interests that transcended quid pro quo equity. If the abrasive austerity in which the "retainer of heaven" lived bred in him a desire for the "elevation of talent," it was his immersion in a rich world of emotional gratification drawn from "ideal" sources that shaped his interest in structuring a society that was in general more provident.

It seems to have been a characteristic of the service strata of Tokugawa samurai that the emotional rewards of their work derived from their belief that their service was for the good of all. Since their material rewards were minimal, many of them measured their own worth in terms of their service to the whole community. Since they really believed that it was their sacred duty to assure the "blessing of the people of which Mencius spoke" (keimin), service for them was the source of a kind of psychological wealth. They received from service a warm feeling of well-being that had little to do with their modest material circumstances. For them the pursuit of the welfare of the society *was* their self-interest. This remarkable attitude was probably shared by a great many of the highly literate service personnel of the late Tokugawa era.

The terms of service an "outer vassal" faced more or less forced him to become an idealist. Although his life held few material rewards, he did reap a rich bounty of "ideal" rewards in the form of symbolic recognition. He was genuinely honored for his services, both by his government and by the culture as a whole. He wore his two swords and his crested *haori* with real pride. This being so, the satisfying social idealism of the Restorationists probably stemmed from another dimension of the same set of institutional conditions that shaped their material class interest.

In the hands of Yoshida Shōin, the wearing conditions common among the service strata were transmuted into an especially satis-fying environment of mythic belief. It was the highly trained and capable but still impoverished and socially inferior administrator that Shōin referred to as a "true gentleman" (kunshi). Thanks to Shōin and others, such men in Chōshū could view themselves as being "sages" (seiken) on whose very shoulders Heaven had placed the sacred obligation of sustaining the well-being of an entire society (ammin) in the realm's time of trouble. These were the kind of men, according to Shōin, who should be given positions of responsibility and consulted on matters of government policy, and whose moral authority transcended even that of rulers.

It was in this sphere that Yoshida Shōin's impact on the Resto-ration was greatest. Yoshida created in his followers perceptions and ideal goals that were both more nourishing and more compel-ling than the prospect of immediate personal well-being. He more than others cultivated the spirit and mentality not only of maxi-mum awareness of public affairs but also of maximum self-tran-scendence and of undistracted engagement.

The ideal vision that the Restorationists had of themselves goes far to explain their readiness to risk their lives month after month and year after year. They believed that their cause represented the good of all, and that the good of all justified perseverance. Al-though some of the reforms they sought were shaped by narrow, class-based goals, the self-sacrificial desperation that characterized the movement during most of its existence meant that only men whose commitment transcended self-interest could bring them-selves to participate. For petty opportunists, the Sonjuku group's 50 percent casualty rate held little appeal.

Corresponding to the ideal role that the activists entertained of themselves was the other of the two broad principles that informed their program. They saw that the society of which their institution-al service roles made them the stewards had crying needs that could be met only by applying most of the surplus wealth that had tra-ditionally gone to an aristocratic few. Actually accomplishing this complex task for the people's benefit was a mission for the sage. Consequently, in addition to seeking the "elevation of talent," the reformers relentlessly insisted on a widespread reallocation of social resources. Nobiliary prodigality, *sankin kōtai* and the rest, should be stopped, they argued, and the realm's resources should be invested instead in universal education, in the acquisition of the amazing new medical and manufacturing techniques of the West, and in improved defense: changes that would soon benefit everyone. Objectives like these were informed primarily by the activists' sense of social responsibility, an attitude that derived in turn from their mythic identity and from the deeply seated ideal obligations that that identity implied.

THE SOCIAL ORIGINS OF THE RESTORATION MOVEMENT

Virtually all of the Chōshū restorationists were drawn from the han's small, modestly provided-for service stratum. This was true of Yoshida, Kusaka, and Takasugi, as we have seen, and it was also true in varying degrees of almost the entire movement. In order to evaluate information relating to the social identity of the movement more generally, it is important first to be aware of the contours of social ranking in Chōshū. The han supported 11,400 families of samurai. About 2,700 of these were samurai proper, or shi; some 3,000 were foot soldiers, or sotsu; and the remaining 5,700 samurai were rear vassals, or baishin, of the ranking shi. The shi group—Chōshū's highest-ranking 2,700 samurai families—had several characteristics that are of interest to us. Shi were further broken down into seventeen ranks, among which incomes varied widely, from a generous 16,000 koku at the top down to a scant 10 koku at the bottom. Some 1,900 of the shi families had incomes of less than 100 koku, which means that in income most of them were much closer to the bottom than to the top.

Although no good sociometric study on officeholding in Chōshū is currently available, the writings and careers of Bakumatsu leaders consistently indicate that while several hundred families at the top of the shi hierarchy were assured entry into the han's most prestigious offices, the lesser offices below these were meted out on a basis of competition among several thousand families—especially shi of less than 200 koku. This 200-koku level seems to have been the essential dividing line below which the service condition was general. It was at this lower level that samurai began earnestly studying the Chinese classics, the Dutch language, or mathematics. They had to cultivate challenging skills in order to assure the survival of their houses. No matter how great their success at sustaining those skills, however, and no matter what the psychological cost of doing so, they were nevertheless excluded by feudal custom from access to the higher offices and incomes in the domain.

Yoshida Shōin was a victim of this pattern. He had a stipend of only 57 koku in the shi scale of 10 to 16,000. Although his academic performance and conceptual knowledge were unsurpassed in his generation, he was still expected to pass the rest of his days as a minor instructor at the han academy, with an income that did not compare favorably with that of a tatami matmaker. He lacked the means even of supporting a family, and it was for this reason that his forbears had not married for many generations, and rather had perpetuated their family line in the chillingly economical way of adopting single collateral relatives.

About half of the Shōka Sonjuku's membership consisted of professionalized shi who like Yoshida received less than 200 koku of income. Another third were foot soldiers, and the remainder were commoner physicians, townsmen, and priests, in that order of frequency. Those students who were not shi were thus also drawn from groups that were wholly or partially professionalized. The Aumeisha group of reformist bureaucrats shared these same characteristics. The Aumeisha began as a discussion club of young scholars at the Meirinkan and came to dominate Chōshū clique politics as active allies of the Sonjuku until the execution of many of them in 1864. With one exception, the twenty-four Aumeisha men had incomes of 173 koku or less. They were for the most part modestly stipended shi, with an income range virtually identical with that of the shi in the Sonjuku.

The rank and file of the Chōshū movement's Western rifle companies, the shotai, also had an unexpectedly strong professional character. Typically, these units were made up of 25 to 40 percent modestly stipended samurai, 3 to 15 percent priests, and 40 to 60 percent other commoners. Up to a third of the commoners were drawn from a class of highly educated rural administrators, the shōya. Some 5 percent of these units were regional schoolmasters, and many of the troops were not improbably their students. In short, educated, professional elements were present in the shotai in much greater proportion than they were present in the society at large, while nonprofessional commoners were underrepresented.

At the time of the Chōshū civil war, the Sonjuku group could count on the help of sympathizers in the capital as well as in the field. A moderate pro-Sonjuku coalition that called itself the Peace Council emerged in Hagi in the early months of 1865. The Peace Council had an income range of 23 to 363 koku, and a mean income of 171 koku. This range fell between that of the Sonjuku and that of its antagonists in the Sempōtai.

The leadership of the only group violently and uncompromisingly opposed to the reformist movement in Chōshū, the Sempōtai, were not drawn from the professional service strata but from the higher reaches of the overarching feudal aristocracy. Their income range was 223 to 1332 koku, and their mean income was 652 koku. (The Sonjuku income range was 10 to 160 koku, and the Sonjuku mean was 50 koku.) These vast incomes placed the Sempōtai leaders squarely in the ranks of the sumptuously provided-for "inner vassal." There was no common ground between the Sempōtai and Sonjuku groups.

Comparison of the incomes of the Sonjuku, Peace Council, and Sempōtai leaders even makes it possible to characterize supporters and opponents of Chōshū activism in a meaningful way by precise income categories. Persons of less than 200 koku of income were most likely to support it. Persons of over 400 koku were most likely to oppose it. Persons of between 200 and 400 koku could go either way. These income categories of under 200 koku and over 400 koku almost certainly corresponded to two different institutional conditions, that of the competitive professional servant and that of the leisured aristocrat of birth. (There were only two small groups in

Chōshū whose political loyalties did not correspond in a predictable way to their rank and income levels—the Justice elders and the Mundane Views faction. Although it is fairly apparent why they conducted themselves as they did, further study of these groups would be most interesting and instructive.[5])

In spite of these minor exceptions (which on closer scrutiny may confirm the rule), the overwhelming majority of the restorationists sprang from the same distinctive social class, the educated service intelligentsia. They were administrators, scholars, and priests, with a high level of education and loyalty but little income or opportunity. Their adversaries were "inner vassal" aristocrats.

THE ORIGINS OF THE MEIJI REFORMS

The Restoration reforms were carried out swiftly after the "imperial army" entered Edo in 1868. These reforms went smoothly because the principles behind the programs, and even the programs themselves, were understood by many, long before 1868. The Meiji reforms of the 1870's grew out of reformist interests that were already being articulated by political thinkers in Chōshū in the 1850's and even earlier. This is a matter of crucial importance for any analysis of the Meiji Restoration, yet one that historians have tended to overlook.

Virtually all of the later Meiji reforms were guided by two broad principles used by Chōshū thinkers early in the 1850's to justify major departures from the institutional status quo. These were, first, the substitution of preferment by merit for preferment by birth and, second, the redirection of the realm's institutional energies to better meet the people's actual needs in the present and to eliminate lavish expenditure on the empty ritual practices of the past. These principles were developed by local reformers who were trying to overcome organizational contradictions that had long plagued the institutional life of their own domains, especially contradictions associated with university training. By the 1850's these same thinkers had come to realize that solutions that were desirable at the local level would be still more desirable if implemented nationally. Perry's sudden appearance had made such a reconstruction seem not only more useful but also more likely of achievement. Moreover, as the years wore on, the reformers had reached an anguished understanding that the old society could not tolerate the kinds of changes they wanted. In order to stabilize their reforms, they would have to impose them everywhere in a manner that would change permanently the center of gravity of public life.

We have seen that Yoshida Shōin demanded rigorous merit recruitment for the Chōshū academy in 1848. Once Yoshida had developed his basic reformist concepts in the institutional microcosm of the Chōshū university, he was able to apply them rapidly to a broad spectrum of institutional practices that reached far beyond the walls of the local academy. By 1858 he was applying his reformist approaches to the larger task of reordering national institutions. Having reached this point, however, Yoshida was executed before he could take the next step, which was to apply his innovative ideas to the problem of radically reorganizing the apparatus of the central authority itself.

Kusaka Genzui converted his mentor's many discrete proposals into a plan for Restoration by taking this last step. In 1862 he recommended that the Bakufu in its national responsibilities be replaced altogether by a new merit bureaucracy centered on the court. Kusaka substantially described in 1862 the institutional pattern that would be realized by his closest friends and followers in 1868.

The Meiji reforms rested not only on twenty years of reformist articulation but also on ten years of actual experimentation within Chōshū. W. G. Beasley has referred to these developments as a "Meiji Restoration in miniature."[6] By the mid-1860's, Chōshū had already instituted a large degree of merit selection in government posts, the elimination of almost all rank considerations in favor of ability in han-sponsored education,[7] the nucleus of a Western-style infantry and navy composed of commoners as well as samurai, and a significantly streamlined bureaucracy.[8] This pattern of Chōshū as bellwether continued even after 1868. The abolition of autonomous han, announced in 1871, was piloted by

222   *Idealism and Revolution*

the voluntary surrender of privileges to the Tokyo government by Chōshū and three other reformist han in 1869.

There is another instructive case of the reformers' tendency to use Chōshū as an experimental forerunner. On 12/2/68 Chōshū's activist-controlled government slashed samurai stipends of 1,000 koku or more by 90 percent, and even stipends between 100 and 1,000 koku were all reduced to 100. At the same time, stipends of less than 100 koku were left entirely untouched. Fiscally, this bold stroke was the end of the "men of large stipend" who had been the perennial target of Yoshida Shōin's complaints in the 1850's.[9] This act was a prelude, of course, to the restorationists' abolition of these and other feudal privileges on a national scale several years later.

It is meaningful, then, to speak of the Meiji reforms of the 1870's as representing a well-developed version of the political goals sought by the Chōshū intelligentsia even before they became involved in the activism of the mid-1860's. Rationalizing reforms like those carried out in the 1870's had been the object of the Chōshū activists' study, petitioning, and experimentation for decades.

CHŌSHŪ AND JAPAN

If the motives behind the Restoration movement were a consequence of class identity, the questions remain of whether the movement was in evidence in domains besides Chōshū and of why the movement was more fully developed in Chōshū than elsewhere.

There is considerable evidence that reformist interests were present among the service strata in many domains besides Chōshū. In the Bakumatsu period and even before, talented and knowledgeable men in a number of domains had called for reforms similar to those advocated by the Chōshū activists. Fujita Tōko, Takano Chōei, Yokoi Shōnan, and Sakuma Shōzan all belonged to this group. Like the Chōshū reformers, these men were almost invariably scholars, teachers, physicians, or experts in Western studies. Many of them actually had close personal ties with the Chōshū activists. Similarly, during the fighting of 1864 and 1866, hundreds of members of Chōshū's paramilitary shotai were conscientious students from other han who had left the two capitals to fight in the armies of Chōshū for the reformist cause.[10]

The broader presence in Japan of reformist perceptions and sympathies was evident also in the fact that after 1868, men of ability from other han like Ōkuma Shigenobu and Katsu Kaishū entered the Restoration government without difficulty. Almost every han acquiesced in the authority of the new government and was able to comprehend and smoothly implement its directives, which suggests that an influential group of informed sympathizers was present in each domain. Fukuzawa Yūkichi has indicated that the Restoration led to a rapid takeover of the government by "lower samurai" of reformist sympathies in Nakatsu han. George Moore in his recent study of Kumamoto han has described a strikingly similar phenomenon taking place there.[11] Something like this may have happened in most of the domains. When the balance of power in Edo, which previously favored local conservatives, suddenly shifted toward reform, the delicate balance that existed in every han tipped in favor of the frustrated reformers who had always been there.

Although it is not entirely clear why the Restoration movement should have developed more vigorously in Chōshū than elsewhere, the reasons for this were probably two. First, because of reformist activity going back several generations, Chōshū, more than other domains, had a strongly developed meritocratic system of educational preparation and administrative recruitment. These arrangements tended to generate an unusually numerous and vital service intelligentsia within the domain. (It should be remembered, of course, that Chōshū's traditional meritocratic arrangements were well developed only by comparison with other domains. They were still marginal compared to the fully meritocratic practices set up after Meiji.) Second, the han's flexible pattern of policy-making by rival vertical cliques, more fully developed in Chōshū than elsewhere, made it possible for the restorationists to win and maintain control of the entire governmental apparatus by more or less peaceful and legitimate means. (The only exception was in the winter of 1864, when Bakufu intervention brought violence to Chōshū politics for the first time, and then only briefly.) This meant that in Chōshū, but not elsewhere, the ruling structures in their entirety could be captured with relative ease as an instrument of radical reformism.

Reformism had sympathizers everywhere, but it was only in Chōshū that they could enjoy unqualified success.

MODERN IDEALISM AND WORLD REVOLUTION

It has sometimes been claimed that the Meiji Restoration was sui generis, a type of revolutionary transformation unique to Japan. Although it is true that the Restoration does not resemble the familiar "bourgeois" and "proletarian" archetypes of revolutionary change, there are elements of similarity linking the Meiji experience with the "great" revolutions of the West. Consideration of such similarities may yield some interesting comparative insights. I will try to highlight some of these by applying to Western revolutions the Japanese paradigm that emerges in the pages above, instead of the reverse approach that has been more common. I will sketch the paradigm, then apply it. I will argue that the utopian goals and ideal motives that distinguished the Chōshū restorationists have been present in most of the great revolutionary upheavals of recent history.

Late Tokugawa society represented a neofeudal or "absolutist" stage of development, characterized by sophisticated social organization and considerable surplus wealth. This was so especially in the vicinity of the country's national and regional metropolises. Much of this wealth went to the lavish support of a politically powerful but functionally noncontributive aristocracy. Coexisting with these privileged few was a more numerous service class, who held only minor aristocratic perquisites. These persons, literate and resourceful, actually managed and produced the growing social wealth, while absorbing little of it themselves.

This inequitable state of affairs was stable, because it was sanctioned by custom and tradition, and because confident aristocratic elements used their political power boldly to protect privilege, whereas the service strata lacked leverage, confidence, and traditional sanction.

This stable traditional pattern was shaken by the sudden intrusion of a formidable external threat: Commodore Perry. The traditional assumptions justifying aristocratic social organization were thus critically undermined causing a shift of the center of political gravity toward the service classes. Service elements enjoyed two advantages that allowed them to parlay this security crisis into a large-scale social reconstruction: ideological competence and paramilitary opportunity. The basic conceptual tools needed to plan and legitimize a new society had been forged a generation and more before Perry, and so were readily available to many when the moment came. In addition, the reformers were fortunate in being able to mobilize an effective army, relying on a combination of service-class loyalties and various forms of sentimental nationalism.

The restorationists' determined ideological activity, combined with their military power, enabled them in time to overwhelm the old order. They then appropriated the country's large aristocratic surpluses as planned and invested them in new forms of socially creative activity, including industrialization. The result was a new regime with startling advantages. The new society was more equitable, orderly, and provident for everyone.

Absolutist society is tormented by a paradox: its means have become modern, but its ends are still feudal. Its wealth is generated by firm, modern institutions, but gathered in by a small class of aristocratic grandees and financial notables. This leads to other paradoxes, namely, a tremendous artificial disparity between rich and poor in general, and the emergence of a disciplined service intelligentsia that selflessly creates and harvests all the growing wealth, but is nonetheless excluded, like the ordinary people, from its major benefits. Two other circumstances, if added to this milieu, will produce a revolutionary reconstruction: a widespread ideological preparation for change among the public, to which is added a national security crisis (or sense that the national interest is being compromised). This is what happened in the Japanese case.

Let us consider the origins of the innovative class that brought the Restoration about. It had arisen as a consequence of the increasingly sophisticated institutional growth that characterized much of the long Tokugawa era. Its ranks included scholars, administrators, physicians, clerics, military technicians, and even a few poets. Although it had come into existence gradually over the course of the preceding two centuries, this group already represented a substantial and active minority in the society of perhaps 10 to 15 percent of the population.

The Meiji Restoration can be understood as a revolution carried out by this modern social class, which found itself oppressed by the institutional configurations of the late feudal status quo. It bears a resemblance to one of the four social classes described by Max Weber. In the middle ground between small merchants and persons "privileged through property," Weber identified a social class that consisted of "propertyless intelligentsia," "specialists," and "civil servants." The intelligentsia, Weber maintained, was a major social category, essentially distinct, in both its social attributes and its political interests, from other social groups.[12]

In other words, the Japanese intelligentsia was a modern social class that had emerged from a long process of institutional evolution. This modernizing evolutionary process is that described by Weber as "rationalization" and "bureaucratization." (It was in this connection that Weber once asserted that the Christian monk was the first modern man.) The restorationists were a class produced by this Weberian dynamic of institutional rationalization and increasing social efficiency, and who had an interest both in carrying that process further, and in terminating the lingering neofeudal (or "patrimonial") misappropriation of its hard-won benefits.

Although this group was obviously interested in a more equitable distribution of material rewards, ideal values must nevertheless be regarded as the key to the distinctive identity and conduct of this class. Their selfless dynamism, in both service and rebellion, is hard to explain without reference to ideal interests and rewards. The realm's disciplined new intelligentsia was prepared to give much yet take little because it was motivated not by simple quid pro quo advantages, but rather by "loyalty" (*chūkō*), or what Weber called "vocation." They were encouraged throughout to respond to ideal values, not material values. Thus the high social cost of service functions of modern quality was borne at first in such a way as not to undermine the premises of aristocratic social organization, by the remarkable expedient of paying for it with "ideal" rewards. (This pattern also dictated the necessity of extreme thrift as a value in the private lives of much of the service class, thus imparting a "puritanical" quality to the ethos of that class.) The immense advantages for an aristocratic elite that could perpetrate such an arrangement on its ablest servants are obvious. Yet it would not be proper to assume that the servants themselves were simply exploited by this. They, after all, had the highest gratification of all: doing right (or believing that they did).

The cultivated idealism of the intelligentsia by and by came to have a momentum of its own, however. The intellectual capabilities of the service classes and their idealist values eventually combined to yield utopian goals. It occurred to philosophers of the service echelon that the selfless rationality by which they gathered the new surplus wealth might also be applied to the allocation of that wealth in such a way as to create a more dynamic society and general enrichment. The loyalties of the service class eventually shifted, from the transitional absolutist institutions that had brought them into being, toward the more modern forms that were still only imagined. A satisfying utopian program, a strong ideal interest in the well-being of all, and consequently a very high tolerance for personal risk, are the essential characteristics of modernizing intelligentsia-based revolution that distinguish it from political agitation on the part of other interest groups. Modern idealism is the hallmark of service revolution.

Recent work by the Japanese scholar Ueyama Shumpei suggests that the phenomenon of service revolution was not unique to Bakumatsu Japan, and that elements of it can be found in the French Revolution. Ueyama observed close institutional similarities between the minor royal officials and priests who made up the revolutionary majority in France's Estates General in 1789 and the "lower-class samurai" who brought about the Meiji Restoration. He found close parallels in the language of the revolutionary ideologist Abbé Sieyès and the Mito scholar Fujita Tōko regarding the unsatisfactory relationship between public service echelons and the privileged minority.[13]

Ueyama's analysis is directly supported by the work of Alfred Cobban, John McManners, and others. In his *Myth of the French Revolution*, Cobban pointed out that the "bourgeois" revolution in 1789 is hard to find, and suggested that the essence of the revolutionary phenomenon in France may have been something very different, namely, a rebellion of "minor officials." The militant leaders and followers of the Third Estate, whether from the church, the military, or the royal administration, fell overwhelmingly into this category. In Cobban's words, "a class of officials and professional men moved up from the minor to the major posts in government and dispossessed the minions of an effete Court: this was what the bourgeois revolution meant."[14]

There were, of course, enormous differences in the respective ideologies and forms of violence that emerged in the Meiji Restoration and in the French Revolution. Nevertheless, the French case, like the Japanese case, sprang from many decades of growing awareness among the nation's leading thinkers that a better world was possible. From the days of Montesquieu and Voltaire on, Enlightenment philosophers began with growing excitement to hammer out among themselves what liberty and equality could really mean. Ideas were everywhere for reconstructing every conceivable institutional practice.

When in 1789 only a courageous stand was needed to bring these ideas into reality, thousands stood up for revolution without looking back. In the French Revolution as in the Japanese Restoration, privileges relating solely to birth were aggressively eliminated, and in both cases, thousands of career opportunities were suddenly opened to "talent." Both cases involved sudden and conscious institutional reform in the direction of radical bureaucratization, and other structural ameliorations that would lead quickly to a phenomenal increase in general welfare and prosperity.

The European revolution most explicitly associated with intelligentsia activity is the Russian Revolution of 1917. Ideologies and forms of violence once again differed markedly from other cases. Still, the leadership role of the intelligentsia was unmistakable. Beginning with Alexander Herzen on the institutional side and Bakunin and Kropotkin on the theoretical side, Russian thinkers were embarked for much of the nineteenth century on a quest for new utopian values and needed structural reforms. Although even discussing these matters involved great risk, many proponents of a new Russia were soon going beyond this to sacrifice themselves in lone terrorist assaults on the living symbols of old regime authority. These thinkers and activists were the *raznochintsy*, and their ranks were filled primarily by "clergy" and "the minor professional and bureaucratic classes." Martin Malia has seen the Russian intelligentsia as a "class" with its own autonomous interests. The boundaries of that class, as in the French and Japanese cases, were defined institutionally, that is, by university experience and institutional condition.[15]

The upheaval of 1917 led to a "rational" restructuring of Russian society leading among other things to large-scale industrial development. Thousands of careers were suddenly open to talent, while aristocratic privileges, material and political, were swept away. The intelligentsia itself did benefit from this, but the Russian masses were perhaps the greatest beneficiaries, and there is no doubt that many of the revolutionaries shared idealistic motives.

A few years ago, Michael Walzer published a well-received study entitled *Revolution of the Saints*. Walzer argued that England's seventeenth-century revolution against monarchical authority was carried out by a "Puritan intelligentsia." These men had the kind of Calvinist calling described by Weber, but it was not directed at economic activity. Rather it was aimed at political activity, such that in the evolutionary course of things they had as a group finally come to wield more power in the state than the prince and the peerage. Moreover, they achieved success by engaging in a disciplined form of "radical politics," leading Walzer to characterize puritanical "radicalism" as a "general historical phenomenon." He has suggested the need for a "systematic comparison of Puritans, Jacobins, and Bolsheviks."[16]

The utopian dimension was prominent in the English Revolution. Francis Bacon in his *New Atlantis* of 1626 had described a perfect land in the Americas where philosophers in the House of Solomon would assure the health and welfare of the people. Many Puritan intellectuals in Bacon's day believed that with God's inspiration they could remake society and create a paradise on earth. (The contemporaneous rise of modern science was one consequence of this attitude.) This was an exhilarating prospect for them, and in the political upheaval and Great Migration to North America that followed, many of the institutional reforms they envisioned came true.[17]

Service revolution deriving from a Weberian evolutionary dynamic may be more than a Japanese idiosyncrasy. Rebellion of the service intelligentsia for its own reasons may have been a powerful or even decisive factor in each of the great revolutions of Europe. In Japan as in Europe, and now in new nations as ideologically diverse as Vietnam and Israel, the Weberian, or organizational, transformation has preceded the large-scale industrial, or Marxist, transformation. In each case, the transformational upheaval has generally been carried out by service elements, often with minor aristocratic perquisites of their own, operating in the name of utopian values against a powerful aristocratic (or colonial) stratum, in circumstances of a widely perceived external threat to the national welfare.

In the typical Third World case, impoverished proletarians are nowhere to be seen. Rather, students, professors, clergymen, technicians, teachers, young officers, and the like join to demand reform in the name of transcendent social values. Despite great risk, they strive relentlessly against a small class of estateholders and financial grandees who are thought to enjoy close ties with foreign interests. The reformers' insurgency has often been focused on a monarch figure who derives lavish personal income from public functions owned by himself, and who serves as the absolutist guarantor of a larger system of social privilege. Signs of this dynamic have been apparent in recent years in Nicaragua, Ethiopia, Iran, and elsewhere. The insurgent group may seek to organize ordinary people for paramilitary activity, and always fashions a judicious combination of traditional folk belief and modern social philosophy such as will accommodate both the demands of sentimental nationalism and the insurgents' program of social rationalization. This kind of pattern conforms closely to the assumptions of service revolution.

In both European and non-European cases, the dynamics of idealist service revolution have gone largely unnoticed in the past, because so little attention has been paid to developing the theoretical paradigms against which they could be perceived. Careful scrutiny of the Meiji Restoration, where the dynamic of service revolution is so clearly present, may provide the essential contours of such a paradigm.

REFERENCE MATTER

Notes

COMPLETE citations are given in the Bibliography, pp. 247–53. The following abbreviations are used in the Notes.

BKS   Suematsu Kenchō, *Bōchō kaitenshi*, 2 vols. (Tokyo, 1967 [1921])
IS   *Ishinshi*, ed. Ishin shiryō hensan jimukyoku, 6 vols. (Tokyo, 1941)
SIKG Fukumoto Yoshisuke, ed., *Shōka sonjuku no ijin Kusaka Genzui* (Tokyo, 1934)
TSI   *Tōgyō sensei ibun*, ed. Tōgyō gojūnensai kinenkai, 2 vols. (Shimonoseki, 1971 [1916])
TTS   *Tōgyō Takasugi Shinsaku*, ed. Takasugi Tōgyō sensei hyakunensai hōsankai (Shimonoseki, 1966)
YSZ   *Yoshida Shōin zenshū*, ed. Yamaguchi ken kyōiku kai, 12 vols. (Tokyo, 1940)

CHAPTER 2

1. *YSZ*, 1: 69–72.
2. *Ibid.*, pp. 3–4.
3. See, for example, Naramoto, *Yoshida Shōin*, pp. 34–35.
4. *YSZ*, 1: 6–7.
5. *Ibid.*, pp. 9–10.
6. *Ibid.*, p. 13.
7. *Ibid.*, pp. 13–14. Shōin's paper, the "Meirinkan osaikō ni tsuki kizuki sho," appears *ibid.*, pp. 221–44.
8. In later years Shōin would become an articulate proponent of travel as an educational experience. See *ibid.*, 5: 161–62.
9. Shōin's journal of the trip is called the "Seiyū nikki" and appears *ibid.*, 10: 19–99.
10. Shōin's list of his Hirado readings appears *ibid.*, pp. 52–54.
11. *Ibid.*, 1: 17–18. The full text of the memorial appears *ibid.*, pp. 263–87.
12. *Ibid.*, 8: 98.
13. *Ibid.*, pp. 65–70.

14. Shōin's journal, "Tōhokuyū nikki," appears *ibid.*, 10: 187–328.
15. *Ibid.*, pp. 196–202.
16. *Ibid.*, pp. 259–60.
17. *Ibid.*, pp. 284–85.
18. *Ibid.*, 1: 21.
19. *Ibid.*, 11: 267–71.
20. *Ibid.*, 10: 380–81, 385–86.
21. *Ibid.*, pp. 386–92.
22. This memorial appears *ibid.*, 1: 297–313.
23. Chang, *From Prejudice to Tolerance*, pp. 112–13.
24. *Ibid.*, p. 114; *YSZ*, 1: 24–25 and 10: 405–13. For the text of Sakuma's poem, see *ibid.*, 1: 375.
25. *YSZ*, 10: 417–35. For Shōin's account of the events of the night of 3/27/54, see his "Sangatsu nijū-shichi yoru no ki," *ibid.*, pp. 459–66. For the American account, see Hawks, *Narrative of the Expedition of an American Squadron*, 1: 420–23.
26. *YSZ*, 10: 435–36.
27. *Ibid.*, pp. 436–44, 451–52; Chang, *From Prejudice to Tolerance*, p. 115.
28. The "Yūshūroku" appears in *YSZ*, 1: 329–71. Sakuma's comment appears on p. 369.
29. *Ibid.*, p. 26. See Naramoto, ed., *Yoshida Shōin shū*, p. 131, for the poetry writing en route and two of the poems.
30. *YSZ*, 1: 26–27.
31. The bibliographies that Shōin kept from 10/54 to 12/55 are called the "Noyama-goku dokushi" and constitute pp. 1–26 in *YSZ*, vol. 11.
32. *Ibid.*
33. *Ibid.*
34. The "Record from Prison" is found *ibid.*, 1: 329–71. The letters are in 8: 276–482, and the miscellaneous essays in 2: 261–321.
35. *Ibid.*, 1: 28.
36. Naramoto, ed., *Yoshida Shōin shū*, pp. 91–93.
37. *Ibid.*
38. *YSZ*, 4: 176–80.
39. *Ibid.*, 11: 26–70, 105ff, and 1: 29–34.
40. *Ibid.*, 4: 19–20.
41. Quoted in Ikeda, *Takasugi Shinsaku to Kusaka Genzui*, p. 28.
42. *YSZ*, 4: 141–43.
43. *Ibid.*, pp. 151–54.
44. *Ibid.*, 12: 200–202. The entire recollections of Watanabe Kōzō are recorded *ibid.*, pp. 200–211.
45. *Ibid.*, pp. 205–7.
46. *Ibid.*, pp. 208–11.
47. *Ibid.*, pp. 200–202, 208–11.
48. *Ibid.*, p. 189. This is drawn from a memoir on the Sonjuku by the student Amano Gomin (1841–1903). The whole memoir appears in *YSZ*, 12: 187–200.
49. *Ibid.*, pp. 190, 200–202, 208–11.

50. *Ibid.*, p. 190.
52. *Ibid.*, pp. 203–4, 207.
54. *Ibid.*
56. *Ibid.*, pp. 205–7.
58. *Ibid.*, p. 202.
60. *Ibid.*, p. 196.

51. *Ibid.*, p. 199.
53. *Ibid.*, p. 191.
55. *Ibid.*, pp. 200–202.
57. *Ibid.*, pp. 208–11.
59. *Ibid.*, p. 198.

61. Based on *ibid.*, 5: 99–100, editor's notes; *BKS*, 1: 13–14; and Kimura, "Hagi," p. 34.

62. *YSZ*, 11: 165–75.

63. Umihara's comprehensive list of Sonjuku students appears in Umihara, *Meiji*, pp. 131–34.

64. Based on Umetani, "Meiji ishin shi ni okeru Chōshū han no seijiteki dōkō," in Sakata, ed., *Meiji*, p. 325.

65. Letter to Kusaka Genzui, 7/18/56, *YSZ*, 4: 153–54.

66. Letter to Kusaka Genzui, 6/2/56, *ibid.*, pp. 142–43. Bracketed insertion mine.

CHAPTER 3

Many of the passages of Yoshida Shōin's writings mentioned in this chapter appear in more literal translation in Thomas Huber, "Chōshū Activists in the Meiji Restoration" (Ph.D. dissertation, University of Chicago, 1975), pp. 54–91.

1. *YSZ*, 1: 223–25.
3. *Ibid.*, 3: 40–41.
5. *YSZ*, 1: 223.
7. *Ibid.*, 5: 396–97.
9. *Ibid.*, pp. 341–49.
11. *Ibid.*
13. *Ibid.*, pp. 137, 141.
15. *Ibid.*
17. *Ibid.*, 1: 223–25.
19. *Ibid.*, 5: 98–99.

2. *Ibid.*, pp. 240–41.
4. *IS*, 5: 527–31.
6. *Ibid.*, pp. 226–29.
8. *Ibid.*, 1: 303–5.
10. *Ibid.*, 5: 162–64.
12. *Ibid.*, pp. 155–56.
14. *Ibid.*, 1: 345.
16. *Ibid.*, 5: 141.
18. *Ibid.*, p. 301.

20. Compare the incomes of Sonjuku students given in Table 3 above with Yamamura, *Samurai Income*, pp. 120–21, 126, 132.

21. See Fukuzawa, "Kyūhanjō," *Monumenta Nipponica* 9: 1, p. 313.

22. Yamamura, *Samurai Income*, pp. 103–9; *YSZ*, 1: 68–72.

23. *YSZ*, 4: 20.

24. *Ibid.*, 3: 243–44, 246, 251.

25. Compare *ibid.*, 1: 299–301 and 5: 103–6.

26. *Ibid.*, 3: 249, 251.
28. *Ibid.*, 11: 1.
30. *Ibid.*, 5: 388, 400–402.
32. *Ibid.*, 8: 214.

27. *Ibid.*, 1: 389–90.
29. *Ibid.*, p. 238.
31. *Ibid.*, 3: 39–42.

33. Shōin's letter to Yamagata Taika inviting his comment on the *Kōmō yowa* appears *ibid.*, 4: 75–77.

34. *Ibid.*, 3: 536–38, *passim.* The entire text of Yamagata Taika's critique, with Shōin's counter critique, appears *ibid.*, pp. 523–611.
35. See *ibid.*, 1: 226, 241, 242.
36. *Ibid.*, pp. 297–98.
37. *Ibid.*, pp. 298–99.
38. See, for example, *ibid.*, 1: 332 and 5: 143.
39. *Ibid.*, 3: 58–59.
40. Najita, "Structure and Content in Tokugawa Thinking," pp. 45, 49.

CHAPTER 4

1. *YSZ*, 1: 33, 36–37; *SIKG*, p. 31; Tokutomi, ed., *Kōshaku Yamagata Aritomo den*, 1: 85, 118–23.
2. See, for example, *YSZ*, 9: 27–28, for some of the contacts Shōin furnished to Kusaka Genzui in Kyoto, including Umeda Umpin and Yanagawa Seigan, and *SIKG*, p. 31, for some of the contacts he furnished to Genzui in Edo and elsewhere, including Sakuma Shōzan.
3. *YSZ*, 12: 198, 205–7.   4. *Ibid.*, 5: 154.
5. *Ibid.*, pp. 189–96.   6. *Ibid.*, pp. 198–206.
7. *Ibid.*, p. 204.   8. *Ibid.*, 1: 35–36.
9. *Ibid.*, 5: 249–54.
10. Naramoto, *Yoshida Shōin*, pp. 124–27.
11. *BKS*, 1: 160.
12. These two letters appear in *YSZ*, 9: 125–28.
13. *Ibid.*
14. Tokutomi, ed., *Kōshaku Yamagata Aritomo den*, 1: 155–56. For the order restoring Shōin's credentials, see *YSZ*, 11: 323–24.
15. Naramoto, *Yoshida Shōin*, p. 60.
16. *YSZ*, 5: 320–22.
17. The order for reimprisonment appears *ibid.*, 11: 325.
18. *Ibid.*, 5: 322–23.
19. *Ibid.*, pp. 322–24.
20. *Ibid.*, p. 324.
21. *BKS*, 1: 161; *YSZ*, 1: 37. Also see *BKS*, 1: 160 for the struggle between Sufu and Shōin in 11/58.
22. *YSZ*, 5: 298–302, 1: 37–38; *BKS*, 1: 161.
23. This letter appears in *SIKG*, pp. 475–76.
24. *YSZ*, 9: 191–93.
25. See *SIKG*, pp. 210–11, for the text of this request.
26. Naramoto, ed., *Yoshida Shōin shū*, p. 69.
27. *YSZ*, 1: 40–41.
28. *Ibid.*, 9: 294–97; *SIKG*, p. 36.
29. *YSZ*, 9: 344.
30. *Ibid.*, pp. 379–81. For the prison-break plan see *TTS*, p. 323.
31. *YSZ*, 9: 381–82.

32. The authorizing han order Nagai bore from Edo to Hagi appears *ibid.*, 11: 333-34.

33. *Ibid.*, 1: 42; Naramoto, *Yoshida Shōin*, p. 149.

34. This account is from a letter to Takasugi Shinsaku, dated 7/9/58, in *YSZ*, 9: 410-11.

35. *Ibid.*, p. 419.

36. *Ibid.*, p. 462.

37. Matsumoto, ed., *Yoshida Shōin*, p. 8.

38. *IS*, 2: 660.

CHAPTER 5

1. *SIKG*, pp. 23, 28; Ikeda, *Takasugi Shinsaku to Kusaka Genzui*, pp. 25, 26.

2. Yoshida Shōin was a proponent of travel as a broadening experience. See *YSZ*, 5: 161-62. For the importance of the grand tour as practiced in han besides Chōshū, see Dore, *Education in Tokugawa Japan*, pp. 111-12.

3. *SIKG*, pp. 29, 30. The 42 poems are reproduced *ibid.*, pp. 681-87. For Yoshida's address, see *YSZ*, 5: 109-11.

4. *SIKG*, p. 31.

5. *YSZ*, 9: 27-28.

6. *SIKG*, pp. 32-33; also see p. 677.

7. *Ibid.*, pp. 474-75.

8. *Ibid.*

9. *Ibid.*, p. 53.

10. Tokutomi, ed., *Kōshaku Yamagata Aritomo den*, 1: 156-57.

11. *SIKG*, pp. 475-76; Craig, *Chōshū*, p. 161. The other signers were Iida Seihaku, Onodera Shinnojō, and Nakatani Masasuke.

12. *SIKG*, pp. 210-11.

13. *Ibid.*, p. 35.

14. *Ibid.*, p. 36. Also see the frontispiece of Matsumoto, ed., *Yoshida Shōin*.

15. *YSZ*, 9: 483.   16. *SIKG*, p. 488.

17. *TSI*, p. 69.   18. *SIKG*, pp. 36-37.

19. *Ibid.*, pp. 34-36.

20. *Ibid.*, p. 39; *Shōkiku Kido-kō den*, 1: 100. Kusaka recorded in his diary that he met with Sufu eight times between the seventh and ninth months of 1861. See Inoue, "Chōshū," p. 313.

21. *Nagai Uta*, pp. 1-2.

22. See the "Taisaku ichido" in *YSZ*, 5: 136-43.

23. Sufu's draft of 3/28/61 appears in *BKS*, 1: 252-54. This understanding of Sufu's draft as critically different from Nagai's is based on the analysis of the Association to Honor Nagai Uta, in *Nagai Uta*, pp. 11-12 and 20-23. The Association considered but rejected the view argued in Nakahara Kunihei's *Nagai Uta yōden* that Nagai's drafts of

the *Kōkai enryaku-saku* and Sufu's were identical. Over Nakahara's view, the Association regards as more reliable the work of the prewar scholar Sugi Binkai, who, after meticulously comparing Sufu's and Nagai's versions, found that they were opposite in intent. Sugi determined that the substantive points in Nagai's three drafts (to the Chōshū government in 3/61, to Sanjō Sanetomi of the court on 5/23/61, and to *rōjū* Kuse Hirochika of the Bakufu on 12/8/61, this last in *BKS,* 1: 257–59) were:

(i) We should approve of the Bakufu's treaty while illuminating its effectiveness.

(ii) We should restrain the arguments of the court.

(iii) We should not regard violation of the decree as a problem.

(iv) We should not recognize the indignation of the "men of high purpose" (*shishi*), as they are persons who do not know the ways of public affairs.

(v) We should judge that "breaking the treaty and expelling the aliens" (*hayaku jōi*) would be a reckless policy inviting certain defeat, and we should assert that there is no route other than opening the country (*kaikoku*).

The substantive points in Sufu's draft, however, were these:

(i) We should honor the will of the court.

(ii) We should not recognize the Bakufu's humiliating treaty.

(iii) We should regard this as the violation of an imperial decree.

(iv) We should sympathize with the indignation of the "men of high purpose."

(v) We should not draw back even from warfare in the cause of "breaking the treaties and expelling the aliens."

24. Kusaka's memorial appears in *Kusaka Genzui ibunshū,* 1: 306–7. Kido Kōin was complaining to Sufu about Nagai's policies at the same time. See Ōe, *Kido Kōin,* p. 98.

25. *SIKG,* p. 40; *Shōkiku Kido-kō den,* 1: 101–2. See Ōe, *Kido Kōin,* pp. 62–64, for Kido Kōin's regret over Sufu's dismissal, as expressed in a letter to Sufu on 10/27/61, and for Kido's own threatened resignation.

26. *Kusaka Genzui ibunshū,* 1: 319.

27. All of the above material on the Aumeisha is drawn from Umihara, *Meiji,* pp. 56–59.

28. See *SIKG,* pp. 501–2, and p. 464, respectively, for these two letters.

29. *Ibid.,* pp. 42–43.   30. *Ibid.*

31. *Ibid.,* pp. 467–68.   32. *Ibid.,* pp. 507–8.

33. Inoue, "Chōshū," p. 48.

34. *SIKG,* p. 45; *Itō Hirobumi den,* 1: 54–55; Ōe, *Kido Kōin,* pp. 70–72.

35. *SIKG,* pp. 45–46; Ikeda, *Takasugi Shinsaku to Kusaka Genzui,* pp. 113–14.

CHAPTER 6

1. These two memorials appear in *SIKG*, pp. 412–37.
2. *Ibid.*, p. 424.
3. *Ibid.*, pp. 432–35.
4. *Ibid.*, p. 46.
5. Naramoto, *Meiji ishin jimbutsu jiten*, p. 140.
6. *SIKG*, p. 53; Tanaka, *Meiji*, p. 116.
7. *BKS*, 1: 319*ff.*
8. *SIKG*, pp. 52–53; *BKS*, 1: 441–42.
9. *BKS*, 1: 452–55.
10. *TTS*, pp. 256–58; *SIKG*, p. 54.
11. See *TSI*, "Shokan," pp. 106–7; Hayakawa, ed., *Kiheitai nikki*, 1:85.
12. This and other data on the early Kiheitai can be found in *BKS*, 1: 453*ff.*
13. Craig, *Chōshū*, p. 134.
14. *TTS*, pp. 61–63.
15. *SIKG*, pp. 55–56.
16. The circumstances of the coup of 8/18/63 are recounted in *IS*, 3: 548–80. For the emperor's personal position, see *ibid.*, pp. 551–53, 642.
17. *BKS*, 1: 540–45.
18. The above material on the Shōkenkaku is drawn from Hirao, *Nakaoka Shintarō*, pp. 57–65.
19. Naramoto, *Meiji ishin jimbutsu jiten*, p. 226.
20. *BKS*, 1: 548, 556–58.
21. *IS*, 4: 10–12, 27; *BKS*, 1: 583.
22. Tanaka, *Meiji*, p. 119.
23. *IS*, 4: 27; *SIKG*, p. 64.
24. *SIKG*, p. 65; *BKS*, 1: 606.
25. *BKS*, 1: 609–12.
26. *Ibid.*, pp. 618–22.
27. *Ibid.*, pp. 623–26.
28. This account of the Kusaka-Kijima debate is based on the reports of Kusaka's aide Minami Tesuke and of Nomura Wasaku. These appear in *SIKG*, pp. 666–68.
29. All of the above on the convergence of the four forces on Kyoto is drawn from *IS*, 4: 86–92.
30. Ōe, *Kido Kōin*, pp. 145–46.
31. *BKS*, 1: 636.

CHAPTER 7

1. *TTS*, p. 222.
2. Naramoto, *Takasugi*, p. 15.
3. Ikeda, *Takasugi Shinsaku to Kusaka Genzui*, pp. 36–37.
4. *YSZ*, 12: 203.
5. Ikeda, *Takasugi Shinsaku to Kusaka Genzui*, p. 39.
6. *YSZ*, 5: 113.
7. *Ibid.*, pp. 211–12.
8. *TSI*, "Shokan," p. 18.

9. Naramoto, *Takasugi*, pp. 51–53.
10. *Ibid.*, p. 57.
11. *TSI*, "Shokan," p. 36.
12. *Ibid.*, p. 69.
13. Naramoto, *Takasugi*, pp. 77–80.
14. Takasugi's daily account of this trip appears in *TSI*, "Nikki oyobi shuroku," pp. 6–26.
15. *TSI*, "Shokan," p. 77.
16. Naramoto, *Takasugi*, pp. 83–85.
17. *Shōkiku Kido-kō den*, pp. 68*ff*; Naramoto, *Takasugi*, p. 99.
18. Takasugi's complete journal of the Shanghai voyage appears in *TSI*, "Nikki oyobi shuroku," pp. 72–124. For a more detailed account in English, see Huber, "Chōshū Activists," pp. 195–99.
19. *TSI*, "Nikki oyobi shuroku," p. 79.
20. *Ibid.*, "Tōgyō sensei nempu," p. 6.
21. *Ibid.*, "Shokan," pp. 88–89.
22. Ikeda, *Takasugi Shinsaku to Kusaka Genzui*, p. 149.
23. This episode is related in Naramoto, *Takasugi*, pp. 130–31, and in *TTS*, p. 252. The poem Takasugi composed to explain his new name, which is rich in literary significance, and a note relating to the circumstances behind it, appear in *TSI*, "Shikabunsho," pp. 9–10.
24. See Naramoto, *Takasugi*, p. 135; *TTS*, p. 253.
25. *TSI*, "Shokan," pp. 106–7.   26. *BKS*, 1: 344–45, 355.
27. *Ibid.*   28. *IS*, 4: 10–14.
29. *Ibid.*, pp. 12–13.
30. *TSI*, "Nikki oyobi shuroku," p. 126.
31. *Ibid.*, pp. 127–34.
32. *Ibid.*, pp. 136–37.
33. *TTS*, p. 265.
34. *TSI*, "Nikki oyobi shuroku," p. 132.
35. *TTS*, p. 265; Ōe, *Kido Kōin*, p. 141.
36. *Itō Hirobumi den*, 1: 105, 119–30. For a Western account of the Four Nation Fleet incident, see Satow, *A Diplomat in Japan*, pp. 95–109, 116–25.
37. *Itō Hirobumi den*, 1: 148–51; *IS*, 4: 248–49.
38. *Itō Hirobumi den*, 1: 157–58.
39. Naramoto, *Takasugi*, p. 165.   40. *TTS*, p. 97.
41. *Ibid.*, pp. 100–101.   42. *Ibid.*, pp. 104–5; *IS*, 4: 259.
43. Tokutomi, ed., *Kōshaku Yamagata Aritomo den*, 1: 431. Bracketed insertions mine.
44. The above material on the passage of authority from Justice to Mundane Views hands is drawn from *IS*, 4: 160–70. These events are also recorded in *BKS*, 1: 686–99.
45. *TTS*, pp. 120–21.
46. *Ibid.*, p. 124.
47. The circumstances of the Hagi-Bakufu negotiations related here are drawn from *IS*, 4: 172–86, where they are set forth in greater detail.

CHAPTER 8

1. *IS,* 4: 191.
2. *TTS,* pp. 129–30. A description of this entire council of 12/13, as well as Takasugi's speech, appears on these pages.
3. *TTS,* pp. 132–33. 4. *IS,* 4: 186.
5. *Ibid.,* p. 427. 6. *BKS,* 2: 762.
7. All of the above on shotai funding and Nomura's activities in the South is drawn from Tanaka, *Meiji,* pp. 166–69, and *TTS,* pp. 137, 139.
8. Umihara, *Meiji,* pp. 131–36.
9. *TTS,* p. 137.
10. All of the above on the armed struggles around Isa and Oda, as well as material on the council of 1/18, is drawn from *TTS,* pp. 136–40.
11. See Tanaka, *Meiji,* p. 123; Craig, *Chōshū,* p. 95.
12. *IS,* 4: 431–38; *TTS,* pp. 141–42.
13. *TTS,* pp. 142–45. One of the daimyo's traditional tasks was to keep peace in the han by selecting policy officials who were acceptable to all of the powerful elements in his government. To exercise this function he had to maintain absolute impartiality and have a sure sense of the han public. His job was to do what elections are now expected to do, namely, to gauge changes in public opinion and in the location of real power, and to place officials on the basis of those changes, thus allowing transfers of power without violence. In dealing with a recalcitrant fringe group, the daimyo sometimes resorted to taking its leaders aside and simply lecturing them back into line. When the daimyo completely failed to satisfy one group or another, that group would threaten violence, thus signaling to the daimyo either that his sense of the public had been in error or that the group in question was being irresponsible, a judgment he had to make.

Over the long term of Chōshū's history, this system of transferring power seldom did deteriorate into violence, indicating not only that the daimyo-referee was usually perceptive and honest, but that a high level of self-discipline was exercised by all elements of the han public. Yet from 12/15/64 to 1/16/65 Chōshū was torn by civil war. This crisis meant, among other things, that Takachika had failed in his traditional duty of keeping the peace. Perhaps it was for this reason that Takachika was extremely energetic in trying to prevent further bloodshed after the Hagi army was finally pushed out of Akamura on 1/16, an event that clearly indicated where the military balance lay. The daimyo personally went back and forth between the leaders of the shotai and the leaders of the Mundane Views faction, urging restraint and conciliation, while putting the government firmly in the hands of the former. The daimyo's offices culminated in a festival celebrating the "reunification of opinions within the han" (*hanron tōitsu*), held from 2/22 to 3/3 at the Reisha shrine in the castle, and observed simultaneously by the shotai in Yamaguchi. It was largely because of these efforts on the daimyo's part and the integrity of Chōshū's public traditions that, after the military point had been made on 1/16, the transfer of power in the government was effected with almost no further violence.

14. See in Chapter 1 above, pp. 32–37.

15. The figures for the Kiheitai in Table 6 are taken from *TTS*, pp. 442–44. The figures for the Yōchōtai and the Second Kiheitai in Tables 7 and 8 are taken from Tanaka, *Meiji*, p. 129.

16. Tanaka, *Meiji*, p. 129.

17. *TTS*, pp. 442–44.

18. Umihara, *Meiji*, pp. 14, 26, 32–33. The *Nihon Kyōiku-shi shiryō* lists 904 juku and terakoya as having been established in Chōshū between 1829 and 1868.

19. Umihara, *Meiji*, p. 239.

20. *Ibid.*, pp. 214–15, 236–37.

21. *Ibid.*, pp. 131–36.

22. *YSZ*, 1: 33.

23. *TTS*, p. 142.

24. Umetani, "Chōshū," p. 340.

25. *Ibid.*

26. Tanaka, *Meiji*, pp. 185, 213–18.

27. Itoya, *Ōmura Masujirō*, pp. 53, 174–76.

28. Dore, *Education in Tokugawa Japan*, p. 222.

29. Compare *BKS*, 1: 261. The Chōshū daimyo had avoided sankin kōtai since the Forbidden Gate as too hazardous.

30. Shibahara, *Meiji*, p. 284. These data are compiled by Shibahara from *BKS*, 2: 810–11, and Tanaka, *Meiji*, pp. 187–89.

31. Ōe, *Kido Kōin*, pp. 156–57.

32. Naramoto et al., eds., *Yoshida Shōin to sono monka*, p. 144.

33. *TTS*, pp. 148–52.

34. *Ibid.*, pp. 293–94.

35. *Ibid.*, pp. 171–73.

36. *Ibid.*, pp. 76–77.

37. For a detailed and authoritative treatment of the Satchō alliance and the long months of troubled negotiations leading to it, see *Shōkiku Kido-kō den*, 1: 492–96, 557–64, 594–97, 603.

38. Shibahara, *Meiji*, p. 285; Tanaka, *Meiji*, pp. 217–18.

39. For a good account of events within the Bakufu relating to Chōshū in the years 1865 to 1866, see *IS*, 4: 373–425.

40. *BKS*, 2: 989–92.

41. *TTS*, pp. 182–83.

42. *Ibid.*, pp. 186–88.

43. *Ibid.*, pp. 189–91.

44. *Ibid.*, pp. 304–5.

45. *Ibid.*, pp. 191–200, 205, 207.

46. For a detailed description of the Hamada and Aki fronts, see *IS*, 4: 506–13.

47. *TTS*, pp. 307–10.

48. *Ibid.*, p. 327.

CHAPTER 9

1. Hall, "The Ikeda House," in Hall and Jansen, eds., *Studies in Institutional History of Japan*, p. 87.

2. Fukuzawa, *Autobiography*, p. 309.

3. *Ibid.*, pp. 309–21.

4. *Ibid.*, p. 312.

5. One of these two groups consisted of the han elders, whose hereditary rank was second only to that of the daimyo himself. Three of Chōshū's six elders worked in close cooperation with activist leaders. The elders Masuda Danjō, Fukuhara Echigo, and Kunishi Shinano were ultimately executed because of their collaboration with the Sonjuku movement. On the activist side, Yoshida Shōin regularly went out of his way to exempt these men from his attacks on upper officialdom, and referred to the sympathetic elders with praise. In his "Four Urgent Tasks" memorial of 7/19/58, for example, Yoshida wrote the following in the context of advising the daimyo about his tutorial readings: "You should put in charge of readings men who are neither pages nor official Confucianists, but men holding the rank of common samurai. You should order them to read before you every night. Then when necessary you should call out men like Masuda Danjō and Fukuhara Echigo, and other men who are really in functional offices" (*YSZ*, 5: 392). The reason for the unexpected political proximity of the elders to the lower-level reformists is to be found in the above passage. Like their socially humbler contemporaries, the elders were "really in functional offices." The hard decisions of state in Chōshū were made not by the daimyo, but by the han elders. These, in conjunction with the leaders of whichever of the two bureaucratic factions was dominant, had to make all final decisions on policy. Accompanying the elders' extraordinary perquisites were extraordinary burdens of responsibility, which was not the case for those holding the many well-endowed sinecures below them. Both the Justice elders and the lower-level service operatives with whom they worked spent their daily lives under a certain amount of stress toiling for the good of the han. This condition gave rise to common political perceptions and interests.

The other group of Chōshū samurai whose political loyalties did not correspond in a thoroughly predictable way to their rank and income levels was the Mundane Views faction. The leaders of this faction in the bureaucracy had ranks, incomes, and educational backgrounds similar to those of the Aumeisha and Sonjuku leaders, and yet opposed the cause of Chōshū reformism. (See Craig, *Chōshū*, pp. 110–11, 261.) It is my view that although the two factions represented comparable amounts of power, their power bases were different. The Mundane Views faction represented the interests of a few hundred well-born families who held superior posts. The daimyo, ceremonially burdened, neutral and passive, was not included in this interest group, nor were all of the han elders, because of the burdens of state that they uniquely bore. The Justice faction, then, represented the several thousand modestly stipended families who held subordinate posts. Holding a configuration of power together in the complex corridors of the Chōshū administration was a difficult task. The Mundane Views leaders thus seem to have been recruited from the ablest of the modestly stipended shi by the elite "inner vassals" to do this work for them. A few modestly stipended shi of ability seem to have been willing to accept such a task in disregard of their own long-term class interests because it was lucrative in posts and emoluments, but also because it was an honor. Only a few of the ablest were chosen.

6. Beasley, *Meiji Restoration*, p. 234.

7. See Dore, *Education in Tokugawa Japan*, pp. 210–11.

8. Although this study has not dwelled on the "streamlining" theme in Yoshida, it is developed by him in his "Four Urgent Tasks" memorial of 7/10/58. See *YSZ*, 5: 381–402. A case of the implementation of this streamlining is touched on above in the section of Chapter 8 entitled "The Postwar Government in Chōshū," pp. 192–97.

9. *IS*, 5: 727–31.

10. See Hirao, *Nakaoka Shintarō*, pp. 57–65.

11. Fukuzawa, *Autobiography*, pp. 322–25; Moore, "Kumamoto and the Meiji Restoration."

12. Weber, *Economy and Society*, 1: 305.

13. See Ueyama, *Meiji*, pp. 20–22.

14. Cobban, *Myth of the French Revolution*, p. 20. See also in this vein Eisenstein, "Who Intervened in 1788?," *AHR*, 71, no. 1 (Oct. 1965): 77–103; McManners, *French Ecclesiastical Society*, pp. 138–39, 212ff.

15. Malia, "What Is the Intelligentsia?," in Pipes, ed., *Russian Intelligentsia*, pp. 4, 11, 15.

16. Walzer, *Revolution of the Saints*, pp. 2ff, 306–7, 317.

17. Webster, *Great Instauration*, pp. xiii–xvi, 11, 45, 518–20.

Bibliography

IT HAS BEEN SAID that the writing of history is cumulative, and to this truism the present study is no exception. A rich literature on the Meiji Restoration now exists in English. Marius Jansen has provided stimulating insights into the activities of the Tosa *shishi*. Robert Sakai has described the social condition of samurai in Satsuma. W. G. Beasley has provided an extremely useful comprehensive study covering the whole Restoration period. John Hall, Conrad Totman, Richard Chang, John Dower, Bernard Silberman, and many others also have shed important new light on the events of the Restoration.

Specialists will immediately see that my study covers some of the same ground as Albert Craig's well-known monograph, *Chōshū in the Meiji Restoration*. Some will say that it is above all an effort to challenge Craig's main conclusions, and it is true that this study seeks to offer meaningful alternative explanations of Chōshū's remarkable role. At the same time, some of my premises represent a further development of innovative ideas that Craig introduced, namely the importance of existing institutional roles and the crucial part played by "rational bureaucrats." I have extended the rationality that Craig adduced to embrace a much broader spectrum of Chōshū public life, and have transformed it, from being only a means of accommodating particular han loyalties, as Craig would have it, into a motive and an end in itself. This modification makes it possible to view much of the standard information available on Chōshū in a very different light.

The perceptions that led to my making a major departure from existing interpretations were mediated by several other evocative studies. Foremost among these was Harry D. Harootunian's article *"Jinsei, Jinzai, and Jitsugaku."* Also extremely helpful in this regard were Thomas C. Smith's well-argued "Merit as Ideology" essay and R. P. Dore's revealing *Education in Tokugawa Japan*.

It is my hope that future historians may find as much instruction and excitement in my work as I have found in the scholarship mentioned here, and in some of the other works that are listed on the following pages.

Aizawa Yasushi. *Shinron.* Tokyo, 1970 [1825].
Beasley, W. G. "Councillors of Samurai Origin in the Early Meiji Government, 1868–9," *Bulletin of the School of Oriental and African Studies,* 20 (1957): 89–103.
————. *The Meiji Restoration.* Stanford, Calif., 1972.
Bellah, Robert N. *Tokugawa Religion: The Values of Pre-industrial Japan.* Glencoe, Ill., 1957.
Bitō Masahide. *Nihon hōken shisōshi kenkyū.* Tokyo, 1973.
Bōchō fūdo chūshinan. Edited by Yamaguchi ken monjokan. Yamaguchi, 1962. 2 vols.
Bolitho, Harold. *Treasures Among Men: The Fudai Daimyō in Tokugawa Japan.* New Haven, Conn., 1974.
Brown, Sidney D. "Kido Takayoshi." Ph.D. diss., Univ. of Wisconsin, 1952.
Chang, Richard. *From Prejudice to Tolerance: A Study of the Japanese Image of the West, 1826–64.* Tokyo, 1970.
Chigiri Kōsai. *Utsunomiya Mokurin.* Tokyo, 1942.
Cobban, Alfred. *The Myth of the French Revolution.* London, 1954.
Craig, Albert. *Chōshū in the Meiji Restoration.* Cambridge, Mass., 1961.
Craig, Albert, and Donald Shively, eds. *Personality in Japanese History.* Berkeley, Calif., 1970.
Dai-Nihon ishinshi shiryō. Edited by Ishin shiryō hensanjo. Tokyo, 1939.
"Dattai kankei shiryō." Unpublished manuscript, Yamaguchi Prefectural Archives (vol. 10, sec. 2, no. 113, in the *Mori bunko kiroku mokuroku*). Material relating to desertion from the Chōshū *shotai.*
DeBary, W. Theodore, ed. *Sources of Japanese Tradition.* New York, 1964. 2 vols.
Dore, Ronald P. *Education in Tokugawa Japan.* Berkeley, Calif., 1965.
Dore, Ronald P., ed. *Aspects of Social Change in Modern Japan.* Princeton, N.J., 1967.
Dower, John, ed. *Origins of the Modern Japanese State.* New York, 1975.
Earl, David M. *Emperor and Nation in Japan.* Seattle, Wash., 1964.
Eisenstein, Elizabeth. "Who Intervened in 1788?," *American Historical Review,* 71, no. 1 (Oct. 1965): 77–103.
Frank, Joseph. *The Beginnings of the English Newspaper, 1620–1660.* Cambridge, Mass., 1961.
Fukumoto Yoshisuke, ed. *Shōka sonjuku no ijin Kusaka Genzui.* Tokyo, 1934.
Fukuzawa Yūkichi. *The Autobiography of Yūkichi Fukuzawa.* Translated by Eiichi Kiyooka. New York, 1972 [1899].
————. "Kyūhanjō," translated by Carmen Blacker, *Monumenta Nipponica,* 9, no. 1 (Apr. 1953): 304–29.
Furukawa Kaoru. *Bakumatsu Chōshū no butai ura.* Tokyo, 1971.
Fuse Yaheiji. "Edo jidai ni okeru kakyū shinshoku," *Hōgaku kiyō,* 9 (Oct. 1967): 9–25.
Gesshō. *Seikyō iko.* Edited by Amaji Tetsuo. Kyoto, 1917. 2 vols.

Hackett, Roger F. *Yamagata Aritomo.* Cambridge, Mass., 1971.
Haga Noboru. *Bakumatsu shishi no seikatsu.* Tokyo, 1970.
Hagi han batsu-etsu roku. Edited by Yamaguchi ken monjokan. Hōfu, 1967. 4 vols.
Hall, John W. "The Confucian Teacher in Tokugawa Japan," in Nivison and Wright, eds., pp. 268–301.
Hall, John W., and Marius B. Jansen, eds. *Studies in the Institutional History of Early Modern Japan.* Princeton, N.J., 1968.
Haraguchi Torao, Robert Sakai, et al., eds. *The Status System and Social Organization of Satsuma.* Honolulu, Hawaii, 1975.
Harootunian, Harry D. "*Jinsei, Jinzai,* and *Jitsugaku*: Social Values and Leadership in Late Tokugawa Thought," in Silberman and Harootunian, eds., pp. 83–119.
———. "The Samurai Class During the Early Years of the Meiji Period in Japan, 1868–1882." Ph.D. diss., Univ. of Michigan, 1957.
———. *Toward Restoration: The Growth of Political Consciousness in Tokugawa Japan.* Berkeley, Calif., 1970.
Hashimoto Bunsō and Matsumoto Sannosuke, eds. *Kindai Nihon seiji shisōshi.* Tokyo, 1971.
Havens, Thomas R. *Nishi Amane and Modern Japanese Thought.* Princeton, N.J., 1970.
Hawks, Francis L. *Narrative of the Expedition of an American Squadron to the China Seas and Japan.* Washington, D.C., 1856. 3 vols.
Hayakawa Junzaburō, ed. *Kiheitai nikki.* Tokyo, 1970 [1918]. 4 vols.
Hayashi Kuniō. "Yoshida Shōin no fukken o megutte." *Mainichi shimbun yūkan,* Mar. 15–16, 1973.
Hirao Michio. *Kaientai shimatsu ki.* Tokyo, 1968.
———. *Kiheitai shiroku.* Tokyo, 1944.
———. *Nakaoka Shintarō.* Tokyo, 1971.
———. *Ryōma no subete.* Tokyo, 1966.
———. *Shinsengumi shi.* Tokyo, 1928.
———. *Yamanouchi Yodō.* Tokyo, 1961.
Hirose Yutaka. *Yoshida Shōin no kenkyū.* Tokyo, 1944.
Huber, Thomas M. "Chōshū Activists in the Meiji Restoration." Ph.D. diss., Univ. of Chicago, 1975.
Ikeda Satoshi. *Takasugi Shinsaku to Kusaka Genzui.* Tokyo, 1966.
Inoue Isao. "Chōshū han sonjō undō no naibu kōzō," *Shigaku zasshi,* 75, no. 3: 29–64.
Inoue Kiyoshi. *Meiji ishin.* Tokyo, 1966.
———. *Saigo Takamori.* Tokyo, 1970. 2 vols.
Inoue Tetsujirō. *Nihon shushigakuha no tetsugaku.* Tokyo, 1924.
Ishin shiryō kōyō. Edited by Tōkyō daigaku shiryō hensanjo. Tokyo, 1966 [1937]. 10 vols.
Ishin Tosa kinō shi. Edited by Zuizankai. Tokyo, 1897.
Ishinshi. Edited by Ishin shiryō hensan jimukyoku. Tokyo, 1941. 6 vols.
Itō Hirobumi den. Edited by Shumbō-kō tsuishō-kai. Tokyo, 1940. 3 vols.

250   *Bibliography*

Itoya Toshi. *Ōmura Masujirō.* Tokyo, 1971.
Jansen, Marius B., ed. *Changing Japanese Attitudes Toward Moder-nization.* Princeton, N.J., 1965.
——. *Sakamoto Ryōma and the Meiji Restoration.* Princeton, N.J., 1961.
——. "Takechi Zuizan and the Tosa Loyalist Party," *Journal of Asian Studies,* 18, no. 2 (Feb. 1959): 199–212.
Kanezashi Shōzō. "Chōshū han Yūgekitai yowa," *Nihon rekishi,* 278 (Jul. 1971): 54–57.
Kano Masanao, ed. *Bakumatsu shisō-shū, Nihon no shisō,* vol. 20. Tokyo, 1969.
——. *Nihon kindai shisō no keisei.* Tokyo, 1956.
Kawakami Tetsutarō. *Yoshida Shōin.* Tokyo, 1968.
Keene, Donald. *The Japanese Discovery of Europe: Honda Toshiaki and Other Discoverers, 1720–1798.* London, 1952.
Kido Takayoshi monjo. Edited by Nihonshi sekkyō kai. Tokyo, 1971. 8 vols.
"Kiheitai kiroku." Unpublished manuscript, Yamaguchi Prefectural Ar-chives (vol. 10, sec. 2, no. 114, in the *Mori bunko kiroku mokuroku*).
"Kijima Matabei-shū." Microfilmed letters, Meiji Bunko Collection, Tokyo University.
Kimura Motoi. "Hagi han zaichi kashin dan ni tsuite," *Shigaku zasshi,* 62, no. 8 (Aug. 1953): 27–50.
Kitajima Masamoto. *Umeda Umpin.* Tokyo, 1943.
Kobayashi Shigeru. *Chōshū han Meiji ishinshi kenkyū.* Tokyo, 1968.
Konishi Shirō. *Kaikoku to jōi, Nihon no rekishi,* vol. 19. Tokyo, 1971.
Kumura Toshio. *Yoshida Shōin.* Tokyo, 1936.
——. *Yoshida Shōin no shisō to kyōiku.* Tokyo, 1942.
McEwan, J. R., ed. *The Political Writings of Ogyū Sorai.* Cambridge, Eng., 1962.
McManners, John. *French Ecclesiastical Society in the Ancien Regime.* Manchester, Eng., 1960.
Mannheim, Karl. *Ideology and Utopia.* New York, 1936.
Maruyama Masao. *Nihon seiji shisōshi kenkyū.* Tokyo, 1971.
——. *Studies in the Intellectual History of Tokugawa Japan.* Trans-lated by Mikiso Hane. Princeton, N.J., 1974.
Malia, Martin. "What Is the Intelligentsia?," pp. 1–18 in Richard Pipes, ed., *The Russian Intelligentsia.* New York, 1961.
Matsumoto Sannosuke, ed. *Yoshida Shōin.* Tokyo, 1973.
Matsuura Rei. *Katsu Kaishū.* Tokyo, 1968.
Matsuura Rei, ed. *Sakuma Shōzan to Yokoi Shōnan, Nihon no meicho,* vol. 30. Tokyo, 1970.
Moore, George. "Kumamoto and the Meiji Restoration." Paper presented at the Colloquium of the Center for Japanese and Korean Studies, University of California, Berkeley, February 9, 1977.
Murata Minejirō. *Shinagawa shishaku den.* Tokyo, 1911.

————. *Takasugi Shinsaku.* Tokyo, 1914.

Murata Seifu zenshū. Edited by Yamaguchi ken kyōiku kai. Yamaguchi, 1963. 2 vols.

Nagai Uta. Edited by Nagai Uta kenshō kai. Hagi, 1962.

Najita, Tetsuo. "Restorationism in the Thought of Yamagata Daini," *Journal of Asian Studies,* 31, no. 1 (Nov. 1971): 17–31.

————. "Structure and Content in Tokugawa Thinking on Political Economy." Paper presented at the Conference on the Comparative Uses of Japanese Studies, Mexico City, Sept. 15, 1974.

Nakahara Masao. *Shiraishi Shōichirō.* Tokyo, 1970.

Naramoto Tatsuya. *Kinsei hōken shakaishiron.* Kyoto, 1948.

————. *Kinsei Nihon shisō-shi kenkyū.* Tokyo, 1965.

————. *Meiji ishin jimbutsu jiten.* Tokyo, 1968.

————. *Meiji ishinron.* Tokyo, 1968.

————. "Nagai Uta—mō hitotsu no Meiji ishin," *Nihon no shōrai,* 20 (Jan. 1971): 206–17.

————. *Nihon no hankō.* Kyoto, 1970.

————. *Nihon no shijuku.* Kyoto, 1969.

Naramoto Tatsuya and Matsuura Rei, eds. *Senkusha no shisō.* Tokyo, 1966.

Naramoto Tatsuya. *Shōka Sonjuku no hitobito.* Tokyo, 1960.

————. *Takasugi Shinsaku.* Tokyo, 1965.

————. *Yoshida Shōin.* Tokyo, 1951.

Naramoto Tatsuya, ed. *Yoshida Shōin shū, Nihon no shisō,* vol. 19. Tokyo, 1969.

Naramoto Tatsuya et al., eds. *Yoshida Shōin to sono monka, Rekishi dokuhon.* Tokyo, 1973.

Nigori Tsuneaki. *Tenchū gumi Kawachi-zei no kenkyū.* Tokyo, 1966.

Nihon kyōiku-shi shiryō. Edited by the Mombushō. Tokyo, 1892. 9 vols.

Nihon kyōiku-shi shiryō sho. Edited by Kokumin seishin bunka kenkyūsho. Tokyo, 1937. 5 vols.

Nivison, David S., and Arthur F. Wright, eds. *Confucianism in Action.* Stanford, Calif., 1959.

Norman, E. Herbert. *Japan's Emergence as a Modern State.* New York, 1940.

Nunobiki Toshio. "Bakumatsu Chōshū han hisabetsu burakumin shotai no katsudō," *Nihonshi kenkyū,* 122 (May 1970): 60–76.

Nunome Tadanobu. *Yoshida Shōin to Gesshō to Mokurin.* Kyoto, 1942.

Ōe Shigenobu. *Kido Kōin.* Tokyo, 1968.

Ogawa Tsuneto. "Teradaya kimmon ryō hen to Maki Izumi no tachiba," *Geirin,* 17, no. 1 (Jun. 1966): 2–24.

Oka Yoshitake. *Yamagata Aritomo.* Tokyo, 1971.

Ōhira Kimata. *Sakuma Shōzan.* Tokyo, 1959.

Okutani Matsuharu. *Shinagawa Yajirō den.* Tokyo, 1940.

Ōmura Masujirō. Edited by Ōmura Masujirō sensei denki kankō. Tokyo, 1944.

Saeki Nakazō. *Umeda Umpin narabini den.* Tokyo, 1929.

Sakai, Robert. "Feudal Society and Modern Leadership in Satsuma Han," Journal of Asian Studies, 16, no. 3 (May 1957): 365–76.

Sakata Yoshio. Meiji ishinshi. Tokyo, 1960.

Sakata Yoshio, ed. Meiji ishinshi no mondaiten. Tokyo, 1962.

Sakata Yoshio, and John W. Hall. "The Motivation of Political Leadership in the Meiji Restoration," Journal of Asian Studies, 16, no. 1 (Nov. 1956): 31–50.

Sansom, George B. The Western World and Japan. A Study in the Interaction of European and Asiatic Cultures. New York, 1950.

Satō Seizaburō. "Seiyō no shōgeki e no taiō," in Shinohara and Mitani, eds., pp. 3–69.

Satow, Ernest M. A Diplomat in Japan. The Inner History of the Critical Years in the Evolution of Japan When the Ports Were Opened and the Monarchy Restored. London, 1921.

Shibahara Takuji. Meiji ishin no kenryoku kiban. Tokyo, 1965.

Shibusawa Eiichi. Tokugawa Yoshinobu-kō den. Tokyo, 1967 [1918]. 4 vols.

Shinohara Hajime and Mitani Taichirō, eds. Kindai Nihon no seiji shidō, seijika kenkyū II. Tokyo, 1965.

Shōkiku Kido-kō den. Edited by Kido-kō denki hensanjo. Tokyo, 1927. 2 vols.

"Shotai senshi-sha." Unpublished manuscript, Yamaguchi Prefectural Archives (vol. 10, sec. 2, no. 88, in the Mori bunko kiroku mokuroku). Lists the names and places of origin of the combat dead in the shotai.

Silberman, Bernard S. Ministers of Modernization: Elite Mobility in the Meiji Restoration, 1868–1873. Tucson, Ariz., 1964.

Silberman, Bernard S., and Harry D. Harootunian, eds. Modern Japanese Leadership: Transition and Change. Tucson, Ariz., 1966.

Smith, Thomas C. The Agrarian Origins of Modern Japan. Stanford, Calif., 1959.

———. "Japan's Aristocratic Revolution," Yale Review, 50 (1961): 370–83.

———. "Merit as Ideology in the Tokugawa Period," in Dore, ed., pp. 71–91.

Suematsu Kenchō. Bōchō kaitenshi. Tokyo, 1967 [1921]. 2 vols.

Tahara Shirō, ed. Yamaga Sokō. Tokyo, 1971.

Tanaka Akira. Bakumatsu no Chōshū. Tokyo, 1971.

———. Bakumatsu no hansei kaikaku. Tokyo, 1965.

———. "Chōshū han ni okeru Keiō gunsei kaikaku," Shirin, 42, no. 1 (1959): 104–24.

———. Meiji ishin seijishi kenkyū. Tokyo, 1965.

Tanaka Sōgorō. Ōmura Masujirō. Tokyo, 1938.

Tōgyō sensei ibun. Edited by Tōgyō gojūnensai kinenkai. Shimonoseki, 1971 [1916]. 2 vols.

Tōgyō Takasugi Shinsaku. Edited by Takasugi Tōgyō sensei hyakunensai hōsankai. Shimonoseki, 1966.

Tokutomi Sōhō. Baku-Chō kōsen. Tokyo, 1937.

Tokutomi Sōhō, ed. *Kōshaku Yamagata Aritomo den.* Tokyo, 1933. 3 vols.

Tokutomi Sōhō. *Yoshida Shōin.* Tokyo, 1893.

Totman, Conrad. "*Fudai* Daimyo and the Collapse of the Tokugawa Bakufu," *Journal of Asian Studies,* 34, no. 3 (May 1975): 581–93.

———. *Politics in the Tokugawa Bakufu, 1600–1843.* Cambridge, Mass., 1967.

Tōyama Shigeki. *Meiji ishin.* Tokyo, 1951.

Tsukahira, T. G. *Feudal Control in Tokugawa Japan: The Sankin-Kōtai System.* Cambridge, Mass., 1966.

Tsumaki Chūta. *Ijin Sufu Masanosuke-ō den.* Tokyo, 1931.

———. *Kido Takayoshi den.* Tokyo, 1927.

Tsumaki Chūta, ed. *Kido Takayoshi monjo.* Tokyo, 1930. 8 vols.

Tsumaki Chūta. *Kurihara Ryōzō den.* Tokyo, 1940. 2 vols.

Tsumaki Chūta, ed. *Kusaka Genzui ibunshū.* Tokyo, 1944. 3 vols.

Tsumaki Chūta. *Maebara Issei den.* Tokyo, 1934.

———. *Yoshida Shōin den.* Tokyo, 1928.

———. *Yoshida Shōin no yūreki.* Tokyo, 1942.

Ueyama Shumpei. *Meiji ishin no bunseki shiten.* Tokyo, 1968.

Umetani Noboru. "Meiji ishin ni okeru Kiheitai no mondai," *Jimbun gakuhō,* 3 (Mar. 1953): 27–36.

———. "Meiji ishin shi ni okeru Chōshū han no seijiteki dōkō," in Sakata, ed., pp. 307–54.

Umihara Tōru. *Meiji ishin to kyōiku.* Tokyo, 1972.

Wakamori Kisaburō. "Bakumatsu ishinki ni okeru kakyū kōmuin no chinage undō ni kansuru shiryō," *Nihon rekishi,* 267 (Aug. 1970): 54–58.

Walzer, Michael. *The Revolution of the Saints.* New York, 1969.

Webb, Herschel. *The Japanese Imperial Institution in the Tokugawa Period.* New York, 1968.

Weber, Max. *Economy and Society.* Translated by Talcott Parsons et al. New York, 1968. 3 vols.

Webster, Charles. *The Great Instauration.* London, 1975.

"Yakunin chō." Unpublished manuscript, Yamaguchi Prefectural Archives, Reference Collection. 18 vols. Lists the names, posts, and dates of tenure of Chōshū officials.

Yamaguchi monjokan shiryō mokuroku ichi, Mori-ke bunko mokuroku dai-ichi bunsatsu. Edited by Yamaguchi monjokan. Hōfu, 1963.

Yamamura, Kōzō. *A Study of Samurai Income and Entrepreneurship.* Cambridge, Mass., 1974.

Yanagawa Seigan zenshū. Edited by Yanagawa Seigan zenshū kankō kai. Gifu, 1958. 5 vols.

Yoshida Shōin zenshū. Edited by Yamaguchi ken kyōiku kai. Tokyo, 1940. 12 vols. Other editions of this work have been published in 1935, 1944, and 1972.

Yoshida Shōin bunsho mokuroku. Edited by Yamaguchi kenritsu toshokan. Yamaguchi, 1954.

Index